SIMPLY GREEN

DIE STADT BEGRÜNEN

Manual for Building Greenery

EINFACH GRÜN

GREENING THE CITY

Handbuch für Gebäudegrün

Hilde Strobl
Peter Cachola Schmal
Rudi Scheuermann (Hg./Ed.)

Inhalt
Content

BEGRÜNT EUCH! REALISIERTE GRÜNBAUTEN
GET GREENED! EXISTING GREENED BUILDINGS

IM GESPRÄCH MIT ...
IN CONVERSATION WITH ...

Why building greenery?
Because it is high time!

Warum Gebäudegrün? Weil es an der Zeit ist!

Selten waren Grünräume derart gefragt wie seit Beginn der COVID-19-Pandemie und der damit einhergehenden Konfrontation mit einem eingeschränkten Bewegungsradius. Vor allem in den Großstädten fehlt vielen Menschen die Möglichkeit, in unmittelbarer Nähe raus aus der häuslichen Enge ins Grüne zu flüchten. Nicht nur steigt die Nachfrage auf dem Immobilienmarkt nach Wohnungen mit Balkonen oder Gärten erheblich, auch Parks und öffentliche Grünflächen sind seither stärker frequentiert. Vieles, was bislang in geschlossenen Räumen stattgefunden hat, wird aus Sicherheitsgründen ins Freie verlegt, vom Treffen mit den Großeltern bis zu Social-Distancing-gerechten Teammeetings im Park. Der Begriff der „gestressten Stadt" wird seither auch auf Stadtparks als „gestresstes Grün" erweitert.[1] Umso mehr sind gegenwärtig Alternativen gefragt, die über die bodengebundenen Grünflächen hinaus grüne Erholungsräume anbieten, wie private und öffentliche Dachgärten. Realisierte Beispiele wie der Dachpark der Universitätsbibliothek Warschau, die Grünflächen auf dem Moesgaard Museum in Aarhus, dem Hypar Pavilion in New York oder dem Frankfurter Skygarden zeigen sich als übertragbare innerstädtische Lösungen – ebenso wie die sich entwickelnde Urban-Farming-Kultur auf den Dächern von Paris oder Brooklyn.

Rarely have green spaces been as much in demand as since the beginning of the COVID-19 pandemic, which has confronted people with a restricted radius of movement. In big cities, above all, many people do not have the opportunity to flee the confines of their homes into green spaces in the immediate vicinity. Not only is demand in the property market booming for apartments with balconies or gardens, but parks and public green spaces have also seen much-increased foot traffic. Much of what previously took place indoors has been shifted for safety reasons into the world outside, be it gatherings with grandparents or team meetings in parks to comply with social distancing regulations. The concept of the "stressed city" has since been expanded to include urban parks as "stressed greenery".[1] At present, there is all the more demand for alternatives that provide green spaces for rest and recreation over and above the ground-based green areas – such as private and public roof gardens. Existing examples such as the roof park of the Warsaw University Library, Poland, the green spaces on the Moesgaard Museum in Aarhus, Denmark, the Hypar Pavilion in New York and Frankfurt's Skygarden are all downtown solutions that could easily be emulated elsewhere – as can the evolving urban-farming culture on the roofs of Paris and Brooklyn.

Call for Projects, Mehrfamilienhaus, Köln/*Apartment building, Cologne*
Aachener Siedlungs- und Wohnungsgesellschaft mbH, Benjamin Marx
Photo: Benjamin Marx

———

1 Judith Lembke, Bloß raus! In der Pandemie haben wir den Außenraum neu entdeckt. Was bleibt von der Liebe für Gärten. Parks und öffentliche Plätz, in: Frankfurter Allgemeine Sonntagszeitung, 6.12.2020.

Die Urbanisierung schreitet immer weiter voran – die Städte werden nicht nur dichter, sondern greifen dabei immer weiter aus. Vor allem in den Millionenstädten zeichnen sich immer stärker die Folgen des Klimawandels ab. Sie sind zunehmend mit erhöhten Feinstaubwerten und Lärmentwicklung sowie Überhitzung (heat island effect) konfrontiert. Neueste Studien belegen sogar eine Korrelation zwischen Bevölkerungsdichte, Hitzeinseln und der Häufigkeit von COVID-19-Infektionen.[2] Dennoch ist es keine Alternative, so Richard Sennett in „Die offene Stadt", aufgrund der Klimaveränderungen nicht zu bauen, sondern es sollte auf Anpassung und Reparatur der Stadt fokussiert werden.[3] Die Begrünung der Gebäudehülle ist eine Möglichkeit, die Stadtlandschaft zu reparieren. Zahlreiche Studien belegen die messbare Veränderung stadtklimatischer Faktoren, sobald Grün über die Parks, Höfe und Vorgärten hinaus die Architektur erobert.

Das „unkalkulierbare Grün" – so die Einschätzung vieler Architekten – bringt zugleich Vorteile und Herausforderungen mit sich. Den kursierenden Vorurteilen wie hohe Herstellungs- und Pflegekosten stehen relativierende, in Zahlen nachweisbare positive Auswirkungen gegenüber: So wirken begrünte Dächer und Fassaden auf das Gebäude selbst wie auch auf die unmittelbare Umgebung. Darüber hinaus ist die Begrünung von Gebäudehüllen entgegen der verbreiteten Einschätzung im Hinblick auch auf ökonomische Aspekte in der Langzeitwirkung durchaus positiv zu bewerten.

---

2   Anne-Marie Hitipeuw, Heat waves and COVID-19 – the silent killer, Beitrag zur Tagung / contribution to the conferene: Cities on the Frontline. COVID-19, Den Haag / The Hague, Juni / June 2020.
3   Richard Sennett, Die offene Stadt. Eine Ethik des Bauens und Wohnens, Berlin / München / Munich 2018 / Richard Sennett, Building and Dwelling: Ethics for the City, London 2018.

Call for Projects
Dachgarten Wohnprojekt,
Wien, Österreich / *Vienna, Austria*
Verein für nachhaltiges Leben,
einzueins architektur ZT GmbH
Photo: Marko Mestrovic

Urbanization continues apace – cities are not only becoming ever more densely built up but expanding outwards, too. The consequences of climate change are becoming increasingly apparent, above all in the megacities, which are confronted to an ever greater extent with higher levels of pollution with fine particulate matter and noise, not to mention the stress of heat islands (heat island effect). The latest studies even show there is a clear correlation between population density, heat islands, and the frequency of COVID-19 infections.[2] Nevertheless, it is not an alternative, as Richard Sennett writes in "Building and Dwelling", his ethics for the city, not to build as a result of changes in the climate; instead, the focus should be on adapting and repairing the city.[3] Greening building envelopes is one way of repairing the city fabric. Countless studies demonstrate there is a quanti-fiable change in the factors influencing the urban climate as soon as green conquers architecture beyond the realm of parks, courtyards and front gardens.

"Unpredictable green", so many architects suggest, offers both advantages and challenges. The prevailing prejudices (such as the high costs of installation and maintenance) as regards building greenery are outweighed by the demonstra-ble positive impacts such new green has: Greened roofs and façades favorably influence both the building itself and the immediate environment. Moreover, and contrary to an oft-voiced opinion, greened building envelopes are decidedly positive in the long run in economics terms, too.

Das Handbuch „Einfach Grün – Greening the City" richtet sich über die Interessensgruppe der Architekten- und Bauherrnschaft hinaus an die Stadtgesellschaft und stellt Argumente für die Begrünung der Gebäudehülle zusammen, und dies nicht nur auf dem Wege der wissenschaftlichen Analysen. Das Buch liefert vielmehr praxisorientierte Hinweise zur Stadtreparatur durch begrünte Fassaden und Dächer, seien es Initiativen an Bestandsgebäuden oder im Neubau.

Dass die Gebäudebegrünung längst zu einer deutschlandweiten Bewegung geworden ist, belegen die Ergebnisse eines Call for Projects, der im Vorfeld der Ausstellung ausgeschrieben wurde und während ihrer Laufzeit fortgesetzt wird. Die zahlreichen Einreichungen zeigen das weite Spektrum der Möglichkeiten, von Gemeinschaftsgärten und Topflandschaften auf Dächern bis zu begrünten Garagendächern und Hauswänden mit Pflanzregalen und Kletterpflanzen. Von außen oft wenig einsehbar, verändern sie dennoch den Stadtraum – atmosphärisch und auch klimatisch.

Viele innovative Techniken bewegen sich auf einem Hightech-Modus – doch ebenso viele unmittelbare Anwendungen beweisen, dass mit dem Einsatz der passenden Mittel und Methoden auf einem Low-Level-Modus ebenfalls wirksame Maßnahmen umgesetzt werden können. Weltweit realisierte Grünbauten von Düsseldorf über Mailand bis Singapur zeigen bereits erprobte und völlig neue Entwicklungen. Auf politischer Ebene sind die Forderungen und Fördermaßnahmen für Gebäudegrün in den jeweiligen Ländern völlig unterschiedlich. In Deutschland setzen die Großstädte auf kommunale Förderprogramme. Architektur- und Ingenieurbüros wie WOHA, Arup, ingenhoven architects, Stefano Boeri Architetti oder Vo Trong Nghia Architects haben spezifische Abteilungen eingerichtet, die sich auf Gebäudegrün spezialisieren. Damit treiben sie Entwicklung und Forschung voran und engagieren sich auch beratend dafür. Die Herausforderung ist klar und längst keine Vision mehr: Je mehr Grünbauten sich über einen längeren Zeitraum etablieren und von Nutzern, Bauherren und der Stadtgesellschaft positiv bewertet werden, desto deutlicher ist die Botschaft. Es ist an der Zeit – viele Beispiele in Deutschland und weltweit demonstrieren eindrücklich, dass es möglich ist!

The manual on "Simply Green – Greening the City" is aimed not just at architects and developers as the interest group directly involved but at civic society as a whole. It offers many arguments for greening building envelopes – and not just in the form of scientific analysis but also in the guise of many practically-oriented tips on how to repair our cities by greening façades and roofs, be it on existing buildings or new builds.

The responses to our "Call for Projects" made prior to the exhibition and which continued during it show that the greening of buildings has long since become a nationwide movement in Germany. The countless entries show the broad spectrum of possibilities, ranging from communal gardens and potted plant gardens on roofs through to greened carport roofs and the walls of houses with plant shelves or climbing plants. Often as good as invisible from the outside, they nevertheless change urban space – both atmospherically and climatically.

Many innovative techniques are truly high-tech in character, and yet just as many other applications demonstrate that the use of the appropriate low-tech means and methods can likewise achieve effective results. Greened buildings world-wide, from Düsseldorf to Milan or Singapore, provide examples of tried-and-tested methods and of completely new ideas. At the political level, the standards set for building greenery and the range of possible grants and subsidies vary greatly from one country to the next. In Germany, large cities are relying on financing programs at the local authority level. At the same time, architecture practices and engineering offices such as WOHA, Arup, ingenhoven architects, Stefano Boeri Architetti or Vo Trong Nghia Architects have long since set up specialist departments dedicated to greening buildings, in this way driving R&D and providing welcome advice on the subject. The challenge is clear and has long ceased to be a futuristic vision: The more green buildings are established over a longer period of time and are rated favorably by users, developers and civic society alike, the clearer the message will be: It is high time for greened buildings! And the many examples in Germany and the world over demonstrate most impressively the many ways in which they are possible.

HILDE STROBL
PETER CACHOLA SCHMAL
RUDI SCHEUERMANN

WARUM, WIE UND WOFÜR GEBÄUDE-GRÜN?

BUILDING GREENERY – WHY, HOW, AND TO WHAT END?

Das Stadtklima und die Folgen - ökologische Aspekte

*The urban climate
and its impact –
ecological aspects*

Wie entwickelt sich das Stadtklima in den deutschen Großstädten? Sind die Initiativen zur Begrünung von Gebäuden sprichwörtlich ein Tropfen auf dem heißen Stein?

Das Stadtklima in deutschen Großstädten ist heute geprägt durch Überwärmung und Luftverschmutzung. Beide Einflüsse treten nicht flächendeckend auf, sondern sind jeweils an hohe Bebauungs- und Kfz-Verkehrsdichten gebunden. Es wird vor dem Hintergrund des globalen Klimawandels davon ausgegangen, dass unsere Städte in zunehmendem Maße Wärme und Hitze ausgesetzt sein werden, wodurch auch die Luftqualität beeinträchtigt wird. Maßnahmen zur Reduzierung der Überwärmung sind hauptsächlich in der Ausweitung der sogenannten blau-grünen Infrastruktur zu sehen. Denn Pflanzen und Wasserflächen können zum Abbau der Übertemperaturen durch Verdunstung und Beschattung beitragen. Neben den flächenbezogenen Begrünungsmaßnahmen fällt der Gebäudebegrünung eine besondere Bedeutung zu, da sie platzsparend angebracht werden kann. Fassaden- und Dachbegrünung stellen nicht nur einen erheblichen klimatischen Wert für ein bepflanztes Gebäude dar, sondern können auch die thermischen Verhältnisse in einer Straßenschlucht verbessern, wenn eine Vielzahl von Häusern bepflanzt wurde. Nicht nur im Sommer, sondern auch im Winter werden hierdurch Energietransporte durch die Gebäudehülle verringert: Im Sommer bedeutet das angenehme

The urban climate in Germany's big cities is shaped by overheating and air pollution. Both factors are not blanket phenomena but linked respectively to high building and high traffic densities. Against the background of global climate change the assumption is that our cities will be increasingly exposed to warmth and real heat, something that will also impair air quality. Measures to reduce overheating mainly entail the expansion of so-called blue-green infrastructure. Because plants and water surfaces can contribute to reducing excessive temperatures by evaporation and shade. Alongside surface-related greening measures, building greenery has a key role to play as it can be deployed without using much space. Façade and roof greenery not only constitutes a considerable climatic asset for a greened building, but can also improve thermal conditions in the street canyon if numerous buildings are greened. Not just in summer but also in winter this reduces energy transmission through the building's outer skin: In summer it spells pleasant cooling for the interior and in winter good insulation against the cold outside. In addition, in particular greened façades are to a not inconsiderable degree effective as filters against air pollution in the form of gases and particulates, meaning the air quality benefits.

Kühlung für den Innenraum, im Winter gute Isolierung vor Kälte des Außenraums. Hinzu kommt, dass insbesondere Fassadenbegrünungen in erheblichem Maße filterwirksam gegenüber gas- und partikelförmigen Luftverunreinigungen sind, wovon auch die Luftqualität profitiert.

Alongside the improvement in thermal conditions, water storage is a key factor for decentral water management in cities in particular the water stored by roof greenery. Since the climate projections for the near and distant future assume that the frequency of torrential

How is the urban climate evolving in Germany's big cities? Are initiatives to green buildings but the proverbial drop in the ocean?

Neben der Verbesserung der thermischen Verhältnisse ist die Wasserspeicherung insbesondere von Dachbegrünungen für ein dezentrales Regenwassermanagement der Städte von besonderer Bedeutung. Da die Klimaprojektionen für die nahe und ferne Zukunft davon ausgehen, dass die Starkregenhäufigkeit auch in Städten zunehmen wird, können insbesondere extensive Dachbegrünungen durch Speicherung des Regenwassers dazu beitragen, Niederschlagsspitzen zu kappen. Dadurch wird einerseits die Kanalisation entlastet, andererseits das Wasserreservoir auf dem Gebäudedach aufgefüllt. Das gespeicherte Wasser wird dann sukzessive über die Verdunstung des Dachbodensubstrats und über die Transpiration der Pflanzen abgegeben, wodurch Überwärmung und Hitze in ihrer Intensität und Dauer verringert werden können.

Dach- und Fassadenbegrünung sollte überall dort realisiert werden, wo dies bautechnisch möglich ist, denn beide sind wichtige Mosaiksteine in der Durchsetzung unserer Städte mit blau-grüner Infrastruktur.

rainfall will also increase in cities, in particular extensive roof greenery can, by storing rainwater, contribute to capping peak rainfall volumes. On the one hand, this eases the load on the municipal drainage system and, on the other, fills roof-top water reservoirs. The water thus stored can be released gradually via evaporation from the roof soil substratum and by the plants' transpiration, which can serve to lower the intensity and duration of excess warmth and heat.

Roof and façade greenery should be realized wherever this is possible in terms of the building structure, as both are important elements in creating blue-green infrastructure in our cities.

WILHELM KUTTLER

ist ein im Ruhestand stehender Hochschullehrer der Stadtklimatologie mit zahlreichen Veröffentlichungen auf diesem Fachgebiet. Lehrbeauftragter an der Universität Duisburg-Essen für Hydroklimatologie. Vorsitzender des Ausschusses Klima im Fachbereich Umweltmeteorologie des Vereins Deutscher Ingenieure (VDI) sowie Vorsitzender der Sektion Rheinland der Deutschen Meteorologischen Gesellschaft (DMG SR). Träger verschiedener nationaler und internationaler Auszeichnungen der Klimatologie/ Meteorologie.

is a retired professor on urban climatology with numerous publications on the topic to his name. Lecturer at Universität Duisburg-Essen for Hydro Climatology. Chairman of the Climate Committee in the Dept. of Eco-Meteorology at Vereins Deutscher Ingenieure (Association of German Engineers) and Chairperson of the Rhineland section of Deutsche Meteorologische Gesellschaft (German Meteorological Society). He has received various national and international awards for climatology/ meteorology.

Wie steht es um die klimatischen Bedingungen in Deutschland? Wie heiß ist es wo?

What are the climatic conditions in Germany like? How hot is it where?

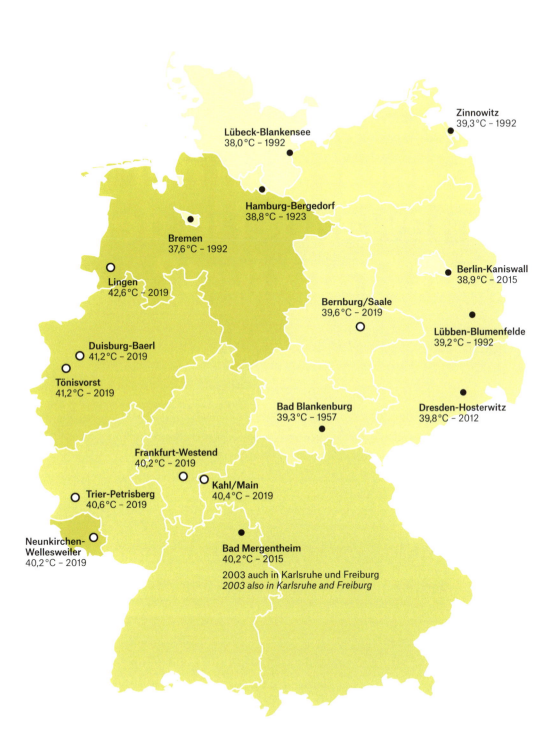

Spitzentemperaturen Sommer 2019
Peak temperatures summer 2019

Wie zeigt sich der Klimawandel in der Stadt Frankfurt?

Einer Prognose des Deutschen Wetterdienstes aus dem Jahr 2011 zufolge wird das Thermometer in Frankfurt am Main bis 2050 kräftig steigen – damals wurde prognostiziert, dass die Anzahl der Sommertage, an denen die 25°C-Marke überschritten wird, bis 2050 auf bis zu 72 steigen und die Zahl der heißen Tage mit Höchstwerten über 30°C auf über 25 steigen könnte. Die Realität übertraf die Prognose bereits 2018: Es wurden 108 Sommertage und 43 heiße Tage registriert – das verdeutlicht die rasante Entwicklung und demonstriert, wohin die Reise geht.

Frankfurt ist seit 2018 die heißeste Stadt Deutschlands mit einem Durchschnittswert von 12,9°C. Mit einem Höchstwert von 40,2°C ist Frankfurt seit 2019 auch die heißeste Stadt Hessens. Es wird in Zukunft deutlich längere und heißere Hitzeperioden geben, und die Jahresniederschläge gehen insbesondere im Sommerhalbjahr deutlich zurück.

In den Jahren 2018/19 fielen in Frankfurt nur noch zwei Drittel der üblichen Jahresniederschläge. 97 Prozent der Bäume in der Stadt sind seither geschädigt. 4.000 mussten im Jahr 2020 allein im öffentlichen Raum gefällt werden. Neben der Wasserknappheit machen aber auch immer häufigere und wesentlich heftigere Unwetter mit Sturm, Hagelschlag, Starkregen und Überflutungen der Stadt und ihren Bürgern zu schaffen.

A German Meteorological Office forecast from 2011 suggests the temperature will surge in Frankfurt/Main through 2050 – back then, the prediction was that the number of summer days when the temperature climbs past the 25°C mark would rise to as many as 72 by 2050 and the number of hot days when the temperature exceeds 30°C could rise to over 25. Reality had already outstripped the forecast by 2018: A total of 108 summer days and 43 hot days were recorded – this illustrates the rapidity of developments and indicates the direction in which things are going.

What signs of climate change are there in the city of Frankfurt?

Since 2018, Frankfurt has been the hottest city in Germany with an average temperature of 12.9°C. With a peak figure of 40.2°C, Frankfurt has also been the hottest city in the state of Hessen since 2019. In future, there will be far more prolonged and hotter heat periods, while annual precipitation will plummet, particularly in the summer half-year.

In the 2018/19 period, Frankfurt saw only two thirds of the usual volume of rain for the year. Since then, 97 percent of the trees in the city have been damaged and in 2020 alone no fewer than 4,000 in public spaces had to be felled. Alongside the scarcity of water, the ever more frequent and far more severe bouts of bad weather with storms, hailstones, heavy rain, and flooding are taking their toll on the city and its inhabitants.

HANS-GEORG DANNERT

Wo sind die Hitzeinseln in Frankfurt?

Die Hotspots der hochsommerlichen Hitzebelastung in Frankfurt finden sich besonders im Innenstadtbereich, innerhalb des Anlagenrings, aber auch in den anschließenden Gründerzeitquartieren, dem Messequartier, den Gewerbegebieten im Westen und Osten der Stadt und z.T. auch schon in den Ortskernen der Stadtteile. Kurzum: überall dort, wo hohe Versiegelung und Bebauungsdichte auf fehlende Belüftung z.B. vom Main, der Nidda oder aus der Wetterau trifft.

Where are the heat islands in Frankfurt?

In Frankfurt, the hotspots during the heat load of high summer are primarily to be found downtown, inside the inner-city ring road, but also in the adjacent quarters dating from the turn of the 20th century, in the area around the trade fair grounds, the commercial estates in the west and the east, and in part even in the core sections of the outlying districts. In short, wherever there is a high incidence of sealed surfaces, high-density building, and a lack of wind, e.g., from the Main, the Nidda or the Wetterau.

HANS-GEORG DANNERT

Frisch- und Kaltluftentstehungsgebiet
Fresh and cold-air production zones

Frischluftentstehungsgebiet
Fresh-air production zone

Misch- und Übergangsklimate
Mixed and transitional climate

Überwärmungspotenzial
Potential for overheating

Moderate Überwärmung
Moderate overwarming

Starke Überwärmung
Strong overwarming

Karte / *map:*
frankfurt.de/themen/klima-und-energie/stadtklima/
klimaplanatlas

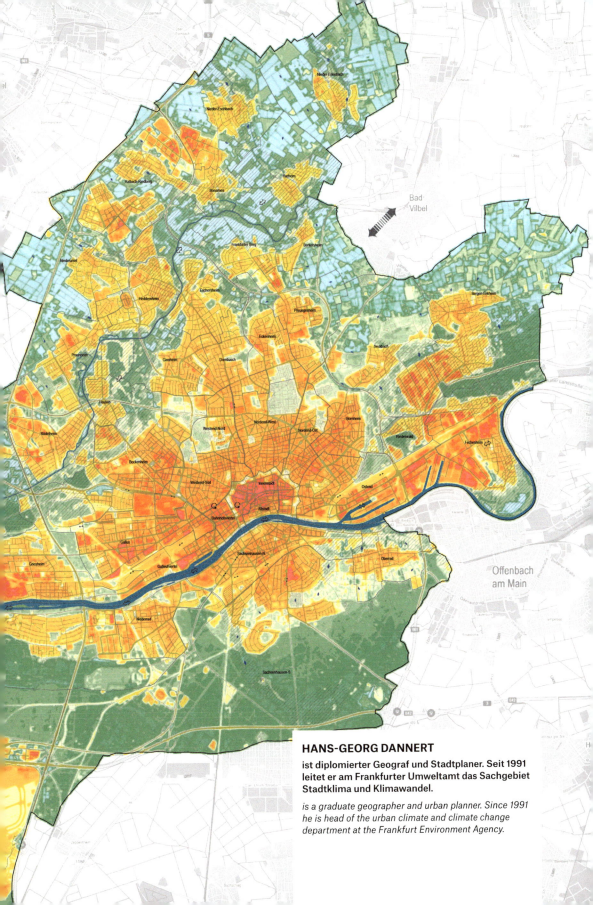

HANS-GEORG DANNERT

ist diplomierter Geograf und Stadtplaner. Seit 1991 leitet er am Frankfurter Umweltamt das Sachgebiet Stadtklima und Klimawandel.

is a graduate geographer and urban planner. Since 1991 he is head of the urban climate and climate change department at the Frankfurt Environment Agency.

Der Nutzen von Gebäudegrün für die Stadt und ihre Bewohner - von bezifferbar bis lebenswert

The benefits of building greenery for the city and its inhabitants - from the quantifiable to the feelgood factor

Infrastrukturelles Grün in den Städten

Warum Gebäudegrün?

RS   Bäume, Büsche und Pflanzen sind nicht nur dekorativ, sondern beeinflussen das Kleinklima einer Stadt – daher auch die Bezeichnung als infrastrukturelles Grün. Die Städte werden nach wie vor immer dichter mit Straßen, Parkplätzen und Gebäuden bebaut, sodass andere Flächen als der Boden aktiviert werden müssen, um lebenswerten Stadtraum zu gestalten. Die Gebäudehülle bietet ungefähr fünfmal so viel Fläche an wie der bebaute Grund. Ein Schritt wäre schon, 100 Prozent zurückzugeben und zu bepflanzen. Das können Dachflächen sein, Brüstungen oder auch mal eine geschlossene Giebelwand.

Die Vorteile für die Stadtbewohner sind vielfältig. Neben dem Kühleffekt durch die Verdunstungskühlung, die die innerstädtische Aufheizung reduziert, übernehmen die Pflanzen auch eine Filterfunktion für den Feinstaub aus dem Verkehr. Wo viel Verkehr ist, gibt es viel Feinstaub. Außerdem wachsen Fassadenbegrünungen in der Regel auf Substrat. Und dieses Substrat – in Kisten, in Regalen, in Pflanztrögen – hilft wiederum, den Umgebungslärm zu dämpfen – mehr als

Why building greenery?

RS   *Trees, bushes and plants are not just decorative, they also influence the microclimate in cities – which is why the term infrastructural green is used. Cities continue to see densities increase, with streets, parking spaces and buildings being erected such that other areas have to be activated as ground in order to create urban spaces worth living in. The outer skins of buildings offer roughly five times as much surface area as built-over land. One step would be to return 100 percent of that footprint to nature by planting on it. The area could be greened roofs, parapets or perhaps the entire area of a closed gable.*

There are many advantages for city dwellers. Alongside the cooling effect through evaporation cooling that serves to reduce heating of downtown areas, plants also filter out fine particulate matter created by traffic. Where there is a lot of traffic, there is also a lot of fine particulate matter. Moreover, façade greenery, as a rule, grows in substrate – substrate in boxes, on shelves, in planters. And that substrate helps in turn to dampen ambient noise – more than do the plants themselves. In this way, to a certain extent windows can be left

die Pflanzen selbst. Dadurch kann es teilweise wieder möglich sein, an frequentierten Straßen mit geöffneten Fenstern zu leben. Natürliche Lüftung wiederum ermöglicht es, mehr und längere Zeiten im Jahr ohne Klimatisierung zu betreiben – und das bedeutet: kein Energieverbrauch. Energie wird derzeit noch in großen Teilen mit fossilen Brennstoffen erzeugt. Die Argumente für Gebäudegrün in der Stadt bauen direkt aufeinander auf und zielen nicht zuletzt auch auf CO_2-Neutralität. Ein nicht zu unterschätzender Aspekt ist zudem die Funktion von Gründächern und Pflanzen bei den Starkregenereignissen der letzten Jahren in vielen Städten. Denn Gründächer absorbieren Regen wie ein Schwamm. Sie saugen das Wasser auf, verdunsten es teilweise und geben es verzögert in die Entwässerung ab, wodurch die akute Überlastung des Abwassernetzes vermindert wird.

open even on highly frequented streets. Natural ventilation, in turn, means that buildings can be used more and for longer periods without air conditioning – and that spells no energy consumption. At present, energy is still in large part generated by fossil fuels. The arguments for building greenery in cities interlock and are geared not least to being CO_2-neutral. One aspect that should not be underestimated is the function of greened roofs and plants when it comes to the bouts of heavy rain many cities have seen in recent years, because greened roofs absorb rain like a sponge. They suck up the water, in part evaporate it, and release it slowly into the drain system, serving to reduce the acute over-burden on the sewer network.

Infrastructural green in cities

In wessen Verantwortung liegt die Förderung von Gebäudegrün?

Who is responsible for promoting building greenery?

RS   Auch wenn es in der Verantwortung von Architekten und Planern liegt, Konzepte zu entwickeln, muss die Politik entsprechende Rahmenbedingungen und Regelwerke schaffen, die zum Beispiel festlegen, dass Flachdächer oder andere Gebäudeteile begrünt werden müssen. Die Benefits von Gebäudegrün sind auch Investoren bewusst. Sie setzen das grüne Image gezielt ein, zumal mittlerweile von einer generellen Akzeptanz ausgegangen werden kann. Wer seinem Gebäude einen nachhaltigen Wert geben und auch langfristig Qualität schaffen möchte, der denkt sehr wohl darüber nach.

RS   *Even if it is the responsibility of architects and planners to develop concepts, it is up to the politicians to create the corresponding framework and regulations that, for example, dictate that flat roofs and other parts of buildings must be greened. Investors are also aware of the benefits of building greenery. They make conscious use of the green image especially, since this now seems to be generally accepted. Anyone wanting to give a building sustainable value and seeking to create long-term quality should most definitely consider building greenery.*

Häufig wird ins Feld geführt, dass Fassadenbegrünungen teuer seien und sehr hohe Kosten im Unterhalt mit sich brächten.

RS   Natürlich entstehen Kosten durch die Installation, die Bepflanzung sowie Pflege und Bewässerungs- und Entwässerungssysteme. Doch auch Gärten, Parks und städtische Grünflächen werden gepflegt und unterhalten. Zudem gibt es Grünsysteme, die gepflegt werden wie Barockgärten oder wilder sind, wie ein englischer Garten. Wenn ein Bauherr in eine aufwendige Grünfassade investiert, die einen sehr hohen Pflegeaufwand hat, damit sie eben auch perfekt aussieht, dann finde ich das durchaus legitim und toll. Doch auch üppiges Verwuchern hat seinen Reiz.
Nichtsdestotrotz liegt mir am Herzen, dass sich in weniger privilegierten Stadtteilen oder im sozialen Wohnungsbau Gebäudegrün etabliert. Denn gerade in Gegenden, die als soziale Brennpunkte zu bezeichnen sind, mit hohem Stresslevel und Aggressionspotenzial, tut es Not, den öffentlichen Raum zu verbessern – und dieser wird durch begrünte Fassaden oder grüne Inseln verändert. Sie wirken nicht nur auf das Gebäude selbst, sondern vor allem auf die Umgebung.

A frequent objection is that façade greenery is expensive and entails very high maintenance costs.

RS   Costs arise for the installation, planting, and the care and watering systems. That said, gardens, parks and municipal green zones are cared for and maintained. Moreover, there are green systems that need caring for, such as Baroque gardens, while others are wilder, such as English gardens. If a developer invests in an elaborate green façade that requires a lot of care for it to look perfect, then I think this is quite legitimate and great. Yet opulent rampant greenery is also attractive.
Nevertheless, I think it is important that in less privileged districts of towns or in social welfare housing greenery becomes the norm. Because precisely in districts that are social flashpoints, where stress levels are high and there is major potential aggression, it is imperative that public spaces be enhanced, and this can be achieved with greened façades or green islands. Not only do they have an impact on the building itself, but above all on the surroundings.

Vision städtisch integrierter Grünsysteme
Vision of urban green infrastructures
© Arup, Green Building Envelope
Zeichnung / *drawing:* Eddie Jacob

RUDI SCHEUERMANN

ist Director und Global Leader Building Envelope Design bei Arup. Sein Fokus liegt auf der multidisziplinären Planung von nachhaltigen und energieeffizienten Gebäudehüllen. Er ist seit 2014 Arup Fellow.

is Director and Global Leader Building Envelope Design at Arup. His focus is on the multidisciplinary planning of sustainable and energy-efficient building skins. He has been an Arup Fellow since 2014.

1	**Nutzgarten** *Urban Farm*	**9**	**Nachhaltige Stadtentwässerung** *Sustainable urban drainage*	**17**	**Bioreaktive Fassade** *Bioreactive façade*
2	**Gewächshaus für Nutzpflanzen** *Greenhouses for farming*	**10**	**Naturraumschaffung** *Bioremediation*	**18**	**Grüne Dächer** *Green roofs*
3	**Vertikale Nutzgärten** *Vertical farming*	**11**	**Begrünte Fassaden mit Hängepflanzen** *Green wall top down*	**19**	**Biodiverse Gründächer** *Biodiverse roofs*
4	**Bienenhäuser** *Beehives*	**12**	**Begrünte Fassaden** *Green wall*	**20**	**Retentionsdächer** *Wet roofs*
5	**Biotopverbund** *Wildlife corridors*	**13**	**Begrünte Fassaden mit modularen Systemen** *Modular plant walls*	**21**	**Städtische Vegetation** *Urban vegetation*
6	**Integrierte Lebensräume für Tiere** *Integrated habitat creations*	**14**	**Living Walls, Samenaussaat** *Seeded living walls*	**22**	**Stadtgärten** *City gardens*
7	**Hochwasserresidenz** *Flood residence*	**15**	**Mooswände** *Moss walls*	**23**	**Photovoltaikdächer** *Photovoltaic roofs*
8	**Wasserspeicher** *Water storage*	**16**	**Baumfassade** *Tree façade*	**24**	**Windturbinen** *Wind turbines*

Initiativen für Gebäudegrün dienen der Umfeldver-besserung. Für das Stadtklima und die Artenvielfalt sind sie unbezahlbar.

Es ist schön, in der Stadt zu leben. Doch zugleich gibt es auch negative Effekte des Stadtklimas. Worin liegen diese, und was kann Gebäudegrün in diesem Zusammenhang leisten?

NP   Der Hitzesommer 2003 hat 70.000 Europäer das Leben gekostet.[4] In Zukunft erwarten wir bei fortschreitendem Klimawandel noch häufigere, längere und intensivere Hitzewellen in Deutschland. Falls es uns nicht gelingt uns anzupassen, könnte dies bis zum Ende des Jahrhunderts zu einer Vervielfachung der hitzebedingten Sterblichkeit aufgrund koronarer Herzkrankheiten um den Faktor 3 bis 5 führen.[5]

Die ungefilterte direkte und reflektierte Sonnenstrahlung heizt Dächer und Fassaden, versiegelte Bereiche ungemindert auf. Heiße Thermik baut sich auf, und die natürliche Fensterlüftung bewirkt keine ausreichende

It is great to live in the city. Yet there are also the negative effects of the urban climate. What are they and what can building greenery contribute in this context?

NP   *The hot summer of 2003 cost 70,000 Europeans their lives.[4] In future, as climate change progresses, we expect more frequent, longer and more intense heat waves in Germany. Should we not succeed in adapting, by the end of the century this could lead to an increase in heat-related fatalities owing to coronary diseases by a multiple of 3–5.[5]*

The unfiltered direct and reflected solar irradiation continues to heat roofs and façades, as well as sealed ground. Hot thermals arise and prevent sufficient interior cooling, and the overheating of surfaces can no longer be adequately mitigated by the lesser cooling at night. Full air conditioning with mechanical cooling emerges as a superficial solution but

4   Spiegel online, 23.03.2007: www.spiegel.de/wissenschaft/mensch/statistik-studie-hitze-sommer-2003-hat-70-000-europaeer-getoetet-a-473614.html (10.11.2020).
5   Paul Becker, Vizepräsident/*vice president,* Deutscher Wetterdienst, Juli /*july* 2015:
     www.dwd.de/DE/klimaumwelt/klimawandel/_functions/aktuellemeldungen/150715_hitzetote_klimawandel.html (10.11.2020).

Abkühlung der Innenräume. Der Überhitzung der Flächen kann der verminderten nächtlichen Abkühlung nicht mehr ausreichend entgegenwirken. Vollklimatisierung mit maschineller Kühlung zeigt sich als vordergründige Lösung, verstärkt jedoch infolge der vermehrten Abwärme durch die Umwandlung elektrischer Energie den Effekt der städtischen Aufheizung. Es bilden sich Hitzeinseln (heat island effect). Die Verschattung und Verdunstungskälte der Pflanzen sorgen für einen natürlichen Kühlungseffekt: Der Energieverbrauch für den Wechsel des Aggregatzustands (Wasser zu Wasserstoff und Sauerstoff) führt zur Abkühlung des umgebenden Mediums, zur „Verdunstungskälte". Der Fokus von Städten sollte deshalb auf der Regenwasserverdunstung liegen.

Wie ökonomisch ist Grün in der Architektur?

NP   Gebäudebegrünungen bieten Kostenvorteile auf mehreren Ebenen und in vielfacher Hinsicht. Auf der Gebäudeebene ist vor allem die Reduktion der Energiebedarfe hervorzuheben (z.B. Einsparung Kühlkosten, Wärmehaltung, Vermeidung technischer Verbraucher wie Klimageräte, Wirkungsgraderhöhung von Photovoltaikmodulen, Grauwasserklärung). Hinzu kommt gegebenenfalls eine Reduktion der Niederschlagswassergebühr. Hinsichtlich Materialschutz

serves only to intensify the urban heat owing to the increased heat discharge through the conversion of electrical energy. Urban heat islands form. Shading and evaporation cooling by plants offer a natural cooling effect: Energy consumption for the change in aggregate state (water to hydrogen and oxygen) leads to cooling of the ambient medium, to "evaporation cooling". The focus in cities should therefore be on rainwater evaporation.

How economical is green in architecture?

NP   *Building greenery offers cost advantages at several levels and in many respects. At the level of the individual building, above all the reduction in energy requirements bears emphasizing, e.g., lower cooling costs, heat retention, avoidance of technical consumption such as a/c units, improvement in the efficacy of photovoltaic modules, treatment of grey water). Added to this is potentially a reduction in fees for rainwater runoff into drains. As regards protection of materials and material economics, greenery protects building surfaces against UV radiation as well as temperature and weather extremes, thus prolonging the service life of the materials. The value of a property rises thanks to the appeal of the greenery, – and the expansion in the area that can be used for planting fruit and vegetables thanks to roof greenery spells an increase in*

Initiatives for greening buildings serve to improve the immediate surroundings. They are priceless for both the ambient city climate and species diversity.

Wärmeentwicklung an der Fassade des Doppelhauses Ohlystraße in Darmstadt
Heat accumulation on the façade of a semi-detached house on Ohlystrasse in Darmstadt
Photo: Nicole Pfoser, 2011

und Materialökonomie schützen Begrünungen Gebäudeoberflächen vor UV-Strahlen sowie Temperatur- und Witterungsextremen und erhöhen so deren Materiallebensdauer. Durch die Attraktivität von Begrünungen steigt der Immobilienwert – und die Nutzflächenerweiterung durch Flachdachbegrünungen bewirkt einen Zugewinn an mietaktiven Flächen und Freiraumangebot trotz städtischer Dichte.

Auf der Ebene der Umfeldverbesserung profitieren wir durch die Verdunstungsleistung der Pflanzen und der damit verbundenen Regulierung des kleinen Wasserkreislaufs. Folge sind die Reduktion von Schäden durch Starkregenereignisse, Sturm und Hagel sowie die Kanalentlastung durch den Regenwasserrückhalt, den insbesondere Dach-

active rented areas and open spaces despite urban densities.

At the level of improvements to the surroundings, we benefit from the plants' evaporation and thus the regulation of the minor water cycle. As a result, there is less damage from the occurrence of heavy rain, storms and hailstones, and the drains are not strained in the same way, as rainwater is retained by the greenery in particular on roofs. The contribution to climate protection is also substantial. The increasing overheating of cities leads, among other things, to health problems, to a reduction in labor productivity, to increased energy consumption (e.g., by a/c units), to heat damage (to transportation routes, buildings, computers...), to people migrating from cities and to stress on local R&R zones. Eight of the

begrünungen leisten. Wesentlich ist auch der Beitrag zum Klimaschutz. Die zunehmende städtische Überhitzung führt unter anderem zu Gesundheitsproblemen, zu einer Reduktion der Arbeitsleistung, zu einem erhöhten Energieverbrauch (z.B. durch Klimaanlagen), zu Hitzeschäden (Verkehrswege, Bauwerke, Computer ...), zu Stadtflucht und zur Belastung der Naherholungsgebiete. Acht der neun wärmsten Jahre, die seit 1881 gemessen wurden, haben wir seit dem Jahr 2000 erlebt.[6] Jeder Hitzetag bei Höchsttemperaturen über 30°C bedeutet für Deutschland 40 Millionen Euro gesundheitsbezogene wirtschaftliche Kosten – durch Verlust an Arbeitskraft, durch Krankenhauskosten und Todesfälle.[7]

Die Reduktion der Luftbelastung durch Feinstaubbindung und gegebenenfalls Verstoffwechselung von Luftschadstoffen und die Minderung der Lärmbelastung dienen der Gesundheit, der Sicherung wie auch der Aufenthalts- und Kommunikationsqualität. Sie leisten somit ebenfalls einen ökonomischen Beitrag. Die Verbesserung der Biodiversität durch die Erweiterung des Nahrungs- und Lebensraums und die Vorbeugung des Artensterbens (z.B. durch Sicherung der Nahrungskette und Bestäubung) sind unbezahlbar.

Ich habe den Eindruck, dass intensiver über Gebäudegrün geforscht wird, als Maßnahmen umgesetzt werden. Falls ja, warum ist das so?

NP   Eine umfassende Literatur- und Internetauswertung zur Thematik der Begrünung zeigt das Forschungsinteresse und den Akzeptanzverlauf in typischen Sachzusammenhängen wie sie aus der zeitgeschichtlichen Parallelbetrachtung herzuleiten sind. Signifikant ist der Wandel der Inhalte vom Nahrungsangebot bis zu den klimatischen und ökologischen Leistungs-

nine warmest years measured since 1881 have occurred since 2000.[6] Each hot day during the highest temperatures in excess of 30°C translates into 40 million euros in health-related economic costs in Germany – as a result of lower productivity, hospital costs and fatalities.[7]

The reduction in air pollution through the binding of fine particulate matter and possible metabolization of air pollutants and reduction in noise pollution promote and secure health, while also enhancing residential qualities and communications. In this way they make an economic contribution. Improving biodiversity through expansion of different species' habitats and feeding areas and pre-empting species dying out (e.g., through securing of the food chain and pollination) are priceless contributions.

I get the impression that there is more research going into greening buildings than there are measures being realized. If that is so, why is it happening?

NP   *A comprehensive evaluation of the literature on the topic of greening, along with Internet searches, attests to the research interest and how acceptance has increased in typical factual contexts such as can be gleaned from a parallel historical view. What is significant here is the shift in content from the range of foodstuffs to climatic and ecological performance factors as a response to the wasting of resources and the climate stress we are seeing today. What catches the eye is the rise in media interest in architectural designs with greenery and the surge in research into its potentials.*

Nevertheless, greenery is not yet a matter of course in planning and realizing buildings. Although the numerous advantages and potentials of greening façades and roofs are proven, in practice developers and investors often reject them. The main obstacles here include cost

6   Quelle/*Source*: Deutscher Wetterdienst.
7   Martin Karlsson, Nicolas R. Ziebarth, Population health effects and health-related costs of extreme temperatures: Comprehensive evidence from Germany, in: Journal of Environmental Economics and Management, 01/2018, S./*p.* 93–117;

faktoren als Reaktion auf die Ressourcenverschwendung und Klimabelastung unserer Zeit. Auffällig sind der Anstieg des Medieninteresses an der Architekturgestaltung mit Begrünungen und die zunehmende Erforschung ihrer Potenziale.

In der Planung und Ausführung sind Begrünungen jedoch noch nicht selbstverständlich. Obwohl die zahlreichen Vorteile und Potenziale der Fassaden- und Dachbegrünungen erwiesen sind, stoßen diese in der Praxis bei Bauherren und Investoren häufig auf Ablehnung. Hinderungsfaktoren sind unter anderem Kostenaspekte bei der Herstellung, in der Pflege und Wartung als auch planerischer wie konstruktiver Mehraufwand. Doch auch die Zielkonflikte mit der technischen Gebäudeinfrastruktur behindern zum Teil die Realisierung: rechtliche Aspekte, die Sorge vor möglichen Schäden am Gebäude, die Angst vor Ungeziefer, der Mangel an Fachwissen zur Planung und Umsetzung (Fachkräftemangel) sowie fehlende Auflagen und Förderungen.

Wie wirkungsvoll ist ein durch politische Vorgaben gesteuerter Einsatz von Gebäudegrün? Bringen ambitionierte Richtlinien auch Nachteile mit sich?

NP   Die möglichen Lösungsansätze sind vielfältig, Forderungen sowie direkte und indirekte Förderungen sind dabei denkbar. Die Bandbreite reicht von gesetzlichen Vorgaben zur Begrünung (konsequente Festschreibung im Bebauungsplan, Auslegung von Bebauungsplänen) über finanzielle Zuschüsse für Planung, Konstruktion, Herstellung (Material und Einbau), Pflege und Wartung bis hin zu Anreizprogrammen hinsichtlich Klimaanpassung, energetischer Gebäudeoptimierung und wasserwirtschaftlichen Aspekten (z.B. gesplittete Abwassersatzung).

Zu einer stadtbildprägenden und klimatisch wirksamen Gebietsentwicklung sind überzeugende Vorbildprojekte, gerade auch begrünte öffentliche Gebäude, vertrauens-

aspects as regards making, caring for and maintaining the systems as well as the additional planning and building involved. That said, conflicts with requirements for positioning of technical building facilities in part also prevent greenery being realized, as do legal aspects, concerns at possible damage to the building, fear of pests, a lack of expert knowledge about planning and implementation (a lack of skilled staff), and the absence of regulations and grants.

How effective is the use of building greenery driven by political stipulations? Do ambitious guidelines also pose disadvantages?

NP   *There are many possible routes to solutions, and one could well imagine both requirements being set and direct/indirect grants being made available. The spectrum could range from mandatory stipulations on greening (consistent definition as part of development plans, interpretation of development plans) through financial support for the planning, construction, manufacture (materials and installation), care and maintenance of the systems through to incentive programs associated with climate adaptation, energy optimization of buildings, and aspects relating to water economy (e.g., subdivisions in the waste water statutes).*

Greened public buildings in particular help build confidence and persuade others to follow suit in relation to development of districts in a manner that takes climate trends into account and defines the cityscape. Best-practice examples covering a street or an entire quarter linked to very visible public displays (information panels and/or measured data on what the greenery achieves) highlight the success and help tackle prejudices. This and connecting requirements with grants and support are another way of boosting acceptance and personal initiative.

Independent of concrete requirements and grants and support, there are factors that are key to reducing obstacles. They include, among other things, conscious interaction with developers and investors (PR work), competent

erweckend und zielführend. Best-Practice-Beispiele im Umfang einer Straße oder eines Quartiers, verbunden mit einem öffentlich gut sichtbaren Display (Informationstafeln und/oder Messdaten zu den Begrünungsleistungen) zeigen den Erfolg und helfen, Vorurteile abzubauen. Dies und die Verknüpfung von Forderung und Förderung sind ein weiteres Mittel hin zu Akzeptanz und Eigeninitiative.

Unabhängig von konkreten Forderungen und Förderungen gibt es Faktoren, die zum Abbau von Hemmnissen maßgeblich sind. Zu diesen Faktoren gehören unter anderem der gezielte Austausch mit Bauherren und Investoren (Öffentlichkeitsarbeit), die kompetente fachliche Beratung zu Planung, Ausführung und Pflege, die fachliche Begleitung der Maßnahmen sowie das Nutzen und Kommunizieren des Imagegewinns bei gelungener Umsetzung (Verstetigung der Öffentlichkeitsarbeit). Um diese Faktoren zur Erfolgssicherung gewährleisten zu können, müssen in den zuständigen Verwaltungen und Abteilungen die personellen Ressourcen zur Betreuung, Beratung und Bearbeitung vorhanden sein.[8]

expert advice on planning, implementation and care, expert support for the measures, and utilizing and communicating the enhanced image once realization is successfully completed (solidifying PR work). In order to guarantee that these factors help secure successes, the relevant local agencies and departments must have the human resources to provide support, advice and processing.[8]

NICOLE PFOSER

ist Professorin für Objektplanung an der Hochschule für Wirtschaft und Umwelt Nürtingen-Geislingen, Studiengang Landschaftsarchitektur. Sie forschte am Fachgebiet Entwerfen und Freiraumplanung des Fachbereichs Architektur der Technischen Universität Darmstadt zum Thema „Grün statt Grau: Gewerbegebiete im Wandel" und veröffentlichte Standardwerke zur Gebäudebegrünung wie „Gebäude, Begrünung, Energie – Potenziale und Wechselwirkungen" (Bonn 2014) und „Vertikale Begrünung" (Stuttgart 2018).

is Professor of Property Planning at Nürtingen-Geislingen University in the Dept. of Landscape Architecture. She did research at the Design and Open Area Planning Study Unit in the Dept. of Architecture at TU Darmstadt on the topic of "Green instead of Grey: the Change in Commercial Estates" and has published the standard reference works on building greenery such as "Gebäude, Begrünung, Energie – Potenziale und Wechselwirkungen" (Bonn, 2014) and "Vertikale Begrünung" (Stuttgart, 2018).

8   Jörg Dettmar, Nicole Pfoser, Sandra Sieber, Gutachten Fassadenbegrünung: Gutachten über quartiersorientierte Unterstützungsansätze von Fassadenbegrünungen, Darmstadt 2016: www.umwelt.nrw.de/fileadmin/redaktion/PDFs/klima/gutachten_fassadenbegruenung.pdf (10.11.2020).

Warum wirken Pflanzen wie Klimaanlagen?

Pflanzen haben die Eigenschaft, Wasser aufzunehmen und Wasser wieder zu verdunsten. Zur Verdunstung des Wassers – damit Wasser zu Wasserdampf wird – wird Energie benötigt, welche die Pflanzen aus der Lufttemperatur ziehen. Der Energieverbrauch führt zu einer moderaten Senkung der Lufttemperatur. Die sogenannte Verdunstungskühlung durch Pflanzen und Boden kann je nach Temperaturniveau einen natürlichen Kühlungseffekt von circa 0,5–1,5 °C bewirken. Je größer die begrünte Fläche der Außenfassade, desto höher der Kühlungseffekt auf das Raumklima des Gebäudes selbst und auf die Umgebung.

Why do plants on façades function like air conditioning?

Plants have the property of taking up water and then evaporating it. To evaporate the water, i.e., turn the water into steam, energy is required, and plants draw it from the ambient temperature. This energy consumption leads to a slight drop in ambient temperature. So-called evaporative cooling by plants and the soil can, depending on the temperature level, have a natural cooling effect of approx. 0.5–1.5 °C. The greater the greened expanse of the outside façade, the greater the cooling effect on the ambient climate of the building itself and its immediate surroundings.

RUDI SCHEUERMANN

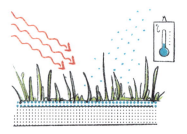

VERDUNSTUNGSKÜHLUNG
EVAPORATION COOLING

Pflanzen nehmen Wasser auf und verdunsten es. Die dazu benötigte Energie ziehen sie aus der Luftwärme, die Luft kühlt dadurch ab.

Plants take up water and evaporate it. The energy they require for this they take from the ambient air, and the air cools as a result.

Illustrationen nach/*Illustrations after*
Pfoser 2018

Illustration nach/*Illustration after*
Kuttler 2011

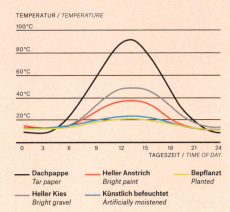

- **Dachpappe** / *Tar paper*
- **Heller Kies** / *Bright gravel*
- **Heller Anstrich** / *Bright paint*
- **Künstlich befeuchtet** / *Artificially moistened*
- **Bepflanzt** / *Planted*

Wie stark können begrünte Dächer Hitze reduzieren?

How do plants change the heat radiation on roofs and façades?

BITUMENDACH / *BITUMEN ROOF*

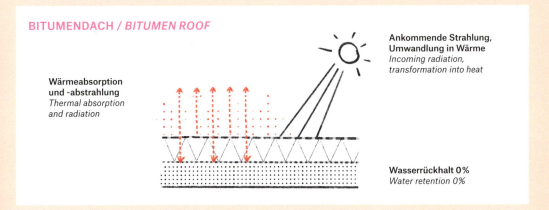

Wärmeabsorption und -abstrahlung
Thermal absorption and radiation

Ankommende Strahlung, Umwandlung in Wärme
Incoming radiation, transformation into heat

Wasserrückhalt 0%
Water retention 0%

RETENTIONSDACH / *RETENTION ROOF*

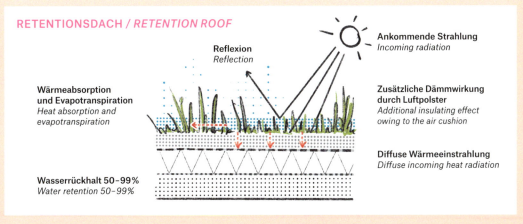

Reflexion
Reflection

Wärmeabsorption und Evapotranspiration
Heat absorption and evapotranspiration

Ankommende Strahlung
Incoming radiation

Zusätzliche Dämmwirkung durch Luftpolster
Additional insulating effect owing to the air cushion

Diffuse Wärmeeinstrahlung
Diffuse incoming heat radiation

Wasserrückhalt 50–99%
Water retention 50–99%

Warum wirken sich begrünte Dächer positiv auf die Leistung und den Energieverbrauch von Klimaanlagen aus?

Viel zu wenig wird beachtet, dass ein Gründach über den eigentlichen Kühleffekt hinaus noch viel weitreichendere Wirkungen mit sich zieht – dies ist ein unglaubliches Potenzial der Energieeinsparung für die ganze Stadt: Die Luftansaugung für eine mechanische Lüftung (Klimaanlage), deren Technik üblicherweise auf dem Dach installiert ist, befindet sich in der Regel circa 3m über dem Dach. Wenn die Luftansaugung für die Klimaanlage über einem Schwarzdach erfolgt, dann hat dieses Schwarzdach im Sommer – wenn die Kühlung am meisten erforderlich ist – schon bei einer Lufttemperatur von 25/26°C eine Oberflächentemperatur von etwa 60/70°C! Um die Luft für die Klimatisierung der Innenräume auf circa 18°C zu kühlen, ist also ein enormer energetischer Aufwand nötig.

Wenn dagegen die Luft über einem Gründach angesaugt wird, dann ist die Oberflächentemperatur durch die Verdunstungskühlung gegebenenfalls sogar etwas geringer als die umgebende Lufttemperatur, also etwa 24/24,5°C. Das heißt, alleine dadurch, dass die Luft über dem Gründach angesaugt wird und nicht über dem Schwarzdach, wird nur ein Drittel der Energie für die gleiche Endtemperatur in den Innenräumen verbraucht.

Far too little attention is paid to the fact that a greened roof not only has a cooling effect but has many other far more decisive effects – offering incredible energy savings potential for the entire city: The air intake for mechanical air conditioning (cooling) – whereby the technology tends to be located on roofs – is, as a rule, installed about 3m above the roof. If the air intake for the air conditioning system occurs over a black roof, then in summer (when cooling is most required) that black roof already has a surface temperature of about 60/70°C when the outside temperature is 25/26°C! A massive amount of energy inputs are required in order to cool the air temperature down to about 18°C inside the rooms.

Why do greened roofs favorably influence the output and energy consumption of air conditioning systems?

If, by contrast, the air intake is positioned over a greened roof, then the surface temperature is possibly even lower than the ambient outside temperature owing to evaporative cooling, meaning about 24/24.5°C. In other words, simply by virtue of the fact that the air intake is over a greened roof and not a black roof means that only a third of the energy is required to achieve the same final temperature in the interiors.

RUDI SCHEUERMANN

**Luftansaugung der Klimageräte
circa 3m über dem Dach**

‣ Angenommene Lufttemperatur von circa 26°C
‣ Lufttemperatur über dem Gründach circa 24°C

**Erforderliche Kühllast für eine gewünschte Kühl-
temperatur von circa 18°C: 6–7°C**

*Air intake of the air conditioning appliances
approx. 3m over the roof*

‣ *Assumed air temperature of about 26°C*
‣ *Air temperature above the green roof about 24°C*

*Required cooling load for a targeted cooling temperature
of about 18°C: 6–7°C*

City Hall Chicago, USA
Photo: Diane Cook, Len Jenshel,
© gettyimages

Luftansaugung der Klimageräte circa 3m über dem Dach

‣ Angenommene Lufttemperatur von circa 26°C
‣ Lufttemperatur über dem Schwarzdach circa 60/70°C

Erforderliche Kühllast für eine gewünschte Kühltemperatur von circa 18°C: 21–22°C

Air intake of the air conditioning appliances approx. 3m over the roof

‣ *Assumed air temperature of about 26°C*
‣ *Air temperature above the black roof about 60/70°C*

Required cooling load for a targeted cooling temperature of about 18°C: 21–22°C

Die Frage ist nicht in Prozent zu beantworten, da es sich um ein komplexes Zusammenspiel mehrerer Faktoren handelt. Sehr viel hängt vom Oberflächenmaterial der Fassade, von der jeweiligen Ausrichtung in eine bestimmte Himmelsrichtung und der damit in Verbindung stehenden Stärke der Sonneneinstrahlung ab. Diese Aspekte wiederum bestimmen den Grad der Erhitzung der thermischen Masse. Je mehr diese durch Pflanzen beschattet wird, desto weniger wird sie erhitzt. Vom Temperaturniveau der Luft hängt ab, wie viel Verdunstungsmenge durch die Pflanzen temperaturabhängig erzeugt werden kann. Auch das Verhältnis von Straßenbreite zu Bebauungshöhe spielt eine große Rolle. Dies beeinflusst je nach vorherrschender Windrichtung die Luftspülung und damit die Abfuhr der erwärmten Luft aus dem Straßenraum.

Um wie viel Prozent können begrünte Fassaden Hitze reduzieren?

By what percentage can a greened façade reduce heat?

The question cannot be answered in percentages, as it involves the complex interaction of several factors. Very much depends on the material used for the façade's surface, its respective orientation toward one of the cardinal points, and the related strength of solar irradiation. These aspects in turn define the degree the thermal mass heats up. The more it is in the shadow of plants, the less it gets heated. The ambient temperature of the air determines what volume of evaporation the plants can produce depending on the temperature. The relationship between the width of the street and the height of the buildings also plays a major role. It influences how the air is replaced depending on the direction of the prevailing wind and thus the extent to which air that is heated up is removed from the street space.

RUDI SCHEUERMANN

Wie verändern Pflanzen die Hitzestrahlung der Wand?

How much do plants change the heat radiation of the façade?

BODENGEBUNDENE BEGRÜNUNG (GERÜSTKLETTERPFLANZEN)
GROUND-BASED GREENERY (TRELLIS CLIMBERS)

WANDGEBUNDENE BEGRÜNUNG, MODULARER AUFBAU
WALL-BASED GREENERY, MODULAR STRUCTURE

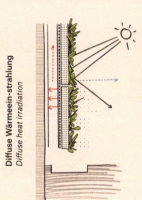

Auf 20 % reduzierte Strahlung
Reduction of up to 20 % in radiation

100 % ankommende Strahlung
100 % incoming radiation

50 % Wärmeabsorption und Evapotranspiration
50 % heat absorption and evapotranspiration

30 % Reflexion
30 % reflection

Verminderte Wärmeabsorption und -abstrahlung der Wandfläche
Lowered heat absorption and heat reflected by the surface of the wall

Diffuse Wärmeeinstrahlung
Diffuse heat irradiation

Ankommende Strahlung
Incoming radiation

Wärmeabsorption und Evapotranspiration
Heat absorption and evapotranspiration

Reflexion
Reflection

←———— **Kühlung durch Verdunstung, verminderte Sonneneinstrahlung und Reflexion** ————→
Cooling by evaporation, reduced solar irradiation and reflection

UNBEGRÜNTE MASSIVWAND
SOLID WALL WITH NO GREENERY

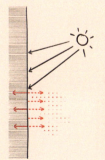

Ankommende Strahlung
Incoming radiation

Umwandlung in Wärme
Transformation into heat

Oberflächenabhängige Wärmeabsorption und -abstrahlung
Surface-dependent heat absorption and reflection

Illustrationen nach/ *Illustrations after*
Pfoser 2018

Warum sorgen Pflanzen für die Reduktion der Hitze nicht nur am Gebäude, sondern allgemein in der Stadt?

Why do plants serve to reduce the heat not only of the building but also in the city in general?

Wenn Sonneneinstrahlung die thermische Masse (Beton, Stein, Mauerwerk …) von Gebäuden trifft, dann wird diese Wärme von der thermischen Masse absorbiert. Diese Wärme wird nach Sonnenuntergang wieder an die das Gebäude umgebende Luft in der Stadt abgegeben und erhitzt das Stadtklima auf Dauer deutlich über die normale Umgebungstemperatur. Dadurch werden unsere Innenstädte viel zu heiß. Weil die Masse über Nacht nicht ausreichend auskühlen kann, steigert sich der den Stadtraum aufheizende Effekt mehr und mehr, Tag um Tag. Das nennt man Hitzeinseleffekt (heat island effect).

Wenn Pflanzen vor der thermischen Masse wachsen, dann verschatten sie diese teilweise und verhindern dadurch das Aufheizen und damit auch die sich daraus ergebende Wärme-abstrahlung. Dadurch wird der Hitzeinseleffekt reduziert. Hinzu kommt, dass durch die Verdunstungskühlung der Pflanzen die innerstädtische Aufheizung zusätzlich vermindert wird.

If solar irradiation encounters buildings' thermal mass (concrete, stone, masonry…) then the warmth is absorbed by the thermal mass. After sundown, the building then releases that heat back into the ambient air of the city and in the long run increases the city's temperature to well above the normal ambient tempe-rature. In this way, our inner cities become far too hot. Because the mass cannot cool down enough at night, the urban space is heated up more and more, day by day. This is termed the "heat island effect".

If plants grow in front of the thermal mass, then they in part cast a shadow over it and in this way prevent it heating up and the subsequent emission of the heat. As a result, the heat island effect is reduced. Moreover, the evaporative cooling by the plants serves to further reduce downtown heat islands.

RUDI SCHEUERMANN

Wie stark kann Gebäudegrün die Luftqualität verbessern?

Wenn in einer Straße circa 20 Prozent aller Gebäude zu 20 Prozent der exponierten Gebäudehülle mit den richtigen feinblättrigen Pflanzen begrünt sind, dann werden 10–20 Prozent der Feinstaubbelastung aus der Luft gefiltert. Dabei ist wichtig, die Fassadenbegrünung in der Nähe der Feinstaubimmission anzubringen – d.h. in der Regel im Bereich der unteren 10 Metern des Gebäudes, im unmittelbaren Umfeld des Verkehrsgeschehens.

Illustration nach/*Illustration after*
Doernach 1982

If, within a street, some 20 percent of all buildings have at least 20 percent of the exposed outer skin greened with the right fine-leaved plants, then 10–20 percent of the fine particulate dust is filtered out of the air. It is important in this context that the façade greenery is close to the sources of the fine particulate, as a rule in the zone covering the lower 10 meters of the building, i.e. the direct vicinity of traffic.

RUDI SCHEUERMANN

How strongly can building greenery improve air quality?

SCHADSTOFFFILTER UND LÄRMSCHUTZ DURCH BÄUME UND FASSADENBEPFLANZUNG
TREES AND FAÇADE GREENERY AS POLLUTANT FILTERS AND NOISE PROTECTION

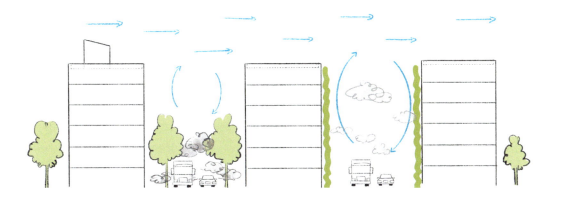

Illustration nach/*Illustration after*
Preiss 2013

Reduzieren Pflanzen an den Gebäuden den Lärmpegel der Stadt?

Hinsichtlich des Stadtlärms sind zwei Arten von Lärm zu unterscheiden: Quelllärm und Umgebungslärm. Der Quelllärm kann nicht reduziert werden: Eine Bohrmaschine, neben der man steht, ist ebenso laut wie der Lärm, den sie verursacht. Da helfen auch keine Pflanzen und kein Pflanzsubstrat. Aber der Umgebungslärm in einer Stadt, also die Summe aller Lärmquellen, die einen Hintergrundlärm erzeugen, kann in der Summe um bis zu 6–8 Dezibel gesenkt werden.

Die Lärmreduktion hängt aber nicht vorrangig von den Pflanzen selbst ab, sondern von der akustischen Masse des Pflanzensubstrats, auf dem die Fassadenbegrünung wächst. 6–8 Dezibel bilden oftmals den kleinen, aber entscheidenden Unterschied, der den gesunden Schlaf bei einer natürlichen Fensterlüftung noch möglich macht. Die Nähe der Fassadenbegrünung zur Lärmquelle des Verkehrs ist dabei sinnvoll und besonders effektiv.

How strongly can plants attached to buildings reduce noise levels in the city and why is this the case?

We need to distinguish between two types of noise in the city: the noise from a source and ambient noise. Noise from a source cannot be reduced: If you stand next to an electric drill then the noise is simply as loud as the noise it emits. No plants or plant substrate will help in such a case. However, the ambient noise in a city, meaning the sum of all noise sources that combine to form background noise, can in total be reduced by 6–8 decibels.

Noise reduction does not depend primarily on the plants themselves but on the acoustic mass of the plant substrate on which the façade greenery grows. A level of 6–8 decibels often forms the small but decisive difference that enables healthy sleep with an open window for natural ventilation. The proximity of façade greenery to the traffic as the source of the noise is key and especially effective.

RUDI SCHEUERMANN

Pflanzen steigern das Wohlbefinden. Wie lässt sich das messen oder erforschen?

Das ist nicht einfach zu messen. Hier gibt es nur Näherungs- und Vergleichswerte. Man kann am ehesten über Umfragen zum Wohlbefinden und gegebenenfalls über Messungen des Stressniveaus von Menschen Auskunft erhalten. Außerdem sind Stresserkrankungen wie Bluthochdruck, aber auch Atemwegserkrankungen durch Feinstaub ein Indikator. Allerdings gibt es kein exaktes Maß, mit dem man den Effekt gezielt und genau ermitteln kann.

Plants enhance well-being. How can that be measured or researched?

This is not something that it is easy to measure. There are only approximations or comparisons that can be made. Information can best be obtained by polling people's sense of well-being and possibly by measuring people's stress levels. Moreover, stress illnesses, such as high blood pressure or pulmonary diseases owing to fine particulates, are another indicator. However, there is no exact yardstick that enables us to define the effect precisely and accurately.

RUDI SCHEUERMANN

Schützen Pflanzen die Bausubstanz?

Ja, sie schützen Dachabdeckungen vor Hagelschlag, Sturm und Extremtemperaturen sowie UV- und IR-Strahlen. Die Lebensdauer der Dachabdichtung verlängert sich um 10–20 Jahre (bei einer gewöhnlichen Lebensdauer von 20–30 Jahren). Das bedeutet: Allein eine extensive Dachbegrünung bewirkt eine Lebensdauer der Dachabdichtung von 40 Jahren.
Auch die Wände werden mittels der Pflanzen vor Sonneneinstrahlung bzw. UV-Belastung und vor Schlagregen geschützt.

Do plants protect the substance of the building?

Yes, they protect roof covers against hail, storm and extreme temperatures, not to mention UV and IR radiation. The service life of roof seals is prolonged by 10–20 years (assuming a customary lifecycle of 20–30 years). That means: already the extensive roof greenery causes the life cycle of the roof covers of 40 years.
Plants protect walls against solar irradiation and UV radiation as well as against driving rain.

GUNTER MANN

„DIE HAUT DER STADT"
"THE CITY'S SKIN"

Die ungeschützte Stadt, überhitzt, laut und mit hoher Feinstaubbelastung der Luft
The unprotected city, overheated, loud and with heavy air pollution by fine particulate matter

Die durch Gebäudegrün geschützte Stadt
The city protected by building greenery

Illustrationen nach/*Illustrations after*
Pfoser 2018

Das primäre Ziel ist die Schaffung ungestörter Lebensräume mit geringem Konkurrenzdruck zur Biotopvernetzung und zur Förderung der Artenvielfalt am Standort. Gebäudebegrünungen haben neben ihren klimatischen, schall- und schadstoff-absorbierenden und gestalterischen Effekten auch das Potenzial, in den überwiegend naturentfernten Stadträumen der Fauna ein Lebensraumangebot zurückzugeben.

Wie reagieren Tiere auf Gebäudegrün in der Stadt?

Faunistische Untersuchungen liefern Ergebnisse zum Deckungsgrad der Begrünung, der Artendiversität der Flora sowie der davon abhängigen Individuenanzahl und -dichte. Ziel ist eine Erfüllung möglichst vollständiger Lebensraumansprüche durch die Einbindung von Bauwerken in Ökosysteme, die Bildung eines „städtischen Grünflächenverbundsystems" unter anderem aus Parkanlagen, Fassadenbegrünungen, Baumalleen und Dachbegrünungen sowie stadtnahen Grünflächen.

How do animals respond to building greenery in the city?

The primary goal is to create undisturbed habitats that are not under strong competitive pressure and that network into biotopes and promote biodiversity on site. Building greenery serves to absorb climatic, noise and toxic influences and harbors design potential whereby the primarily non-natural urban spaces give fauna back a potential habitat.

Study of fauna provides insights into the degree of greenery and floral biodiversity as well as the number of individual species and densities. The goal is to fulfill as many claims to complete habitats as possible by tying buildings into ecosystems, forming an "urban coherent green zone system", consisting among other things of parks, façade greenery, avenues of trees and roof greenery, as well as green zones close to cities.

Je nach Begrünungsform können unterschiedliche Tier-
gruppen und Artenzahlen auftreten: Flache Extensivbegrünungen zeigen temporär unter anderem Spinnen,
Heuschrecken und durch eine geeignete Pflanzenwahl
weitere „Fluginsekten" (z.B. Wildbienen, Schmetterlinge,
Schwebfliegen). So können auch Extensivbegrünungen
ganzzeitige Bienen- und Schmetterlingsweiden darstellen.
Auch für Vögel ist das Gründach ein idealer, vor Katzen,
Hunden, Füchsen usw. geschützter Rückzugsraum.

Fassadenbegrünungen sind Fressplatz, Nistplatz, Fang-
platz, Sonnen- und Schattenplatz, Versteckplatz, Witte-
rungsschutz, Verpuppungsort, Aussichtsplatz und
Paarungsraum zugleich. Sie liefern mit ihrer Blattmasse,
mit dem Nektar, den Pollen und Früchten wertvolle Nah-
rung und Lebensraum für beispielsweise Vögel, Insekten,
Spinnen und Schmetterlinge. Durch die Nahrungskette
stellt sich ein natürliches Gleichgewicht ein.

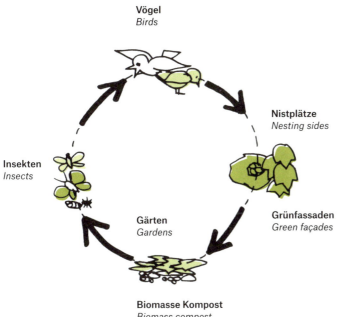

Vögel
Birds

Nistplätze
Nesting sides

Insekten
Insects

Grünfassaden
Green façades

Gärten
Gardens

Biomasse Kompost
Biomass compost

Depending on the type of greenery, different animal groups and numbers of species arise: Flat, extensive greenery attracts – among others and temporarily – spiders, grasshoppers and, if the right plants are chosen, other "flying insects" such as wild bees, butterflies and hoverflies. Extensive greenery can also provide permanent meadows for bees and butterflies. Greened roofs are also ideal for birds as a space protected against cats, dogs, foxes and the like.

Façade greenery is an eating place, a nesting space and a catching place, a sunny or shady space, a hiding space, protection from the weather, a place for pupation, a viewing platform and mating grounds all rolled into one. With its mass of foliage, nectar, pollen and fruit, it provides invaluable nutrition and a habitat for birds, insects, spiders and butterflies, for example. Through the food chain, a natural balance arises.

NICOLE PFOSER

———
Illustration nach/*Illustration after*
Doernach 1982

Argumente für und Ressentiments gegen Gebäudegrün

Arguments for and prejudices against building greenery

Are there specific fears among architects as regards opting for plants?

Gibt es spezifische Ängste in der Architektenschaft hinsichtlich des Einsatzes von Pflanzen?

Für Architekten und Ingenieure ist es eine Herausforderung, mit der relativen Unberechenbarkeit von Pflanzen umzugehen. Wofür planen sie denn: für den Erstbepflanzungszustand, für ein mittleres Wachstum oder für eine späte Wachstumsphase? Außerdem lenkt das Pflanzenwachstum stark von der „Architektursprache" ab, wenn nicht „grüne Architektur" selbst das Gestaltungsziel ist. Denn Landschaftsarchitekten gestalten sehr wohl mit Pflanzen. Unbehagen beim entwerferischen Einsatz von Pflanzen entsteht bei manchen Planern aus Unkenntnis: Es ist eine eigene „Disziplin", auf die man sich einlassen muss. Auch müssen sie die Qualität der Veränderung als Chance begreifen und nicht als Bedrohung. Doch das kann man lernen, wenn man bereit ist, sich darauf einzulassen.

For architects and engineers, it is a real challenge to handle the relative unpredictability of plants. What are they planning for? For the status at first planting or for a later growth phase? Moreover, the plant growth detracts strongly from the "architectural idiom" if the "green architecture" is not itself the objective of the design proposal. After all, landscape architects rely heavily on plants in their designs. The one or other planner feels uncomfortable incorporating plants in proposals out of a lack of knowledge: It is a "discipline" in its own right that is involved. Yet they must accept the quality of change as an opportunity and not as a threat, although that is something you can learn only if you are willing to embark on the journey.
RUDI SCHEUERMANN

Was kann Gebäudegrün gestalterisch im Stadtraum leisten?

RAUMBILDUNG / *CREATING THE SPACE*

Platzabschluss
Outer edges

Zonierung
Zoning

Raumkontur, Raumteilung
Spatial contours and division

Hofbildung
Creating inner courtyard

LENKUNG / *MANAGEMENT*

Zentrierung, Aktivierung
Centering, activation

Markierung, Wegführung
Markings, routes

Initialisierung, Motivation
Initializing, motivating

Zusammenfassung, Blickpunkte
Summary, eye-catchers

WIRKUNG IM STADTRAUM
IMPACT IN URBAN SPACE

Ensemblebildung
Creation of ensembles

Blickpunkt, Fernwirkung
Eye-catchers, effect from distance

Alleinstellungsmerkmal
Unique selling point

Gliederung, Verkürzung der Längenwirkung
Structure, shortening the vanishing point

Blicklenkung, Verkürzung der Tiefenwirkung
Guiding the eye, shortening the sense of depth

Längsgliederung, Verstärkung der Tiefenwirkung
Structuring lengthways, strengthening the sense of depth

Quergliederung, Verstärkung der Höhenwirkung
Cross structuring, strengthening the sense of height

Staffelung, optische Höhenbegrenzung
Staggering, limiting the visual sense of height

What can greened buildings contribute to the design of the urban fabric?

PROPORTION, RHYTHMUS, MODULARITÄT
PROPORTIONS, RHYTHM, MODULARITY

Horizontale Gliederung, Längung
Horizontal structure, lengthening

Vertikale Gliederung, Überhöhung
Vertical structure, creating a greater sense of height

Blockhaft
Block-like

Reduktion der Fläche durch Schraffur
Reduction of the area by cross-hatching

KUBATUR / *VOLUME*

Öffnung des Erdgeschosses, Eingangssituation
Opening out the ground floor, entrance situation

Abschottung des Erdgeschosses
Isolating the ground floor

Stärkung des oberen Abschlusses
Strengthening the upper closed edge

Zwischenhöhe, Vermittelnde Zwischenhöhe
Intermediate level

RAUMBILDUNG, PLASTIZITÄT
CREATING SPACE AND A SENSE OF THREE DIMENSIONS

Sicht- und Sonnenschutz
Sight and sun protection

Schichtung, Tiefe
Layering, depth

Integration
Integration

Balkone, Loggien: Privatheit
Balconies, loggia: privacy

KONTRASTBILDUNG / *CREATING CONTRASTS*

Geometrie/Pflanzen
Geometry/plants

Betonung einer Rhythmik
Emphasizing a rhythm

Signal, Werbezeichen
Signals, advertising symbols

Betonung einzelner Flächen
Emphasizing individual areas

Illustrationen nach / *Illustrations after*
Pfoser 2018

Ist es eine Leistung des Gebäudegrüns, die Grenzen zwischen privat und öffentlich zu verwischen bzw. zu verunklären und neue Wohlfühloasen zu schaffen?

Wenn man so will: ja. Mit dem Blick von oben, aus der Vogelperspektive, gibt es keine Unterschiede zwischen privatem und öffentlichem Grün. Man erkennt grüne Oasen in den Blockinnenbereichen, die man in der Hitze der Sommer-tage nicht erreicht. Die Definition sogenannter teilöffentlicher Räume, die sich eingeschränkt für bestimmte Nutzungen (Park, Café) und bestimmte Tages-zeiten (tagsüber) für die Allgemeinheit öffnen und dann abends wieder aus-schließlich den Anliegern bzw. Anwohnern zur Verfügung stehen, können so das Angebot von erholsamem Grün in der Stadt deutlich erhöhen.

Der Effekt begrünter Fassaden und Höfe wirkt über das Gebäude hinaus in seine Umgebung und damit in den öffentlichen Raum hinein. Die unmittelbare Nachbarschaft profitiert mehr von einer kühlen, grünen Pflanzenwand als von einer wärmespeichernden Marmorfassadenverkleidung und erhöht in der Regel die Aufenthaltsqualität.

Is one achievement of building greenery the fact that it blurs the line dividing the public from the private, or rather makes it unclear, while at the same time creating feel-good oases?

You could say that, yes. Seen from above, i.e., from a bird's eye perspective, there is no difference between private and public green. You can discern the green oases inside the blocks of buildings that are otherwise inaccessible in the heat of a summer's day. The definition of so-called semi-public spaces that are only open to the public to a limited extent for specific usages (parks, cafés) and at certain times of day (daytime) and are then exclusively available to local residents and neighbors in the evening can thus significantly enhance the provision of recreational greenery in a city.

The effect of greened façades and courtyards has a favorable impact not just on buildings themselves but on the vicinity and thus on public space. The immediate neighborhood benefits more from a cool, green wall of plants than it does from heat-retaining marble façade cladding, and as a rule boasts a better quality of life.

HANS-GEORG DANNERT

Wann ist der beste Zeitpunkt für die Planung für Gebäudegrün?

Im Neubau sollte Grün von der ersten Planungssitzung an zusammen mit den Architekten bedacht werden. So kann das Potenzial beider Gestaltungsebenen am besten ausgeschöpft und am kostengünstigsten umgesetzt werden. Bei Architekturwettbewerben zeigt sich eine neue Tendenz: Architekur, Freiraumplanung und Gebäudebegrünung werden von Beginn an als eine Einheit behandelt. Die Begrünung der Gebäudehülle wird zunehmend in die energetischen und klimatischen Berechnungen eingebunden.

When is the best point in time to plan greening a building?

With new builds, the greenery should be considered from the very first planning meeting onwards, in consultation with the architects. In that way, the potential of both levels of design can best be exploited and realized in a cost-effective manner. A new trend is emerging in architecture competitions: Architecture, open space planning and building greenery are being treated as a unit from Day One. The greening of a building's outer skin is increasingly factored into the energy consumption and climate calculations.

GERHARD ZEMP

Ist das nicht teuer? Mit welchen Kosten ist zu rechnen?

Zu den Dachbegrünungen: Wenn wir alle „harten" und „weichen" Faktoren berücksichtigen, dann rechnet sich eine Dachbegrünung durch ihre vielfältigen Leistungen wie z.B. Schutz der Dachabdichtung, Hitze- und Kälteschutz, Verdunstungskühlung, Wasserrückhalt und Entlastung der Kanalisation, – und damit keine kostenaufwendigen Regenüberlaufbecken.

Und mit einem begehbaren Dachgarten ist das schon gekaufte Grundstück ein zweites Mal zusätzlich nutzbar: Ein Quadratmeter Dachgarten (Intensivnutzung) kostet etwa 80–150 € – wo bekommt man noch so günstig ein Grundstück mit Garten!? Eine Extensivbegrünung des Dachgartens liegt bei 20–40 €/m². Die Kosten werden pro Quadratmeter geringer, je größer die zu begrünende Fläche ist. Umgerechnet belaufen sich die Herstellungskosten bei Gebäuden unter sechs Geschossen auf circa 1,5 Prozent der Bauwerkskosten, bei höheren Gebäuden circa 0,4 Prozent.[9]

On greening roofs: If we consider all the "hard" and "soft" factors, then a greened roof pays off thanks to its various characteristics, such as the protection of the roof's seals, thermal insulation, evaporation cooling, water retention, relief of the sewage system – and thus no cost-intensive rain overflow basins.

And a roof garden enables a person to additionally use the plot a second time: A square meter of roof garden (used intensively) costs about €80–150 – where else do you get a plot with a garden so cost-effectively?! Extensive greening of a roof garden costs in the range of 20–40€/m². The larger the greened area is, the more the outlays per square meter fall. The price tag in the case of buildings with less than six stories comes to about 1.5 percent of the construction costs, with the figure dropping to approx. 0.4 percent in higher buildings.[9]

How economic is greenery in architecture?

9   Freie und Hansestadt Hamburg, Behörde für Umwelt und Energie (Hg./*Ed.*), Hamburgs Gründächer. Eine ökonomische Bewertung, Hamburg 2017; ders. (Hg.)/*id. (Ed.)*, Dachbegrünung. Leitfaden zur Planung, Hamburg 2019.

Die Pflegekosten liegen etwa bei 1–3 € bei extensiven und etwa 3–10 € bei intensiven Dachbegrünungen. Einsparungen lassen sich durch den Wasserrückhalt und die Entlastung der Kanalisation erzielen: Schon eine extensive Dachbegrünung kann etwa 40–70 Prozent des Jahresniederschlags zurückhalten und etwa bis zu 30 l/m² im Aufbau speichern. Im Rahmen der gesplitteten Abwassersatzung gibt es oft eine Gebührenminderung von etwa 0,50 €/m², wenn das Dach begrünt ist.[10] Ein Beispiel: 5.000 m² Dachbegrünung können mit Regenwassernutzung und dem Kühlungseffekt bis zu 6.000 € Stromkosten im Jahr einsparen.

Maintenance costs come to about €1–3 for extensive roof gardens and about €3–10 for intensive roof greenery per square meter. Roof greenery offers savings in the form of water retention and less use of the drainage system: Extensive roof greening can itself retain about 40–70 percent of the annual precipitation and store up to 30 l/m² in the superstructure. As part of split waste water levies, fees are often reduced by about 0.50 €/m² if a roof is greened.[10] An example: 5,000 m² of roof greenery can, thanks to the use of rain water and the cooling effect, save up to €6,000 in electricity bills each year.

GUNTER MANN

---

10 Felix Mollenhauer, Gunter Mann, Kosten-Nutzen-Betrachtungen von Dachbegrünungen,
    in: Gebäude-Grün, Berlin 4/2018, S./p. 20–23.

Einsparungen und Kostenreduktion durch Fassadenbegrünung

Saving and costs reductions based on greening façades

TEMPERATUR/*TEMPERATURE*

Vermeidung der Aufheizung der Wand
‣ **Reduktion der Kühlkosten**
Avoidance of heating up the wall and saving of cooling costs
‣ *Reducing cooling costs*

Wärmehaltung durch Reduktion des Wärmeverlusts der Wand
‣ **Reduktion der Heizkosten**
Heat retention by reducing the heat loss from the wall
‣ *Reducing heating costs*

LICHT/*LIGHT*

Sonnenschutz für Wand und Fenster
‣ **Ersatz für technischen Sonnenschutz**
Sun protection for walls and windows
‣ *Substitutes for technical sun protection*

LÜFTUNG *VENTILATION*

Kühlung der Zuluft im Sommer / Pufferwirkung der Zuluft im Winter
‣ **Ersatz für Klimageräte**
Cooling of the supply air in summer / buffer effect of the supply air in winter
‣ *Substitute for air conditioning*

WASSER *WATER*

Nutzung von Regenwasser und Einsparung von Trinkwasser
‣ **Einsparung von Trinkwasser**
Use of rainwater and saving of drinking water
‣ *Saving potable water*

ÖKOBILANZ UND BESTANDS-SCHUTZ/*ECOLOGICAL BALANCE AND PROTECTION OF THE BUILDING STOCK*

Bauteilschutz u.a. vor UV-Strahlung, O_2-Produktion und Feinstaubfilterung
‣ **Lebensdauerverlängerung von Baumaterial**
Component protection, etc. against UV radiation, O_2 production and fine dust filtering
‣ *Extended service life of the construction materials*

Illustrationen nach/*Illustrations after*
Pfoser 2018

Und wer soll das dann pflegen? Welcher Aufwand entsteht in den kommenden Jahren?

And who has to care for it all? What effort is required in future years?

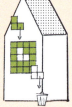

NACHPFLANZUNG
REPLANTING

Pflanzenaustausch ist vermeidbar bei angemessener Versorgung der Vegetation, Auswahl der Pflanzen ist entscheidend
Replacing plants can be avoided if the vegetation is duly supplied with nutrients and water; plant choice is decisive in this regard

BEWÄSSERUNG UND NÄHRSTOFFVERSORGUNG
WATERING AND PROVISION OF NUTRIENTS

Austrocknen und hohe Feuchtigkeit hängen von der Positionierung der Fassade ab. Südseiten oder stark besonnte Fassaden brauchen mehr Wasser und höhere Nähstoffversorgung. Nordseiten und beschattete Fassadenlagen können zu feucht werden und benötigen eine niedrigere Nährstoffversorgung.
Whether plants dry out or receive a lot of moisture depends on the alignment of the façade. South sides or façades strongly in the sun require more water and nutrients. North sides or façades in the shade may become moist and require fewer nutrient inputs.

TRAGLAST
LOAD

Rankhilfe entsprechend der Traglast der Bepflanzung, Nachjustieren bei Materialverfall
Trellises for vines in line with the load posed by the plants; recalibrate if the materials deteriorate over time

---

Illustrationen nach/*Illustrations after*
Pfoser 2018

VERSORGUNG UND ENTSORGUNG BODENGEBUNDENER BEGRÜNUNG
PROVIDING FOR/DISPOSAL OF GROUND-BASED GREENERY

▸ Einfache Versorgung
▸ *Simple provisions*

Wasserversorgung durch gesammeltes Regenwasser (Zisterne), evtl. durch zusätzliches Brauchwasser (Wasseranschluss für künstliche Bewässerung), Laub fällt ab und bildet Nährstoffe für den Boden oder wird kompostiert
Water supply using collected rainwater (cisterns), possibly using additional process water (water connection for artificial watering) Foliage is shed and forms nutrients for the soil or gets composted

VERSORGUNG UND ENTSORGUNG WANDGEBUNDENER BEGRÜNUNG
PROVIDING FOR/DISPOSAL OF WALL-BASED GREENERY

▸ Diverse Versorgungstechniken
▸ *Various different ways of providing*

**Wasser- und Nährstoffversorgung über Systeme, die je nach Gegebenheiten den Verbrauch regeln.
Ableitung des Überlaufwassers
Entsorgung des Grünabfalls
Steuerung durch Sensoren
Stromanschluss notwendig
(gegebenenfalls durch PV-Anlage)**
*Water and nutrient supply using systems that adjust consumption depending on the conditions.
Run-off water drained
Green waste disposed of
Controlled by sensors
Electrical connection needed
(possibly via the PV plant)*

ERREICHBARKEIT
ACCESSIBILITY

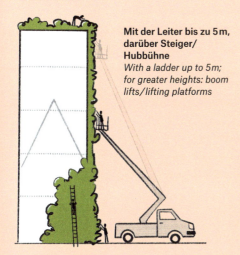

Mit der Leiter bis zu 5 m, darüber Steiger/ Hubbühne
With a ladder up to 5m; for greater heights: boom lifts/lifting platforms

SCHNITT
PRUNING

Entfernen von Totholz und Wildbewuchs an Fenstern, Türen und Dachanschlüssen
Removing dead wood and rampant growth at windows, doors and roof seams/gutters

Grünpflanzen produzieren Grünabfall. Wer soll sich darum kümmern?

Die Blätter der vertikalen Begrünungen an der Fassade sind vergänglich und können absterben. Die Pflanzen müssen zur Erhaltung in Form geschnitten oder verjüngt werden, damit das optische Gesamtbild erhalten bleibt. Die Windlast und der damit verbundene Bruch auf große Grünflächen sowie das Gesamtgewicht sind wichtige und nicht zu unterschätzende Faktoren. Bei regelmäßiger und fachgerechter Pflege stellen diese aber kein Problem dar. Wichtig ist, dass die Arbeiten anhand einer Checkliste und eines regelmäßigen Monitorings überprüft werden. Übrigens: Der Grünabfall ist kompostierbar und fügt sich somit rückstandslos wieder in die Natur ein.

Green plants produce green waste. Who should take care of it?

The leaves of vertical greenery on façades are transient and can die, so the plants need to be trimmed or tapered to retain their shape and thus the overall visual impression. The wind load and the related leaves and branches for large spaces of greenery and the overall weight are all important factors that should not be underestimated but, assuming the correct regular care, these do not present a problem. The key is to regularly monitor the work done by means of a checklist. Incidentally: The green waste can be composted and thus perfectly reintroduced into the natural cycle.

ALEXANDER HILDEBRAND

Und im Winter sieht dann alles fürchterlich aus! Die paar Monate Sommer in Deutschland ...

And everything looks awful in winter! These few summer months in Germany ...

Ganzjähriges Grün gibt es nur in den milden Klimazonen des Mittelmeers, der Tropen und Suptropen. Die Vegetation in Deutschland und ganz Mitteleuropa ist vom Kontinentalklima bestimmt und damit durch die Besonderheit und Schönheit der vier Jahreszeiten geprägt. Eine Methode, um mit dem Laubverlust im Herbst umzugehen, ohne dass sich die gesamte Fassade verändert, ist eine partielle Integration von Pflanzen. Darüber hinaus gibt es Gräser und immergrüne Gehölze z.B. einheimische Wacholderarten, die auch den winterlichen Garten gestalten und ebenso in der Gebäudebegrünung eingesetzt werden können.

Only plants in the mild climatic zones of the Mediterranean, the Tropics and the Sub-Tropics remain green all year round. The vegetation in Germany and all of Central Europe is defined by the continental climate and therefore by the characteristics and beauty of the four seasons. A method of handling the leaf shedding in autumn and prevent the entire façade from changing is to partially integrate plants. Moreover, one can choose grasses and evergreen bushes (for example indigenous types of juniper) that give a fine look to gardens in winter and can likewise be used to green buildings.

GERHARD ZEMP

Wie ökologisch ist
Grün an der
Gebäudehülle?
Wenn man den
Wasserverbrauch
mit einberechnet,
die Substrate,
das Material ...

How ecological
is greenery attached to
the outside of a building?
If one factors the water
consumption into the
equation, the substrates,
the material ...

Nicht weniger ökologisch als andere Baustoffe. Extensive Dachbegrünungen benötigen kein bis wenig Frischwasser, bei Intensivbegrünungen wird viel Regenwasser genutzt. Die eingesetzten Substrate beruhen in der Regel auf natürlichen Materialien und Recyclingstoffen, die Erdenwerke stammen aus der Region, wodurch sich die Transportwege verkürzen. Und die zum Einsatz kommenden Vliese (Polypropylen) stammen in der Regel aus Recyclingmaterial.

No less ecological than other construction materials. Extensive roof greenery requires little to no fresh water; intensive greenery needs a lot of rainwater. The substrates used tend to involve natural materials and recycled materials, while the earth is local, reducing transportation. And the non-wovens used (polypropylene) tend likewise to be recycled material.
GUNTER MANN

Aluminium ist ein gängiges Material zur Herstellung von Fassadensystemen und Dächern. Auch für die Begrünung kann es eine wichtige Rolle einnehmen. Wie steht es um die Nachhaltigkeit von Aluminum im Bauwesen?

Ein traditionell wichtiges Material beim Bau von Gebäudefassaden ist das endlos oft und in gleichbleibender Qualität recycelbare Aluminium – 200.000.000 Tonnen davon stecken heute in Bauwerken weltweit. Gerade vor dem Hintergrund der energieintensiven Herstellung ist es wichtig, die hierfür benötigten Energieträger und Optionen zu betrachten – nachhaltige und zukunftsgerechte Konzepte sind daher gefragter denn je. Genau an dieser Stelle setzt das Aluminiumsystemhaus WICONA mit Hydro CIRCAL 75R an. Diese eigens entwickelte Aluminiumlegierung besteht aus einem Mindestanteil von 75 Prozent End-of-Life-Aluminium (Altschrott). Das bedeutet: Ein Großteil des verwendeten Aluminiums war bereits 30 Jahre oder länger in Fenstern, Türen oder Fassaden verbaut, wurde nach der Demontage gesammelt und der Wiederverwertung zugeführt.

Hydro CIRCAL 75R benötigt bei der Herstellung im Vergleich zu Primäraluminium nur 5 Prozent des Energieaufwands – bei gleich hoher Qualität. In einem speziellen Prozess wird das Aluminium so wiederaufbereitet, dass es zur Produktion neuer, hochwertiger Profilsysteme dient. Seit WICONA 2019 damit begonnen hat, seine Aluminiumprofilsysteme auf diese Aluminiumlegierung umzustellen, konnten bereits über 40.000 Tonnen CO_2 einspart werden[11] – das ist gleichbedeutend mit circa 200 Millionen weniger gefahrenen Autokilometern. Letztendlich lässt sich durch diese Innovation beim Fassadenbau eine deutliche CO_2- und Ressourceneinsparung erreichen. Dies ist vor allem im Sinne der von Investoren und Bauherren verstärkt nachgefragten Nachhaltigkeitszertifizierungen (z.B. DGNB) für ihre Gebäude. Eine ideale Lösung also für das „grüne" und nachhaltige Bauen in der Zukunft.

Aluminum is a traditionally important material in the construction of building façades, which can be recycled endlessly and the quality consistently maintained. 200,000,000 tons of such recycled aluminum are now in use in buildings worldwide. Especially given that producing aluminum is a very energy-intensive process, it is important to consider the energy sources and options required for this – sustainable and future-oriented concepts are therefore in greater demand than ever. This is precisely the starting point for the WICONA aluminum system house which features Hydro CIRCAL 75R. This specially developed aluminum alloy consists of a minimum proportion of 75 percent end-of-life aluminum (old scrap). This means that a large proportion of the aluminum used has already been utilized in windows, doors or façades for 30 years or longer, was collected after dismantling, and then recycled.

Compared to primary aluminum, Hydro CIRCAL 75R requires only 5 percent of the energy inputs for production – while retaining the selfsame high quality. In a special process, the aluminum is reprocessed in such a way that it can be used to produce new, high-quality profile systems. Since 2019, WICONA has been switching its aluminum profiles over to this aluminum alloy, and more than 40,000 tons of CO_2 emissions have already been avoided[11] – which is equivalent to around 200 million fewer car kilometers driven. Ultimately, this innovation in façade construction has resulted in a significant reduction in CO_2 emissions and resource use. This is particularly in line with the increasing wish among investors and developers that their buildings receive sustainability certification (e.g., DGNB). In other words, it is an ideal solution for "green" and sustainable buildings going forward.

WERNER JAGER

Aluminum is a material frequently used for making façade systems and roofs. It can also play a key role in greening buildings. How sustainable is aluminum as a material used in the building industry?

---

11   Vergleich Herstellung von Aluminium-Recyclat/Primäraluminium (European Aluminium 2018 Report):
      a) 2,3 kg CO_2-Emission/kg Aluminium-Recyclat
      b) 8,6 kg CO_2/kg Primär-Aluminium, hergestellt mit EU Energiemix (cradle to gate)
      c) 12,7 kg CO_2/kg, mit WORLD-Energiemix
      d) 20,0 kg CO_2/kg, mit CN-Energiemix
      Comparison production of aluminum recyclate/primary aluminum (European Aluminum 2018 Report):
      a) 2,3kg CO_2 emission/kg aluminum recyclate
      b) 8,6kg CO_2/kg primary aluminum, produced with EU energy mix (cradle to gate)
      c) 12,7kg CO_2/kg, with WORLD energy mix
      d) 20,0kg CO_2/kg, with CN energy mix

Wie viel Wasser benötigt eine Dach- und eine Fassadenbegrünung?

Nachdem eine geschlossene Pflanzendeckung bei einer klassischen Extensivbegrünung stattgefunden hat, erhält sich diese bei „normalen" Witterungsverhältnissen selbst. Voraussetzung ist, dass unter den Pflanzen ein Systemaufbau mit Drainageelement liegt, das Wasser speichert und es im Bedarfsfall durch Diffusion an das darüber liegende Substrat abgibt.

Grundsätzlich hängt der Wassergebrauch vom Gründach- bzw. Fassadenbegrünungsaufbau und vom Witterungsverlauf respektive der Jahreszeit ab. Eine extensive Dachbegrünung verbraucht im Sommer etwa 2–4 l/m² am Tag, eine intensive Dachbegrünung – und so ähnlich auch wandgebundene Fassadenbegrünungen – etwa 4–8 l/m².

How much water does a greened roof/ greened façade require?

If, as in the case of classic extensive greenery, the roof is completely covered by planting, then under "normal" weather it will tend for itself. The key is that beneath the plants there is a systemic structure with drainage elements that stores water and if required releases it by diffusion into the substrate above it.

Essentially, the water consumption of greened roof/façade structures depends on the course of the weather and/or season. Extensive roof greenery consumes about 2–4 l/m² a day in summer whereas intensive roof greenery (and the same applies for wall-bound façade greenery) requires about 4–8 l/m².

GUNTER MANN / JOACHIM STROH

Eine wichtige Frage ist die Bewässerung. Wie lässt sich der Einsatz von Leitungs- wasser reduzieren?

Wird über den natürlichen Niederschlag hinaus eine Bewässerung der Begrü-nung erforderlich, ist nach Möglichkeit ebenfalls Regenwasser einzusetzen. Vorteilhaft ist die Regenwasserzwischenspeicherung in einer Zisterne. Eine Alternative stellt die Nutzung von Grauwasser dar. Hierbei werden gering verschmutzte Abwässer (z.B. aus Dusche, Badewanne, Waschmaschine) in einem unabhängigen Leitungsnetz über einen Grobfilter zum Tanksystem geführt. Dort erfolgt eine zweistufige Reinigung: eine biologische Aufberei-tung durch Mikroorganismen (Abbau organischer Stoffe) sowie die physikali-sche Reinigung durch einen feinen Membranfilter, der Bakterien zurückhält. Eine Trinkwassernachspeisung kommt hinzu. Die Entnahme erfolgt durch eine Pumpe über eine Steuer- und Regeltechnik.

A key question is the watering. How can you reduce the use of mains water?

If the greenery requires watering over and above natural precipitation, then wherever possible rainwater should be used. It is advantageous to store rainwater in a cistern in the interim. An alternative is to use grey water, meaning less sullied wastewater (e.g., from the shower, bathtub, washing machine) that is fed via an independent piping grid and a coarse filter into a tank. There, a two-stage purifi-cation process ensues: biological treatment by micro-organisms (breaking down organic compounds) and physical purification using a fine membrane filter that retains the bacteria. Potable water is also fed into the tank. Control technology then determines when water can be extracted by a pump.

NICOLE PFOSER

Was leistet Dachbegrünung für die Reduktion von Nieder- schlagswasser?

Der Regenwasserrückhalt durch den Einsatz von Gebäudebegrünung wird durch die Stadt oder Kommune finanziell gefördert, indem Abwassergebühren gesenkt werden. Die Gebühren für die Einleitung des Niederschlagwassers werden über die anteiligen Flächen und deren Abflussbeiwert, das heißt den Versiegelungsgrad, auf dem Grundstück bemessen. Die Niederschlagswassergebühr ist ein Teil der gesplitteten Abwassergebühr, die neben dem Einleiten von Schmutzwasser erhoben wird. Flächen wie Gründächer, die keinen oder nur einen geringen Beitrag zum Abfluss des Niederschlagswassers leisten, müssen nicht oder nur anteilig bei der Bemessung der Gebühr angesetzt werden. Bei intensiven Dachbegrünungen beträgt der Wasserrückhalt je nach Aufbau 60–99 Prozent der Niederschlagsmenge bei einer Speicherfähigkeit von 30–160 l/m². Aber auch schon bei extensiven Substraten können im Jahresmittel circa 75–90 Prozent der Gesamtniederschlagsmenge zurückgehalten werden.[12] Hierdurch sind die Voraussetzungen für einen völligen Entfall der Dachwassereinleitung in die Kanalisation verbessert.

---

12   Walter Kolb, Abflussverhältnisse extensiv begrünter Flachdächer, in: Zeitschrift für Vegetationstechnik 3/1987, S./p. 111–115;
     Hans-Joachim Liesecke, Untersuchungen zur Wasserrückhaltung extensiv begrünter Flachdächer, in: Zeitschrift für Vegetationstechnik
     2/1988, S./p. 56–66. Manfred Köhler, Stadtökologie: Ökologische Untersuchungen an extensiven Dachbegrünungen, in: Verhandlungen
     der Gesellschaft für Ökologie, 18/1989, S./p. 249–255.

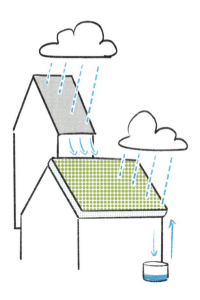

Regen auf ein herkömmlich gedecktes Dach und auf ein begrüntes Dach. Oberflächenabluss, Übertragung des gesammelten Regenwassers auf Dachbegrünung (Retention) und Verdunstungsleistung
Rain on a customary tiled roof and on a greened roof. The surface run-off, the retention of the rainwater thus collected by the roof greenery and the evaporation output.

How does roof greenery reduce precipitation water?

Rainwater retention by means of building greenery is something the municipality or local authority can financially support by lowering sewage charges. The fees for introducing rainwater are calculated according to the pro-rated surface area and the drainage value assigned to them, meaning the degree of sealed surfaces for the plot as a whole. The rainwater charges are a component in the overall sewage fees charged alongside the fees for wastewater. Surfaces such as greened roofs that contribute little or no rainwater to the volume drained need not be included in calculation of the fees, or only to a pro-rated extent. Depending on the structure used, intensive roof greenery can spell retention of 60–99 percent of the rainwater volume with a storage factor of 30–160 l/m². Indeed, the use of extensive substrates alone can already lead to retention on an annual average of some 75–90 percent of the total precipitation volume.[12] This improves the preconditions for complete elimination of any water being fed from the roofs into the drains.

NICOLE PFOSER

Schäden sind nicht primär auf die Begrünung selbst zurückzuführen. Sie können durch eine fehlerfreie Planung und eine regelmäßige pflanzengerechte Pflege und Wartung vermieden werden.

Gebäudevorschäden in Form von Rissen oder Bauweisen mit offenen Fugen verlangen eine sorgfältige Auswahl geeigneter Begrünungstechniken. Massive Außenwände (gedämmt oder ungedämmt), die intakt sind, mit geschlossenen Fugen und pflanzenphysiologisch geeignetem Haftgrund, eignen sich zur Direktbegrünung. Alle anderen Konstruktionen mit Fugen (z.B. Ständer- und Fachwerkbauweise, mehrschalige nicht hinterlüftete oder hinterlüftete Wandaufbauten, Luftkollektorfassaden) erfordern eine separate Pflanzebene (Gerüstkletterpflanzen oder vorgehängt hinterlüftete wandgebundene Begrünungen).

Zerstören Pflanzen Fassaden und Putze?

Begrünungen setzen eine Kosten-Nutzen-Klärung der Erwartungen (Gestaltung, Ökologie, Energie) voraus, ebenso der Bautechnik (Gebäudesubstanz, Begrünungssystem, Statik), der rechtlichen Einbindung (Baurecht, Brandlast, Nachbarrecht, Zugänglichkeit) und der Versorgung der künftigen Begrünung mit Nährstoffen und Wasser. Bestimmte Eigenschaften von Pflanzen, wie zum Beispiel die Wuchsform, Wuchshöhe und Wuchskraft, das End-/Fruchtgewicht, Dickenwachstum und eventuell lichtfliehende Eigenschaften sowie die Pflanzenbedürfnisse (z.B. Sonne/Schatten, Wasserbedarf und -qualität, Bodeneigenschaften) sind bei der Planung zu beachten. Hilfskonstruktionen sollten auf die Lebensdauer des Pflanzenbewuchses ausgerichtet sein. Hingegen schützen fachgerecht ausgeführte und gepflegte Begrünungen sogar die Bausubstanz vor Witterungseinflüssen, UV-Strahlung und Temperaturextremen und verlängern so deren Lebensdauer.

Do plants destroy façades and plaster?

Damage cannot primarily be attributed to the greenery itself and can be avoided with error-free planning and regular care and maintenance aligned to the specific types of plants.

Prior damage to buildings in the form of cracks or structures built with open joints calls for a careful choice of suitable greening techniques. Solid outside walls (insulated or not) that are intact, have sealed joints and a backing that is suitable for plants to attach to are appropriate for direct greenery. All other structures with joints (e.g., post-and-beam and half-timbered buildings, multi-envelope, non back-ventilated or back-ventilated wall structures, or air collector curtain façades) require a separate plant level (plants that climb on trellises or suspended, back-ventilated, greenery attached to the wall).

Greenery must rest on an analysis of the cost/benefits as regards expectations (design, ecology, energy) and likewise of the building technology (built substance, greening system, load-bearing properties), legal conditions (building permission, fire load, rights of neighbors, accessibility) and nutrients and water supply to the future plants. Certain plant properties, such as the shape in which and speed at which they grow, their height, their final weight and/or the weight of fruit, secondary growth and potentially light-receding properties as well as plant needs (e.g., sun/shade, water quantity and quality, soil properties) all need to be factored into planning. Frames and the like need to be designed to last the life of the plants. Duly realized greenery that is properly tended protects the building's substance from the impact of weather, UV radiation and extreme temperatures and thus extends its service life.

NICOLE PFOSER

Was macht der wilde Wein mit dem Putz?

Wilder Wein hat den Ruf, mit seinem Haftscheiben Mauer-
werk zu schädigen. Das trifft meist nur auf alten, porösen
Verputz zu. In der Regel führt er kaum zu Beschädigungen.
Möchte man den Wein allerdings abnehmen, bleiben die
Haftscheiben als kleine schwarze Punkte zurück. Sie
verwittern nur langsam und fallen über die Jahre ab.
Die Jungfernrebe ist kein Selbstklimmer, sondern eine
Rankpflanze – und damit eine Art des wilden Weins, die
Bauschäden ausschließt.

Ist Begrünung schlecht für Allergiker?

Das hängt immer von der Bepflanzung
ab – ganz egal ob am Gebäude oder in
Parks und Gärten.

Virginia creeper has a reputation for damaging masonry with its holdfast pads. That is usually only the case with old, porous plaster. As a rule, there is hardly any damage. However, if you wish to remove the creeper then the holdfast pads remain behind as little black dots. They take time to weather and drop off in the course of the years. The climbing Virginia creeper is not a self-climber, but a climbing plant – and thus a kind of creeper that excludes damage to buildings.

HILDE STROBL

What does Virginia creeper do to the plaster?

Is greening bad for allergy sufferers?

That always depends on the planting – no matter whether on buildings or in parks and gardens.

Pflanzenkunde zum Gebäudegrün

Plant lore for building greenery

Über Stadtpflanzen und Pflanzengesellschaften

Welche Standortfaktoren sind in deutschen Städten ausschlaggebend für die Wahl der Pflanzen zur Gebäudebegrünung?

What location factors in German cities are key as regards choosing the plants for building greenery?

AvB Ausschlaggebend sind zum einen die Klima- und Lichtverhältnisse. Für Pflanzen sind die größten Herausforderungen Wetterextreme wie Hitzestress und Wassermangel in sehr heißen und trockenen Sommermonaten in Abwechslung mit Unwettern. Diese Phänomene treten durch den Klimawandel immer häufiger auf. Die Lage am Gebäude, das heißt die Sonnenausrichtung sowie die Gebäudehöhe in Bezug auf den Wind, sowie Wärmequellen wie die Abluft von Klimaanlagen können verstärkend oder abmildernd auf die Faktoren einwirken. Hinzu kommen die Frostperioden im Winter; besonders gefährlich sind die Früh- beziehungsweise Spätfröste, wenn sich die Pflanzen noch nicht oder nicht mehr in der Winterruhe befinden. Hier haben es tropische Städte wie Singapur mit der hohen Luftfeuchte und milderen Temperaturen leichter.

Ein weiterer Punkt ist der verfügbare Wurzelraum, der den Wasserspeicher, den Nährstoffgehalt und nicht zuletzt den Raum zum Festhalten der Pflanze beeinflusst. Wenn für die Pflanze kein Boden vor einem Gebäude zur Verfügung steht, sind der Substratumfang

AvB Most crucial are the climatic and lighting conditions. For plants, the greatest challenges are extreme weather, such as heat stress and the lack of water in extremely hot and dry summer months, and these alternating with storms. These phenomena occur ever more frequently owing to climate change. Conditions on the building, meaning the alignment to the path of the sun, the height of the building in relation to the wind, and heat sources such as the extractor ducts from air conditioning systems, can intensify or milden the impact of these factors. Then there are frost periods in winter, whereby the early and late frost periods are especially dangerous, since at those points the plants have not yet gone into hibernation. In this regard, tropical cities such as Singapore, with its high humidity and milder temperatures, have an easier time of it.

Another factor is the space available for the roots, as this influences water storage, the nutrition in the soil and not least the space to hold the plants in place. If there is no soil in front of a building for the plant, then the scope of substrate and the planting system to be used have a bearing on the choice of plant.

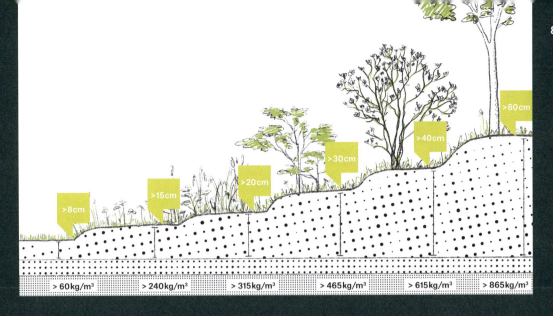

>8cm
>15cm
>20cm
>30cm
>40cm
>60cm

> 60kg/m³   > 240kg/m³   > 315kg/m³   > 465kg/m³   > 615kg/m³   > 865kg/m³

About city plants and plant communities

und das verwendete Pflanzsystem bei der Pflanzenwahl zu berücksichtigen. Standort-nachteile können mit einem entsprechen-den Pflegeaufwand wie Bewässern, Düngen, Verankern und sogar Beheizen ausgegli-chen werden. Hierbei ist zu bedenken, dass dadurch stark vom Menschen abhängige Systeme geschaffen werden und der Kosten-Nutzen-Aufwand relevant ist.

The disadvantages of certain locations can be offset by corresponding care, such as watering, fertilizing, anchoring, and even heating. It bears considering here that this gives rise to systems that depend strongly on human intervention and the cost/benefit ratio needs to be taken into account.

Welche Pflanzen eignen sich besonders für ein begrüntes Dach?

What plants are especially suited to a greened roof?

AvB   Im Prinzip sind hier keine Grenzen gesetzt, wenn die statischen Voraussetzun-gen gegeben sind. Auf überbauten Tief-garagen zum Beispiel können ganze Wälder etabliert werden. Für klassische Hausdächer eignen sich Sedum-Arten, Moose und Gräser. Ausschlaggebend hierbei ist der vorhandene Wurzelraum für die Pflanzen.

AvB   *In principle there are no limits as long as the load-bearing structure is sufficient. For example, entire forests could be planted over underground carparks that are topped with a concrete slab. Plants from the Sedum genus, mosses and grasses are suitable for typical house roofs. What counts here is there being sufficient space for the plant roots.*

Illustration nach/*Illustration after*
benz24.de/aufbau-dachbegruenung

Efeu
Ivy

wächst pro Jahr bis 1 m, Stränge bis 30 m Länge, selbstkletternd, immergrün, wächst im Schatten, über 30 Sorten, karge Böden, blüht ab etwa dem 8. Jahr

Grows by up to one meter a year, strands up to 30m long, self-climbing, evergreen, grows in the shade, over 30 different types, barren soil, blooms from about the 8th year onward

Trompetenwinde
Trumpet vine

sucht guten Boden. Bis 10 m, Triebe mit Halbranken, orange-farbene Blüten von Juni bis September, sonnige und warme Lagen in gutem Boden, Rückschnitt im Winter

Needs good soil. Up to 10m, semi-climbing shoots, orange-colored blooms from June to September, requires a sunny and warm spot with good soil; needs to be cut back in the winter

Pfeifenwinden
Pipevine

lieben einen feuchten Boden. Große herzförmige Blätter, Halbschatten oder Sonne, die Wurzeln brauchen Feuchtigkeit

Loves moist soil. Large, heart-shaped leaves, semi-shady or sunny locations, the roots need moisture

Waldreben
Clematis

sind Pflanzen, die Sonne lieben. Bis 3 m hoch, circa 10 m² pro Pflanze, braucht Rankhilfe und tiefgründigen, kalkigen und humösen Boden, liebt Sonne, Blütezeit: Juni/August

Plants that love the sun. Up to 3m high, about 10m² per plant, needs a trellis and deep, chalky soil with plenty of humus; loves the sun; blossoms from June to August

Brombeeren
Blackberries

sind Rankgewächs bis circa 6 m, immergrün, jede Staude kann bis zu 5 kg Früchte tragen, Spalierpflanze

Climbing plant up to about 6m, evergreen, each bush can bear up to 5kg of fruit, needs a cordon

Winterjasmin
Winter jasmine

blüht bei Kälte. Zweige bis 5 m, überrascht im Winter mit seinen duftenden, gelben Blüten, gebunden oder hängend, muss nach der Blütezeit ein wenig gekürzt werden

Blossoms when it is cold. Branches grow up to 5m, a winter surprise with its fragrant yellow blooms, tied to a trellis or hanging, needs pruning slightly after it has blossomed

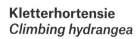

Wilder Wein
Virginia creeper

ist im Winter kahl. Wächst bis 10 m hoch, blattwerfend, flaschengrün im Frühjahr, goldrot im Herbst, braucht kalkigen Lehmboden

Sheds its leavers in winter. Grows up to 10m high, bottle-green in the spring, golden red in the autumn; needs chalky, loamy soil

Kletterhortensie
Climbing hydrangea

blühen mit weißen Dolden. Triebe bis 7 m mit Luft- und Kletterranken, weißen Dolden Juni/Juli, milde Gegenden, lateinische Bezeichnung: Hydrangea petiolaris

Blooms with white cones. Shoots of up to 7m with tendrils and climbing shoots, white blooms from June to July, mild regions, Latin name: Hydrangea petiolaris

Aus/*From*
Doernach 1982

Welche Pflanzen eignen sich im deutschen Raum besonders für eine vertikale Fassadenbegrünung?

AvB   Die kostengünstige Methode ist nach wie vor die Pflanzung von zum Beispiel Kletterpflanzen in den gewachsenen Boden. Man unterscheidet bei Kletterpflanzen zwei Arten: erstens die Selbstklimmer wie zum Beispiel Wilder Wein, der sich durch Haftscheiben an ein Gebäude haftet, oder Efeu, welches mithilfe von Haftwurzeln ein Gebäude emporklimmt. Für Efeu eignen sich nur intakte Fassaden; zweitens die Gerüstklimmer, die je nach Kletterstrategie und Wuchsstärke entsprechende Rankgerüste benötigen. Auch die Verwendung von Spaliergehölzen oder Baumwänden hat sich schon über Jahrhunderte bewährt, zwischenzeitlich sind sie jedoch wieder etwas in Vergessenheit geraten.

Jünger sind die sogenannten Living Walls. Bei diesen wird eine Art miteinander verbundener Pflanztröge eingesetzt, in die Sträucher, Kletterpflanzen, Stauden und Gräser gepflanzt werden können – oder auch Bäume. Das System der Living Walls gibt es ebenfalls als Vorhangfassade. Dieses klassische System, das im Grunde auch im Innenraum Verwendung findet, nutzt zur Bepflanzung Stauden, Gräser und kleinere Gehölze. Eine weitere Variante zur Fassadenbegrünung sind Mooswände. Es ist festzuhalten, dass die ganze Pflanzenbandbreite für eine Fassadenbegrünung umsetzbar ist. Die genaue Auswahl hängt von den Standortvoraussetzungen und der Pflege der Pflanzen ab.

Gibt es heimische, regionale Pflanzenarten, die sich speziell für den Einsatz auf dem Dach oder an einer Fassade eignen?

AvB   Der Einsatz sogenannter Gebietsheimischer, also regionaler Arten, ist natürlich möglich. Hier können Pflanzen aus vergleichbaren Standortbedingungen übertragen werden. Vor allem Arten trockenheitsliebender Pflanzengesellschaften eignen sich. Doch auch das Ansäen einer gebietsheimischen feuchtigkeitsliebenden Wiesenmischungen an der Wand, die an der Hochschule Geisen-

What plants are suitable for the greening of vertical façades in Germany?

AvB   *The cost-effective method remains, for example, to rely on creepers and vines planted in the ground. There are essentially two different kinds of climbers: first, the self-climbing ones, such as Virginia creepers, which adhere to the building by dint of their holdfasts, or ivy, which climbs up a building using its holding roots. Ivy only comes into question for intact façades. Second, there are climbers that require frames that vary according to the plant's climbing strategy and size. The use of trellises and tree walls is a centuries-old strategy, even if it has since been somewhat forgotten.*

A more recent variation is the so-called "living wall". Here, a kind of linked set of planters is used in which shrubs, climbers, bushes and grasses can be planted – or even trees. The living wall system can also take the shape of a curtain wall. This classic system, which can equally also be used in the building's interior too, relies on bushes, grasses and smaller shrubs. Another way of greening a façade is a moss wall. The basic principle in all cases is that the entire range of plants can be deployed to green a façade. The exact choice depends on the conditions on location and how the plants will be tended.

Are there local and regional types of plant that are specifically suited to use on roofs or façades?

AvB   *You can of course use local plants, meaning species from the region. In fact, you can simply take plants that are thriving in comparable conditions. Most suited are above all plant communities that like dry conditions. That said, sowing local, moisture-loving types of meadow grasses has also proved a good strategy, as can be seen from the example of the wall tested at Hochschule Geisenheim. Since the beginning of the year, it has been mandatory to plant regional species in the wide-open outdoors (in areas where there are no settlements, farming or forestry). For this reason, as a rule, nurseries and above all seed manufacturers tend to stock an initial assort-*

heim getestet wurde, hat sich bewährt. Die Verwendung von gebietsheimischen Arten in der freien Natur (nicht besiedelten, land- und forstwirtschaftlichen Bereichen) ist seit Anfang des Jahres verpflichtend. Deshalb sind erste Sortimente in Baumschulen und vor allem bei Saatgutherstellern in der Regel vorhanden. Das Angebot befindet sich jedoch noch im Aufbau.

Viele heimische, regionale Pflanzengesellschaften wie zum Beispiel Trockenrasen beherbergen bedrohte Pflanzen und Tierarten. Die Verwendung heimischer Pflanzenarten im städtischen Raum kann daher durchaus eine sinnvolle Ergänzung sein. Die künstlichen Standorte können aber kein adäquater Ersatz zu den natürlich gewachsenen Pflanzengesellschaften mit ihrem komplexen Zusammenspiel zwischen Standortfaktoren und daran angepassten Lebensgemeinschaften sein. Bezüglich der Verwendung heimischer Arten in der Stadt bedarf es noch weiterer Forschung und der Zusammenarbeit von Naturschutz und Planern. Die Zukunft der städtischen Begrünung liegt in einem gesunden Mix aus Pflanzen unterschiedlicher Herkunft – gebietsheimischer und nicht heimischer Pflanzen, um den komplexen Anforderungen gerecht zu werden.

Gibt es spezielle „Stadtpflanzen"?

AvB   Je nach Verwendungsbereich weisen Pflanzen spezielle Anforderungen auf wie zum Beispiel Salzverträglichkeit im Straßenbereich. Für die Stadt eignen sich sukkulente Arten oder Pflanzen, die sich der Trockenheit anpassen, aber auch wasserliebende Arten mit großen Blättern – je nach Standort. Sie sorgen in erhöhtem Maß für Verdunstungskühle und dienen als Feinstaubfilter. Universell geeignete Pflanzen für die Stadt gibt es hingegen nicht! Die größte Herausforderung ist die Speicherung und pflanzenverwertbare Bereitstellung des gesammelten Regenwassers in der Stadt.

ment of such plants, whereby the range still needs to be expanded.

Many local, regional plant communities, such as dry grassland, are home to endangered species and animals. The use of local plant species can therefore be a meaningful addition to urban spaces. The artificial sites cannot, however, be considered an adequate substitute for plant communities growing in wild nature, with their complex interplay of local factors and communities that have adapted accordingly. More research needs to be done as regards the use of local species in cities, and nature conservationists and planners need to collaborate here. The future of urban greenery lies in a healthy mix of plants of different origins – local plants combined with those from outside in order to do justice to the complex requirements involved.

Are there special "city plants"?

AvB   Depending on the area of application, plants have to possess special properties, for example to be able to tolerate salt if growing close to roadsides. For cities, succulents or plants that adapt to dry conditions are best, as are large-leafed species that love water – it all depends on where they will stand. They increasingly provide evaporation cooling and serve to filter fine particulate matter from the air. By contrast, there are no universally suitable plants for cities! The main challenge is to store the rainwater that collects in a city, and then make it available to the plants.

Geißblatt
Woodbine

wird 4m groß. Auch: Jelänger-jelieber, wächst in der Sonne und auch im Halbschatten, blüht im Juni/Juli

Stalks grow to 4m high, prefers sunny locations or the semi-shade, blooms in June/July

Kletterrosen
Rambling roses

macht ohne Spalier keine Klimmzüge. Bis 4m, gelb, rot, rosa blühend, sehr bewährt „New Dawn" (hellrosa), sonniger Standort, braucht Rankgerüst, muss gebunden werden

Best with an espalier. Climbs up to 4m, yellow, red or rose blooms, "New Dawn" is a light-rose colored favorite, prefers sunny locations, needs a trellis, to which it should be tied

Akebien
Akebia

tragen im Herbst blaubereifte Früchte. Halbimmergrün, duftende, blauviolette Blüte, blaubereifte Früchte im Herbst, lateinisch Akebia

Bears glaucous blue fruit. Semi evergreen, fragrant, violet-blue blooms, glaucous blue fruit in autumn

Klettererdbeere
Climbing strawberries

wachsen bis 3m hoch, sonniger Standort, humöser, guter Boden, Bodendeckung wichtig. (Die Kletterhimbeere rankt bis 8m hoch, nur zweijährige Triebe tragen Früchte)

Grows up to 3m high, prefers sunny locations with humus and good soil, important to have ground cover. (Climbing rasp-berries grow to as high as 8m, only biennial shoots bear fruit)

Strahlengriffel
Actinidia

sind empfindlich. Rankt bis 8m. Weiße Blüten im Frühjahr, dunkelgrün, sonnige und halbschattige Lage, besonders empfindlich gegen Wind und Trockenheit

Is sensitive. Climb up to 8m. white blooms in spring, dark-green leaves, prefers sunny locations or the semi-shade, particularly sensitive to wind and the dry

Blauregen
Wisteria

blüht von Mai bis Juli. Auch: Glyzinie, bis 6m, blauviolettte Blütendolden, Sonne bis Halbschatten, guter, kalkhalti-ger und tiefgründiger Boden

Blossoms from May to July and grows to 6m high, violet-blue conical blooms, prefers sunny locations or the semi-shade and good, chalky, deep soil

Wilder Hopfen
Common hops

zeigt keinen Laubabwurf in milden Lagen. Humulus lupulus (lat.), wird 4–5m hoch, wuchert sehr stark, Standort: lehm-haltiger, nährstoffreicher Boden, keine volle Südlage, im Herbst sterben alle oberirdischen Teile ab

Does not shed its leaves, needs mild climate. Humulus lupulus (lat.) grows to 4–5m high and is very rampant; requires loamy soil with many nutrients, avoid south-facing slopes; in autumn all the parts above the ground die

Knöterich
Knotweed

ist anspruchslos. Stränge bis 10m, ca 4m pro Jahr, im August/September weiße Blütenrispen, sehr genügsam, braucht aber einen Rankträger

Is easy-going. Strands grow to 10m at a rate of about 4m a year; white flower panicles in August to September, very undemanding, requires a trellis

Aus/From
Doernach 1982

Woher beziehe ich die Pflanzen? Sind Qualität und Angebot von Pflanzen aus dem Baumarkt ausreichend?

AvB   Gebietsheimische Arten sind in Baumärkten eher nicht zu finden, und man sollte beachten, dass Pflanzen oft in voller Blüte verkauft werden, das heißt dass Sortimente oft saisonal ausgerichtet sind. So besteht die Gefahr, nicht alle Jahreszeiten entsprechend abzudecken. Die Pflanzung in voller Blüte bedeutet außerdem den größten Stress für die Pflanzen, sie ist bei Topf- oder Containerware und guter Pflege aber möglich. Besser ist jedoch die Pflanzung in der Vegetationsruhe (Frühjahr/Herbst), dann sind die Pflanzen teilweise in den Töpfen noch nicht sichtbar. Die größte Auswahl gibt es in Baumschulen und Staudengärtnereien.

Nach welchen Kriterien sind die Pflanzen auszuwählen? Wer bietet Unterstützung?

AvB   Die Pflanzenauswahl richtet sich nach den Lebensbereichen, und dementsprechend ist sie abhängig vom verwendeten Pflanzsystem, der Lage am Gebäude, den Nutzungsansprüchen, der Gestaltungsidee und der Investition, die man tätigen möchte (Anlage- und Pflegekosten). Hierbei können natürlich Fachplaner wie Landschaftsarchitekten, Garten- und Landschaftsbauer, Staudengärtnereien und Baumschulen helfen. Kontakte können unter anderem auch über den Bundesverband GebäudeGrün e.V. (BuGG) oder auch bei den Städten und Gemeinden angefragt werden, die zum Beispiel Förderprogramme zur Gebäudebegrünung anbieten. Es gibt auch schon fertige Pflanzenmischungen, beispielsweise für extensive Dachbegrünungen (oft von ausführenden Firmen oder Systemherstellern gemischt). Darüber hinaus bietet die zahlreiche Literatur zur Dach- und Fassadenbegrünung die Möglichkeit, sich selbst in das Thema einzuarbeiten.[13]

Where can I procure the plants? Is the quality and range of plants on offer in DIY stores sufficient?

AvB   *DIY stores tends not to stock local species and it bears noting that plants are often sold when in full bloom, meaning the assortment is often very seasonal. There is thus the risk that not all the seasons are accounted for. Planting your purchases when they are in full blossom also involves great stress on the plants but is quite possible in the case of potted or container plants that are then well tended. It is, however, better to plant during dormancy (spring/autumn), when the plants are in part not yet visible in their pots. The largest selection can be found in nurseries and gardening stores stocking perennials.*

What should the criteria be for selecting plants? Who can advise?

AvB   *The choice of plants depends on where they will stand and therefore on the planting system used, the location of the building, the expected uses, the design idea and the investment you want to make (planting and nurturing costs). In this context, specialist planners such as landscape architects, garden and landscape planners, or nurseries for shrubs or trees can all help. Contact details can be obtained, for example, through Bundesverband Gebäude-Grün e. V. (BuGG) or the cities or municipalities, which offer grants for greening buildings. There are also ready-to-go plant combinations, for instance for extensive roof greening (often put together by the companies installing the plants or systems manufacturers). Moreover, there is plenty of literature on roof and façade greening, so you can immerse yourself in the topic, too.[13]*

---

13   U.a./*i.a.* Manfred Köhler, Georg Barth, Thorwald Brandwein, Fassadenbegrünung und Dachbegrünung, Stuttgart 1993; Walter Kolb, Manfred Köhler u.a./*i.a.*, Handbuch Bauwerksbegrünung. Planung – Konstruktion – Ausführung, Köln 2012; Wolfgang Ansel, Petra Reidel, Moderne Dachgärten – kreativ und individuell, München 2012; Walter Kolb, Dachbegrünung – Planung, Ausführung, Pflege, Stuttgart 2016.

Mit welchen Schädlingen oder Umwelteinflüssen werden Pflanzen in den Städten konfrontiert?

AvB   Die extremen Standortbedingungen gekoppelt mit den extremen Wetterlagen – wie trockene Sommer, Unwetter mit Starkregen und Stürmen sowie Frost im Winter – sind Gefahren für die Pflanzen in der Stadt. Außerdem bereiten der hohe Nutzungsdruck und eventuell damit verbundene Beschädigungen (Vandalismus) den Pflanzen Probleme – und derart gestresste Pflanzen sind anfälliger für Krankheiten. Die Anzahl der Schädlinge und Pflanzenkrankheiten nehmen in den letzten Jahren rasant zu. Gründe dafür sind neue Lebensbedingungen für Schädlinge, die durch den Klimawandel entstehen. Durch den zunehmenden Güter- und Personenverkehr erfolgt die Verbreitung rasant schnell und unkontrolliert. Viele Schädlinge werden eingeschleppt, finden geeignete klimatische Voraussetzungen und können sich ohne natürliche Feinde ausbreiten. Die oft großflächige und monotone Pflanzenverwendung einer Art trägt zu dieser Verbreitung bei. Es gibt kaum noch Stadtbaumarten, die frei von Schädlingsbefall sind – vom Befall der Kastanien mit der Kastanienminiermotte über das Ulmensterben bis zum Eschentriebsterben. Die beste Vorbeugung ist, die Pflanzenauswahl an den Standort anzupassen und möglichst artenreich zu gestalten. Dies gilt für alle Bereiche auch außerhalb der Gebäudebegrünung.

Lassen sich Nutzpflanzen, Gemüse und Kräuter auf dem Dachgarten anbauen?

AvB   Es gibt bereits zahlreiche Dachfarmen oder andere vertikale Ideen der Landwirtschaft in, auf oder an Gebäuden. Die Idee ist, möglichst nah am Kunden zu produzieren und möglichst ressourcenschonend zu arbeiten, zum Beispiel mit geschlossenen Systemen, bei denen Gemüseanbau und Fischzucht kombiniert werden. Besonders im Innenbereich funktionieren diese nur unter hohem Einsatz von Know-how und Technik. Aber es gibt auch einfache Umsetzungsmöglichkeiten, so bei Nutzung von Balkonkästen, Terrassenkübeln oder einer essbaren Wand

What pests or environmental factors confront plants in cities?

AvB   The extreme conditions in the planting locations coupled with extreme weather conditions – such as dry summers, storms with downpours, high winds, and frost in winter – are all dangers to plants in cities. Furthermore, the high pressures innate in their use and the possible attendant damage (vandalism) pose problems for the plants – and plants stressed in this way are more susceptible to disease. The number of pests and plant diseases has been rocketing in recent years. Reasons include the new living conditions for pests that climate change is creating. Increasing goods and passenger traffic means that they spread far faster and with no control. Many pests are imported, encounter suitable climatic conditions, and can spread without any natural born enemies. The frequent selection of large expanses of monotonous plants of a single kind contributes to this spread. There are very few urban tree species that are not prone to pest infestation – be it the chestnuts suffering from horse chestnut leaf miner moths, elm diseases, or the death of shoots on ash trees. The best preventative tactic is to adapt the choice of plant to the location and include as many species as possible. This applies likewise to all areas other than building greenery, too.

Can crop plants, vegetables and herbs also be nurtured on roof gardens?

AvB   There are already countless roof farms or other vertical ideas for farming in, on, or attached to buildings. The main idea is to grow produce as close to the consumer as possible and spare as many resources as possible, for example by using closed systems that combine vegetables and fish farming. Especially indoors, such systems require a lot of know-how and technology. However, there are also very simple uses, such as those involving balcony flowerboxes, patio planters or an edible wall on which fruit, vegetables and herbs are planted on your balcony. It is not advisable to grow urban vegetables directly adjacent to a heavily used road as this will lead to a higher incidence of heavy metals in the produce, although if the plants are well washed then levels will hardly be harmful.

14.000 m² landwirtschaftliche Anbaufläche auf den Dächern von
Paris Expo Porte de Versailles, Paris, Frankreich
14,000 m² of farmed area on the roofs of Paris Expo Porte de Versailles, Paris, France
Photo: © Valode & Pistre Architectes/Agropolis

zum Anbau von Obst, Gemüse und Kräutern auf dem eigenen Balkon. Man sollte nur nicht direkt an einer dicht befahrenen Straße Stadtgemüse anbauen, um erhöhten Einträgen von Schwermetallen vorzubeugen. Bei guter Reinigung ist der Anbau in der Regel jedoch unbedenklich.

Sind alle Pflanzen gleich pflegeintensiv?

AvB   Das hängt vom System ab: Besonders substratlose Systeme (Living Walls auf Vlies- oder Steinwollbasis) sind sehr anfällig, wenn zum Beispiel die Bewässerungsanlage ausfällt. Hier kann ein einziger heißer Tag dazu führen, die gesamte Bepflanzung zu schädigen. Auch wirken sich Mangelerscheinungen, hervorgerufen durch pH-Wert-Veränderungen oder einseitige Düngungen, direkt auf die Pflanzungen aus, da keine Pufferwirkung durch Boden oder Substrate erfolgt. Je stärker die Substratschicht oder der durchwurzelbare Boden ist, desto seltener muss gedüngt oder gewässert werden. Zusammenfassend kann man sagen: Je besser die Pflanzen versorgt werden, umso weniger muss gepflegt werden.

Die Pflege steigt mit dem Anspruch an die Pflanzung. Wenn Pflanzen aus unterschiedlichen Lebensbereichen verwendet und zu-

Do all plants require the same amount of care?

AvB   That depends on the system: In particular, systems that use no substrate (living walls that rely on non-woven or rockwool as a backing) are very susceptible to damage if, for example, an irrigation system fails. In such instances, a single hot day can lead to damage to all the plants. Moreover, deficiencies caused by changes in pH value or one-sided fertilizers directly impact the plants as there is no buffer provided by soil or a substrate. The thicker the layer of substrate or the deeper the soil for the roots, the less you will need to use fertilizer or water the plants. In summary, it is safe to say that the better the plants are provided for, the less they will need care.

The more discerning the plant standard, the more tending will be required. If plants from different habitats are grown and a specific appearance is to be maintained throughout, then this will involve maximum tending. The more accurately the choice of plant is geared to the location in the city, the lower the need to tend the plants. This is also the case if a dynamic change in plant combinations is desired, with new ones being added and others spreading more rapidly than others or disappearing. An

gleich ein bestimmtes Pflanzenbild durchgehend bestehen bleiben soll, dann ist dies mit maximalem Pflegeaufwand verbunden. Je besser die Pflanzenauswahl an den vorhandenen Lebensbereich in der Stadt angepasst wird, umso geringer ist der Pflegeaufwand. Er reduziert sich zudem, wenn eine dynamische Veränderung der Pflanzenzusammensetzung erwünscht ist – neue kommen dazu, andere breiten sich stärker aus als andere beziehungsweise verschwinden. An einen intensiven Dachgarten ist – abseits aller ökologischen Vorteile – aufgrund des höheren Anspruchs an die Aufenthaltsqualität und Ästhetik ein entsprechend hoher Pflegeaufwand geknüpft. Eine extensive Dachbegrünung erfordert hingegen wenig Pflege, und auch Kletterpflanzen oder Mooswände müssen so gut wie gar nicht gepflegt werden.

Welche Pflanzen passen gut zusammen und bilden ein gemeinsames Habitat oder Biotop?

AvB   Im Prinzip passen die Arten aus den gleichen Lebensbereichen gut zusammen. Vorbilder der Pflanzenverwendung sind natürliche beziehungsweise naturnahe Pflanzengemeinschaften. Diese Arten mit gleichen Standortansprüchen werden entsprechend der gestalterischen Intention dann für die Stadt zusammengestellt. Auch die Kombination verschiedener Pflanzengesellschaften ist üblich, zum Beispiel die Mischung von heimischen Trockenrasen und Wiesen mit osteuropäischen Steppen und nordamerikanischen Prärien. Dadurch erreicht man sehr lange Blütenzeiten.

Aber auch ruderale Stadtgesellschaften lassen sich mit herkömmlichen Zierarten mischen. Ruderalvegetation reagiert auf durch den Menschen veränderte Voraussetzungen wie Bodenverhältnisse (Aufschüttung, Schotter) und Lebensbedingungen. Dies erfordert jedoch neben einem gestalterischen auch ein ökologisches Verständnis, denn die ruderalen Pflanzen werden in der Regel weniger als Zierpflanzen geschätzt. Zu ihnen zählen Arten wie Brennnessel, Holunder, Rubinie oder Sommerflieder.[14]

intensively greened roof requires a lot of tending over and above the ecological advantages involved, if only because of the higher standards for leisure time and aesthetics. By contrast, extensive roof greenery requires little tending, and climbing plants or moss walls require as little as no tending at all.

What plants go well together and form a shared habitat or biotope?

AvB   *Essentially, species from the same region go well together. The best examples of using plants involve natural or close-to-natural plant communities. These species require the same sort of conditions and are then combined for city use in line with the creative intentions. Combination of different plant communities is also customary, for example mixtures of local dry grasses with East European steppe grasses and those from American prairies. This is also a way to get very long blossoming periods.*

That said, ruderal plants can be mixed with the usual ornamental species. Ruderal vegetation responds to the conditions that have been changed by the presence of humans, such as soil conditions (rubble, gravel) and living conditions. However, this calls not just for a landscaping idea but for ecological knowledge, since ruderal plants are, as a rule, not regarded as favorably as ornamental plants. They include nettles, elderberry, false acacias and butterfly bushes.[14]

ALEXANDER VON BIRGELEN

ist Vizepräsident für Lehre an der Hochschule Geisenheim University und leitet den Lehrstuhl für Freipflanzenkunde und -verwendung. Er ist Gründungsmitglied des Berliner Planungsbüros Strauchpoeten und engagiert sich seit 2005 im bundesweiten Arbeitskreis Pflanzenverwendung.

Alexander von Birgelen is Vice President for Teaching at the Geisenheim University and head of the Chair for Open Plant Science and Use. He is a founding member of the Berlin planning office Strauchpoeten and has been involved in the nationwide plant use working group since 2005.

---

14   Richard Hansen, Friedrich Stahl und Swantje Duthweiler,
     Die Stauden und ihre Lebensbereiche, Stuttgart 2016.

Bepflanzung von Bestands- gebäuden

Planting of existing buildings

Welche Voraussetzungen muss ein Gebäude mitbringen, damit man es begrünen kann?

Es muss durch die Besitzer gewünscht sein, das ist die erste Voraussetzung. Außerdem muss die Statik für eine Dachbegrünung zusätzliches Gewicht tragen können. Eine extensive Dachbegrünung bringt ein zusätzliches Gewicht von mindestens 70 kg/m² aufs Dach, intensive Begrünung entsprechend noch mehr, denn es muss sowohl Substrat und Schichtaufbau als auch darin gespeichertes Wasser berechnet werden. Aus diesem Grund muss ein Statiker anhand der vorhandenen Planungsunterlagen oder mithilfe einer Testbohrung prüfen, wie massiv die Decken und Wände sind.

What preconditions must a building fulfill if it is to be greened?

First and foremost, the owners must want to have the greenery. Moreover, the building must be able to bear the additional load of the greenery. Extensive roof greenery involves additional weight of 70 kg/m² on the roof, intensive greenery correspondingly more, as the total then involves not only the substrate and layering, but also the water stored in it, too. For this reason, the structural engineer must use the existing planning documentation or make a test drill bore to establish the strength of the ceilings and walls.

LARA-MARIA MOHR

Call for Projects
Dachgarten / *Roof garden*
Schottenfeldgasse Wien, Österreich / *Vienna, Austria*
gaupenraub +/-
Photo: Alexander Hagner

As a tenant, do I have any chance of the building owners supporting greening?

Habe ich als Mieter eine Chance, dass der Gebäudebesitzer die Begrünung unterstützt?

Mieter, die an einer Begrünung interessiert sind, sollten dem Vermieter aufzeigen, welche Vorteile eine solche Maßnahme mit sich bringt. Einerseits wird den Vermieter interessieren, dass er gegebenenfalls Kosten einsparen kann. Dabei sind laufende Kosten wie Kühlung oder Dämmung vermutlich eher irrelevant, da sie auf die Miete umgelegt werden, aber die Verlängerung der Lebensdauer könnte durchaus ein Argument sein. Andererseits ist die Attraktivitätssteigerung einer begrünten Immobilie nicht von der Hand zu weisen. Und: Grün schafft Identifikationsräume! Manche Besitzer stehen einer Begrünung zudem positiver gegenüber, wenn das Engagement der Mieter sicher ist und diese sich beispielsweise verpflichten, sich um die Pflege zu kümmern.

Tenants who are interested in greening should draw the landlord's attention to the advantages such a measure has. On the one hand, the landlord should be interested in the potential cost savings. In this context, current costs such as cooling or insulation are probably fairly irrelevant as they can be passed on to tenants, but the extended service life of the building could well be a strong argument. On the other hand, the enhanced appeal of a greened property is quite obvious. And: Greening creates space with which we identify! The one or other owner may be more favorably disposed to greening if the tenants' commitment is certain and they pledge to tend to the greenery, for example.

LARA-MARIA MOHR

What can tenants undertake without the landlord's permission?

Anything is possible if it can grow in a planter and does not really impose on the neighbors. However, in the case of balconies and flat roofs the planters should not exceed a certain weight. Moreover, all measures should be reversible, meaning go for pots and planting sacks!

Was können Mieter ungefragt unternehmen?

Alles, was in Trögen zu pflanzen ist und nicht zu sehr die Nachbarn bedrängt, ist möglich. Bei Balkonen und Flachdächern darf allerdings ein gewisses Gewicht nicht überschritten werden. Auch sollten alle Maß-nahmen reversibel sein. Also: her mit den Töpfen und Pflanzsäcken!

HILDE STROBL

Es gibt zahlreiche Varianten sowohl für die Fassaden- als auch für die Dachbegrünung. Wer sich nicht selbst intensiv damit auseinandersetzen kann oder will, holt sich Expertise aus dem Garten- und Landschaftsbau, der Architektur oder der Dachdeckerinnung.

Wann und wofür brauche ich fachliche Unterstützung, wenn ich ein Bestandsgebäude begrünen will?

Dachbegrünung:
Wichtig ist es, bestimmte Parameter der Dachgegebenheiten mit Spezialisten abzuklären, wie Statik, Wurzelschutz, Dachgefälle, Dachrand, An- und Abschlüsse, Dachdurchdringungen oder Lichtverhältnisse. Daraus ergeben sich die zu verwendenden Systemaufbauten und Vegetationstragschichten ebenso wie die Auswahl der Pflanzen.

Fassadenbegrünung:
Je komplexer der Anspruch, desto mehr fachliche Unterstützung ist nötig. Bodengebundene Selbstbegrünung auf eigenem Grund ist immer möglich, doch helfen Pflanzenfachberater bei der standortspezifischen Pflanzenwahl. Wenn geplant ist, Rankhilfen und zusätzliche Verschattungselemente einzubauen, sollte nicht nur die Brand- und Windlast beachtet werden: Es gibt zahlreiche verschiedene Systeme, je nach Konstitution und Position der Mauer. Sie unterscheiden sich enorm im Hinblick auf finanzielle Aspekte und klimatische Wirkung. Beratung ist wichtig und kann u. a. über den Bundesverband GebäudeGrün (BuGG, www.gebaeudegruen.info) erfolgen. In Frankfurt ist eine Erstberatung im Rahmen von „Frankfurt frischt auf" durch die Kommune möglich.

There are countless variants for greening both façades and roofs. Anyone who does not want to deal intensively with the issues, or cannot so do, will rely on experts from the fields of garden and landscape planning, or on architects or roofing contractors.

When and for what do I need expert support if I wish to green an existing building?

Roof greening:
It is important that you discuss certain parameters of the roof conditions with experts, such as load-bearing properties, protection against roots, angle of slope, roof edge, connections, roof penetrations or lighting conditions. These stipulations will determine what superstructure is to be used as well as what vegetation soil strata, not to mention the choice of plants.

Façade greening:
The more complex the requirements, the more support from the specialists you will need. Ground-based self-greening on your own plot is always possible, but plant specialists will help you chose the right plant for the right place. If you plan to install guides for bines and additional shading elements, then you will need to consider fire protection and wind loads and also the fact that there are countless different systems depending on the constitution and position of the wall. They differ immensely as regards the financial aspects and climatic impact. It is important to get good advice, for example from Bundesverband GebäudeGrün (BuGG, www.gebaeudegruen.info). In Frankfurt, initial advice can be obtained from your local authority in the framework of the "Refreshing Frankfurt/Frankfurt frischt auf" program.

LARA-MARIA MOHR

Wie steht der Denkmalschutz zur Begrünung von Fassaden und Dach?

How do the heritage authorities regard the greening of façades and roofs?

Eine Begrünung denkmalgeschützter Gebäude ist im Einzelfall zu klären. Begrünungselemente wie Spalierobst, die Begrünung von Wuchshilfen und Pergolen waren bereits in der Historie gern verwendete Gestaltungsmittel zur Gliederung von Fassaden, zur optischen Zusammenfassung heterogener Baukörper sowie zur Raumbildung und Schaffung von Privatheit (z.B. Hermann Muthesius, Joseph Maria Olbrich, Heinrich Tessenow).

Whether a heritage-listed building can be greened needs to be assessed on a case-by-case basis. Down through time, greenery elements such as trellised fruit and greenery on frames and pergolas have often been used as a design device to structure façades, visually bracketing heterogeneous volumes, and to create spaces or private spheres (e.g., Hermann Muthesius, Joseph Maria Olbrich and Heinrich Tessenow).

NICOLE PFOSER

„Unsere Häuser stehen nackt. Noch nie gab es so kalte Wände. Kalt und leer und hart. Wände von laufendem Meter. [...] Wieviel misslungene Hinterhöfe, wieviel nackte Brandmauer, wieviel trostlose Garagen und sonstige Häßlichkeiten könnte man mit gutem Bewuchs wieder ansehnlich gestalten."[15] In der berühmten Publikation „Grün kaputt" formulieren die Autoren eine radikale Absage an nackte Häuserwände. Pflanzen an Fassaden wären demnach nicht eine unberechenbare Größe wider die Gestaltung, sondern selbst Gestaltungsmittel. Sie sind hilfreich, weniger attraktive Fassaden zu kaschieren.

Funktionieren Pflanzen wie Schminke an Gebäuden? Zur Frage der Ästhetik von begrünten Fassaden

15   Dieter Wieland, Peter M. Bode, Rüdiger Disko, Grün kaputt, München 1983, S./p. 92.

Bepflanzung von Gebäuden im Bestand
Façade greening of existing buildings
Photo: www.fassadengruen.de

Do plants work like make-up on buildings? The question of aesthetics on greened façades.

"Our buildings are naked. Never before have there been such cold walls. Cold and empty and hard. Meter after meter of walls. [...] How many failed backyards, how many naked fire-walls, how many drab garages and other monstrosities might be made respectable once again with appropriate greening?"[15] In the famous publication entitled "Grün kaputt", the authors put forward a radical rejection of naked building walls. Plants on façades, they say, are not an incalculable dimension counte-ring the design, but rather a means of design in themselves. They are also helpful in masking less attractive façades.

HILDE STROBL

Vertikales Grün

Vertical greenery

Welche Systeme wandgebundener Begrünung gibt es?

Neben den traditionellen bodengebundenen Varianten erlangen Begrünungssysteme ohne Boden- und Bodenwasseranschluss zunehmend Bedeutung. Unterschieden werden diese wandgebundenen Begrünungen in lineare, modulare und flächige Bauweisen.

WANDGEBUNDENE BEGRÜNUNG
WALL-BASED GREENERY

Pflanzen in horizontalen Vegetationsflächen, Pflanzgefäße an Tragkonstruktionen

Plants on horizontal surfaces for greenery, Plant containers attached to support structures

Stauden (u.a. auch Gräser, Farne, bedingt Zwiebel- und Knollengewächse), Kleingehölze; Schlinger, Ranker, bedingt Spreizklimmer

Perennials (including grasses, ferns, to a lesser extent bulb and tuber plants), small shrubs; creepers, climbing plants, to a limited extent spreading climbers

Substrat in Gefäßen
(Einzel- oder Linearbehälter)

*Substrate in containers
(single items or lines of containers)*

**Pflanzen in senkrechten Vegetationsflächen/„Vertikale Gärten"
Modulare Systeme**

*Plants in vertical surfaces for greenery/ "vertical gardens"
Modular systems*

Stauden (u.a. auch Gräser, Farne), Kleingehölze, Moose; bedingt Wurzelkletterer, Spreizklimmer

Perennials (including grasses and ferns), shrubs, mosses; to a limited extent root climbers, spreading climbers

- Substrat in Element-Einheiten aus Körben/Gabionen, Matten, Kassetten
- Substrattragende Rinnensysteme
- Direkt begrünte Kunst- und Natursteinplatten mit begrünungsfördernder Oberflächenrauheit

- Substrate in element units consisting of baskets/gabions, mats, cassettes
- Substrate-bearing trough systems
- Artificial and natural stone panels with coarse surfaces that encourage greenery can be used as the surface on which the plants are set

**Pflanzen in senkrechten Vegetationsflächen/„Vertikale Gärten"
Flächige Konstruktionen**

*Plants in vertical surfaces for greenery/ "vertical gardens"
Surface structures*

Stauden (u.a. auch Gräser, Farne), Kleingehölze, Moose, bedingt Wurzelkletterer, Spreizklimmer

Perennials (including grasses and ferns), small shrubs, mosses; to a limited extent root climbers, spreading climbers

- Textil-Systeme/Textil-Substrat-Systeme
- Metallblech-Systeme mit Öffnungen zu Vegetationsflächen
  (Textil bzw. Substratträger)
- Direktbegrünung auf nährstofftragender Wandschale

- Textile systems /Textile substrate systems
- Sheet metal systems with opening for the planting units (textile or substrate containers)
- Direct greening on wall shells that contain nutrients

BODENGEBUNDENE FASSADEN-
BEGRÜNUNG
GROUND-BASED FAÇADE GREENERY

WANDGEBUNDENE FASSADEN-
BEGRÜNUNG
WALL-BASED FAÇADE GREENERY

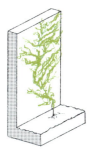 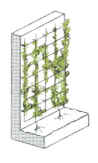   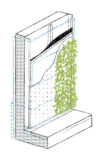

**Direktbewuchs
der Fassade**

*Plants grown directly
on the façade*

**Leitbarer Bewuchs
an separater
Wuchskonstruktion**

*Plants that can be
guided in their growth
on a separate structure*

**Horizontale Vegetations-
flächen, Pflanzgefäße**

*Horizontal planting areas,
plant containers*

**Vertikale Vegetations-
flächen, modular**

*Vertical planting areas,
modular*

**Vertikale Vegetations-
flächen, flächig**

*Vertical planting areas,
across the surface*

What systems of wall-based greenery are there?

*Alongside the traditional ground-based variants,
greenery systems with no contact to the ground or
groundwater are becoming increasingly popular.
A distinction is made here between linear, modular
and surface-based structures.*

NICOLE PFOSER

Illustrationen nach / *Illustrations after*
Pfoser 2018

Konstruktions-kriterien für Begrünungen

Construction criteria for greenery

Die heutige Bandbreite erfolgreicher Begrünungen von vertikalen Flächen umfasst zwei grundsätzlich unter-schiedliche Bauweisen mit jeweils mehreren Varianten: die „bodengebundenen" und die „wandgebundenen" Begrünungstechniken sowie Mischformen beider Bau-weisen.

The range of successful greenery on vertical surfaces today involves two essentially distinct construction types, each with several variants, namely "ground-based" and "wall-based" greening techniques as well as hybrids of the two.

Bodengebundene Begrünungstechniken

Die ursprüngliche und nach wie vor aktuelle Begrünungstechnik für Fassaden, Brandwände, Grenzmauern etc. bezieht ihre Wasser- und Nährstoffversorgung aus dem anstehenden Erdreich beziehungsweise aus einem ersatzweise hergestellten Bodenvolumen. Dabei kann es sich neben gewachsenem Boden auch um ein künstlich bereitgestelltes Bodenmaterial handeln. Entscheidend sind eine pflanzengerechte Bodenqualität bezüglich Zusammensetzung und Masse sowie ein natürlicher Bodenwasseranschluss durch die Zuführung und Speicherfähigkeit von Regenwasser. Bei zu tief liegendem Bodenwasserspiegel, unzureichend beregneten Pflanzorten und anhaltenden Trockenperioden ist eine zuverlässige Ersatzbewässerung (manuell oder automatisch) notwendig. Bodengebundene Fassadenbegrünungen werden in Selbstklimmer und Gerüstkletterpflanzen unterteilt. Wandgebundene Begrünungen werden unterschieden in:
▸ lineare
▸ modulare und
▸ flächige Bauweisen.

Ground-based greening techniques

The original and still very prevalent system for greening façades, firewalls, border walls, etc. relies on water and nutrients from the soil below or from a soil volume put in place for that purpose. Alongside ground that was already in place, the soil involved can be made available artificially. What is decisive is soil quality that is right for the plants in terms of composition and mass as well as natural contact with the groundwater through the introduction and retention of rainwater. If the groundwater level is too deep, or if the plants do not receive enough rainwater and there are prolonged dry periods, then a reliable (manual or automatic) substitute source of water is needed. Ground-based façade greenery is sub-divided into self-climbing plants and trellis-based plants. Wall-based greenery is subdivided into
▸ linear,
▸ modular and
▸ surface-based structures.

Lineare Bauweisen

Horizontal laufende Rinnen (Metall, Keramik) oder lineare Reihungen aus Einzelbehältern werden an einer tragenden Sekundärkonstruktion beziehungsweise auf Auskragungen so auf Distanz übereinandergestapelt, dass die Wuchsgröße der Pflanzenwahl sowie ein geplanter Lichteinfall (vor Glasfassaden und Fenstern) nicht behindert werden. Im Übrigen ist die Pflanzenauswahl kaum eingeschränkt. Die Rinnen respektive Einzelbehälter nehmen als Wasser- und Nährstoffspeicher das Substrat auf. Die nötige künstliche Wasser- und Nährstoffversorgung verläuft frostsicher bis zur Konstruktion, wird in der Sekundärkonstruktion zu den einzelnen Substratlagen geführt, wo sie zum Beispiel mittels Tropfbewässerung das Substrat tränkt. Parallel verläuft eine Entwässerungsleitung.

Modulare Bauweisen

Hier dienen vorgefertigte Quadrat- oder Rechteckmodule als Substratspeicher. Die Einzelmodule haben in der Regel handliche Abmessungen, damit das Versetzen auf der Unterkonstruktion einfach möglich ist. Zwischen den Modulen und der Gebäudewand ist für eine Durchlüftung zu sorgen. In der nicht sichtbaren Unterkonstruktion der Module (Sekundärkonstruktion) verlaufen Versorgungsleitung und Ablaufleitung, sie werden mit den Tropfrohren der Substratpolster verbunden.

Flächige Bauweisen

Hier wird die zu begrünende Gesamtwand mit einer systemtragenden Sekundärkonstruktion verbaut (Abdichtung, Hinterlüftungs- und Installationsraum) und mit einer verrottungsfreien Trägerplatte vollflächig verschalt (verformungssteife Metall- oder Kunststoffplatten). Als pflanzentragende Schicht dienen vorgesetzte Geotextilien, die ganzflächig als Wasserspeicher wirken. Die Pflanzen werden in eingeschlitzte oder aufgeklammerte Filztaschen mit Substrateinlage gesetzt, deren Ort und Pflanzenbestückung allein dem Gestaltungsziel des Entwurfs unter Berücksichtigung des Konkurrenzverhaltens benachbarter Pflanzen dienen. Alternativ kann eine doppelte Filzlage so mit einer Substratzwischenlage versteppt werden, dass Taschenschlitzungen an beliebiger Stelle möglich sind.

Konstruktionskriterien — übliche Fassadenbauweisen und geeignete
Begrünungstechniken (Prinzipschnitte)
*Structural criteria — the customary façade structures and the greening
techniques most suitable (sectional illustration of the principles)*

MASSIVE WANDAUFBAUTEN
SOLID WALL CONSTRUCTIONS

STÄNDER- UND FACHWERKBAUWEISE
POST-AND-BEAM AND HALF-TIMBERED STRUCTURES

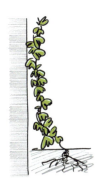 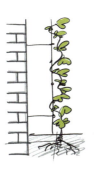

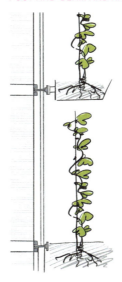

**Bsp. Selbstklimmer
Bodenwasser-Anschluss**

Example – self-climber
Groundwater connection

**Bsp. Gerüstkletterpflanzen
Kletterhilfe und Boden-
wasseranschluss**

Example – climbers on frames
Climbing frame and
groundwater connection

**Bsp. Mischformen
Kombination aus
bodengebundenen und
fassadengebundenen
(Einzel- oder Linear-
behälter) Begrünungen**

Example – hybrid forms
Combination of ground-
based and façade-based
(single units or lines of
containers) greenery

MEHRSCHALIGE, NICHT HINTERLÜFTETE
WANDAUFBAUTEN
*MULTI-LAYER WALL CONSTRUCTION
WITHOUT BACK VENTILATION*

MEHRSCHALIGE, HINTERLÜFTETE WANDAUFBAUTEN
*MULTI-LAYER WALL CONSTRUCTION
WITH BACK VENTILATION*

 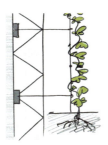

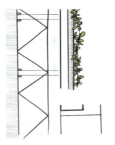 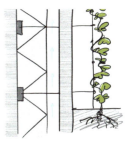

**Bsp. Regelsystem
Begrünung in Einzel-
oder Linearbehältern**

Example – regular system
Greenery in single units
or lines of containers

**Bsp. Gerüstkletterpflanzen
Kletterhilfe und Boden-
wasseranschluss**

Example – frame-based climbers
Climbing frame and ground
water connection

**Bsp. Flächige Kon-
struktionen ohne
Bodenanschluss**

Example – surface-
based structures
With no connection to
the ground

**Bsp. Gerüstkletterpflanzen
Kletterhilfe und Boden-
anschluss**

Example – frame-based
climbers
Climbing frame und
connection to the ground

Illustrationen nach/*Illustrations after*
Pfoser 2018

Linear structures

Horizontal channels (metal, ceramic) or linear rows of individual containers are stacked on a load-bearing secondary structure or projections at such a distance from one another that the growth of the plants and the influx of light (in front of glass façades or windows) is not impeded. There are, incidentally, almost no restrictions as regards the choice of plants. The channels or individual containers are filled with the substrate that provides the water and nutrients. The artificial water and nutrient supply must be frost-proof and run down the secondary structure through to the substrate and its individual layers, where, for example, it moistens the substrate by means of drip irrigation. There must be a drain parallel to this.

Modular structures

Prefabricated square or rectangular modules serve as the substrate containers in this instance. As a rule, the individual modules are of a handy size, so all that is required is simply to place them on the base frame. There must be space for ventilation between the modules and the wall of the building. The invisible base frames for the modules (secondary structures) contain the supply pipes and drains that are linked to the drip pipes for the wedge of substrate.

Surface-based structures

In this case, the overall wall to be greened is covered with a secondary structure that holds the planting system (it includes seals, back ventilation space and the installation space), and is completely covered in a non-rotting backing panel (non-distorting metal or plastic panels). Geotextiles attached to this then function as the layer bearing the plants, while the textile functions throughout as a water retention medium. The plants are set in felt bags with a substrate content slitted into or clamped onto the geotextile; the location of the felt bags is determined solely by the design desired and takes into account competition with neighboring plants. Alternatively, a double layer of felt can have a layer of substrate tacked in between such that bag slits can be positioned wherever desired.

NICOLE PFOSER

Wie steht es um die Brandlast von Rank- und Klettergewächsen? Was ist zu beachten?

Kletterpflanzen sind nicht geregelte „Baustoffe". Jedoch wirkt der Wassergehalt aller lebenden Pflanzenteile feuerhemmend. Die Brandlast (Wärmepotenzial aller vorhandenen brennbaren Stoffe) begrünter Fassaden hängt maßgeblich vom Pflegezustand der Begrünung ab. Die dauerhafte Vitalität der Pflanzen ist die Grundvoraussetzung gegen die Entwicklung der Brandlast. Dafür sind die Bewässerung und Düngung sicherzustellen, und abgestorbene Pflanzenteile (bzw. Totholz) müssen durch regelmäßige Pflege entfernt werden. Alle für die Kletterhilfen verwendeten Werkstoffe müssen mindestens Baustoffklasse B1 (schwer entflammbar) aufweisen.[16] Nach einer Erhebung von 54 Brandfällen an bodengebundenen Fassadenbegrünungen in Deutschland zwischen 2008 und 2014 zeigt sich eine auffällige Dominanz von Efeu. Einerseits aus der häufigen Verwendung hergeleitet, stellen andererseits der hohe Anteil toter, trockener Pflanzenteile und die unsachgemäße Entfernung des Bewuchses durch Abflammen die Hauptursache von Bränden dar.[17]

Climbing plants are classified as non-regulated "construction materials". However, owing to their water content all living plant parts are fire inhibitors. The fire load (heat potential of all flammable materials on site) of greened façades depends critically on how well the greenery is cared for. The enduring vitality of the plants is the basic condition for avoiding a fire load developing. To this end, water and nutrients must be provided regularly and dead plant parts (e.g., dead wood) removed in the course of regular tending. All materials used as climbing frames must be at least class B1 construction material (hardly inflammable).[16] A survey of 54 fires involving ground-based façade greenery in Germany between 2008 and 2014 shows a striking dominance of ivy. The main cause of the fires is attributable on the one hand to the frequent use of ivy, and on the other to the high portion of dead or dry plant parts and their incorrect removable through flaring off.[17]

NICOLE PFOSER

What is the fire load constituted by Virginia creepers and climbers? What needs to be heeded?

16 Stefan Brandhorst, Pflege und Wartung wandgebundener Fassadenbegrünungen, 7. FBB-Symposium Fassadenbegrünung 2014/ *7th FBB-symposium façade greening 2014*: www.gebaeudegruen.info/fileadmin/website/downloads/bugg-symposien/ Fassadenbegruenungssymposium/7_FBB-Fassadenbegruenungssymposium_2014.pdf (10.11.2020).

17 Thorwald Brandwein, Statistisches über Brände mit Kletterpflanzen und Strategien zu ihrer Vermeidung: www.fassadenbegrünung-polygrün.de/wp-content/uploads/2014/11/Text-Brand_Strat_Wien-2014_ISO.pdf (10.11.2020).

Zur Frage der Last: Gewicht und Windlast

SELBSTKLIMMER	SCHLINGER/WINDER
SELF-CLIMBERS	*TWINERS/WINDING PLANTS*

Konstruktionen mit vorwiegend senkrechter Ausbildung
Structure with primarily vertical reach

Lasteinflüsse (Laub/Frucht/Holz): circa 170–2.230kg/Pflanze (bei ungehemmtem Wuchs/tropfnass)	**Lasteinflüsse (Laub/Frucht/Holz):** circa 5–30kg/m² (Gewichtsschätzung bei fachgerechtem Schnitt/tropfnass)
Load factors (foliage/fruit/wood): approx. 170–2,230kg/plant (if allowed to grow unhindered/dripping wet)	*Load factors (foliage/fruit/wood): approx. 5–30kg/m² (weight estimated after expert pruning/dripping wet)*

+ Windlast (abhängig von Polsterdicke/Exposition – erhöhte Windlast in Gebäuderand-/Eckbereichen)
+ Gewichte aus Schnee, Eis

+ Wind load (depends on thickness of padding/exposure — increased wind load at building edges and corners)
+ Weight of snow and/or ice

+ Gewichte Kletterhilfen (abhängig von Werkstoff und Materialeinsatz)
+ Gewichte aus Schnee, Eis (Pflanze/Kletterhilfe – abhängig von örtlichen Bedingungen)

+ Weight of climbing frames (depends on materials used)
+ Weight of snow and/or ice (plant/climbing frame — depends on local conditions)

gegebenenfalls Sicherung

Intakte und pflanzenphysiologisch geeignete Wandfläche/Mauer

Possibly requires securing

Intact wall surface/wall suitable for plant physiology

gegebenenfalls seilparallele Aufleitung (s. rechte Abb. „Starkschlinger")

Ø Seil/Stab: 4–50mm, Abstand zueinander: 20–80cm

Vertikalabstand Abrutschsicherung oder Querstreben: 50–200cm

Feldmaße und Dimensionierung abhängig von natürlicher Endwuchshöhe, Pflanzenstärke und Schlingverhalten

Possibly parallel wire as upward guides (see ill. on the r.: "Strong twiners")

Ø wire/rod: 4–50mm, Distance apart: 20–80cm

Vertical distance for the anti-slip guard or the cross strut: 50–200cm

Field size and dimensions depend on natural final growth height, strength of the plant and how it twines

On load questions: weight and wind loads

RANKER
CLIMBING PLANTS

SPREIZKLIMMER
SPREADING CLIMBERS

Gitter- und netzförmige Konstruktionen
Grid and net-like trellises

Konstruktionen mit vorwiegend waagerechter Ausrichtung oder gitter-/netzförmige Konstruktionen
Structure with primarily horizontal reach or grid/net structure

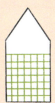

Lasteinflüsse (Laub/Frucht/Holz):
circa 6–21 kg/m² (Gewichtsschätzung bei fachgerechtem Schnitt/tropfnass)

Load factors (foliage/fruit/wood):
approx. 6–21 kg/m² (weight estimated after expert pruning/dripping wet)

Lasteinflüsse (Laub/Frucht/Holz):
circa 7–14 kg/m² (Gewichtsschätzung bei fachgerechtem Schnitt/tropfnass)

Load factors (foliage/fruit/wood):
approx. 7–14 kg/m² (weight estimated after expert pruning/dripping wet)

+ **Windlast (abhängig von Polsterdicke/Exposition – erhöhte Windlast in Gebäuderand-/Eckbereichen) Schwingungsübertragung in die Primärkonstruktion vermeiden**

+ *Wind load (on thickness of padding/exposure — increased wind load at building edges and corners) Avoid vibration transfer onto the primary structure*

+ **Spannungszustände von Kletterhilfen: Temperaturwechsel/Dickenwuchs der Kletterpflanze (insbesondere Starkschlinger)**

+ *Tension of climbing frames: changes in temperature/thickness of main stems of climbers (in particular strong twiners)*

Ø Seil/Stab: 4–30 mm

Maschen-/Gitterweite: B 10–30 cm, H 20–50 cm max.

Feldmaße und Dimensionierung abhängig von natürlicher Endwuchshöhe und Pflanzenstärke

Ø wire/rod: 4–30 mm

Mesh/grid size: b 10–30 cm, h 20–50 cm max.

Field size and dimensions depend on natural final growth height and strength of the plant

Vorzugsweise horizontale Ausrichtung Vertikalabstand untereinander: circa 40 cm

Maschen-/Gitterweite: B 30–50 cm, H 50 cm max.

Feldmaße und Dimensionierung abhängig von natürlicher Endwuchshöhe und Pflanzenstärke

Preferably with a horizontal reach.
Vertical distance apart: approx. 40 cm

Mesh/grid size: b 30–50 cm, h 50 cm max.

Field size and dimensions depend on natural final growth height and strength of the plant

---

Illustrationen nach/*Illustrations after*
Pfoser 2018

Pflanzen in horizontalen Vegetationsflächen an Kragkonsolen oder Vorkonstruktionen

Plants in horizontal growing areas attached to projecting consoles or on-front structures

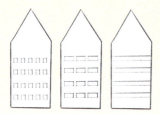

Lasteinflüsse (Pflanzengefäß/ Substrat, wassergesättigt/Pflanzengewicht): circa 450–550 kg/lfdm (Bsp. Kletterpflanzen), Pflanzenhöhe 5 m (inklusive Kletterhilfe)

Load factors (plant container/substrate, water-saturated/plant weight): approx. 450–550kg/continuous meter (e.g. climbers) Plant height 5m (incl. climbing frame)

+ **Gewicht** Kragkonsolen oder Vorkonstruktionen
+ **Windlast** (abhängig von Polsterdicke Pflanzen/ Exposition – erhöhte Windlast in Gebäuderand-/ Eckbereichen), Schwingungsübertragung in die Primärkonstruktion vermeiden
+ **Gewichte** aus Schnee, Eis (Pflanze/Kragkonsolen oder Vorkonstruktionen/Pflanzenbehälter/ Kletterhilfe – abhängig von örtlichen Bedingungen)
+ **Spannungszustände von Kletterhilfen:** Temperaturwechsel/Dickenwuchs der Pflanzen/ Kletterpflanzen (insbesondere Starkschlinger)

+ *Weight projecting consoles or on-front structures*
+ *Wind load (depends on padding thickness/exposure — increased wind load at building edges and corners), Avoid vibration transfer onto the primary structure*
+ *Weight of snow and/or ice (plant/projecting consoles or on-front structures/plant containers/climbing frames — depends on local conditions)*
+ *Tension of climbing frames: changes in temperature/thickness of main stems of climbers (in particular strong twiners)*

gegebenenfalls Sicherung Windsicherung (Gehölze) Kletterhilfe gem. Gerüstkletterpflanzen

Ø Seil/Stab: 4–50 mm
Abstand zueinander: 20–80 cm
Maschen-/Rasterweite: b 10–80 cm, h 20–200 cm

Feldmaße und Dimensionierung abhängig von natürlicher Endwuchshöhe, Pflanzenstärke, gegebenenfalls Schlingverhalten

Possible securing against wind (shrubs) Climbing frames for climbers that require them

Ø *wire/rod: 4–50mm*
Distance apart: 20–80cm
Mesh/grid size: b 10–80cm, h 20–200cm

Field size and dimensions depend on natural final growth height, strength of the plant and how it twines

WANDGEBUNDEN, MODULAR
WALL-BASED, MODULAR

Sekundärkonstruktion mit vertikaler Vegetationstragschicht in Pflanzmodulen

Secondary structure with vertical layer of plant containers in modules

Lasteinflüsse (Sekundärkonstruktion/ Substrat bzw. Substratersatz, wassergesättigt/ Pflanzengewicht):
circa 30–220 kg/m²

Load factors (secondary structure/substrate or substrate substitute, water-saturated/plant weight): approx. 30–220 kg/m²

+ **Windlast** (abhängig von Polsterdicke der Pflanzen/ Exposition – erhöhte Windlast in Gebäuderand-/ Eckbereichen), Schwingungsübertragung in die Primärkonstruktion vermeiden
+ **Gewichte aus Schnee, Eis** (Pflanze/Sekundärstruktion, abhängig von örtlichen Bedingungen)

Flächenmaße und Aufbautiefe Modul systemabhängig

+ *Wind load (depends on padding thickness, plants and exposure — increased wind load at building edges and corners), Avoid vibration transfer onto the primary structure*
+ *Weight of snow and/or ice (plants/secondary structure — depends on local conditions)*

Surface area size and depth of the modules depends on the system used

WANDGEBUNDEN, FLÄCHIG
WALL-BASED, SURFACE

Sekundärkonstruktion mit vertikaler Vegetations-tragschicht an wartungsfreier Primärkonstruktion

Secondary structure with vertical planting containers attached to a primary structure requiring no maintenance

Lasteinflüsse (Sekundärkonstruktion/ Substrat bzw. Substratersatz, wassergesättigt/ Pflanzengewicht):
circa 30–35 kg/m²

Load factors (secondary structure/substrate or substrate substitute, water-saturated/plant weight): approx. 30–35 kg/m²

+ **Windlast** (abhängig von Polsterdicke der Pflanzen/ Exposition – erhöhte Windlast in Gebäuderand-/ Eckbereichen), Schwingungsübertragung in die Primärkonstruktion vermeiden
+ **Gewichte aus Schnee, Eis** (Pflanze/Sekundärstruktion, abhängig von örtlichen Bedingungen)

Flächenmaße und Aufbautiefe systemabhängig

+ *Wind load (depends on padding thickness, plants and exposure — increased wind load at building edges and corners), Avoid vibration transfer onto the primary structure*
+ *Weight of snow and/or ice (plants/secondary structure — depends on local conditions)*

Surface area size and depth of the modules depends on the system used

---

Illustrationen nach/*Illustrations after*
Pfoser 2018

Ab welcher Gebäudehöhe ist eine Begrünung nicht mehr möglich oder sinnvoll?

Kletterpflanzen erreichen Höhen bis zu 30 Metern. Wand-gebundene Begrünungen benötigen keinen Boden- und Bodenwasseranschluss, sind jedoch auf eine technische Versorgung mit Wasser und Nährstoffen angewiesen. Pflege- und Wartungskosten steigen mit zunehmender Gebäudehöhe, vor allem wenn Leitern nicht mehr ausrei-chend sind und auf Steiger zurückgegriffen werden muss.

Eine sinnvolle Integration der Begrünung bereits während der Planung – die Begrünung von Wartungsumgängen, Laubengängen, Balkonen und Loggien – kann hier kosten-sparend wirken. Windsog und Austrocknungen in Rand- und sonnenexponierten Bereichen sind zu beachten, können jedoch vom Fachplaner zuvor berechnet werden.

Climbing plants can reach heights of 30 meters. Greenery attached to walls does not require a connection to the ground or to groundwater but does rely on technical provision of nutrients and water. The higher the building, the higher the costs of caring for the plants and maintaining the system, particularly if ladders cannot be used and walkways/catwalks are required.

As of what height is it no longer possible or meaningful to introduce greenery?

The meaningful integration of greenery as early as the planning stage (the greening of maintenance shafts, covered walkways, balconies and loggias) can serve to save costs here. Factors to consider are wind suction and drying out in sections at the edges or those most exposed to the sun; expert planners can take this into account in advance to mitigate these influences.

NICOLE PFOSER

In den wandgebundenen Fassadenbegrünungssystemen werden in der Regel winterharte Pflanzen eingesetzt, deren Wurzeln den Frost gut überstehen. Dennoch ist es empfehlenswert, die Wurzeln zu schützen, indem z.B. Gefäße mit einem Mindestmaß von 50 cm genutzt oder Dämmstoffe eingesetzt werden. Wurzeln sind empfindlicher als das Holz oder die Blätter immergrüner Pflanzen.

Wie überstehen die Pflanzen Frostperioden?

Bei jedem Projekt müssen die lokalen Eis- und Frosttage berücksichtigt werden. Das heißt, eine Vegetationswand kann auch im Alpenraum auf 2.000 Metern Höhe erfolgreich umgesetzt werden. Hier sind Substratschichtdicke und das gewählte System entscheidend. Die Wasserversorgung muss im Winter angepasst werden, doch auch im Winter und an Eistagen ist die Versorgung der Pflanze mit Wasser wichtig. Sonst verdunsten die Pflanzen bei Sonnenschein, wenn kein Wasser nachgefüllt wird und vertrocknen.

There are potentially periods of frost in the winter months – even if these have become increasingly infrequent in recent years. Wall-based façade greenery systems rely on hardy plants whose roots withstand frost well. All the same, it bears protecting the roots, for example by using planters with a minimum size of 50cm or insulating material. Roots are more sensitive than the wood or leaves of evergreens. Moreover, the water supply should be adjusted in winter.
ALEXANDER HILDEBRAND

The number of local days with frost and ice need to be factored into every project, meaning a vegetation wall can also be successfully realized in the Alps at an altitude of 2,000 meters. Decisive here are the thickness of the substrate layer and the system chosen. The water supply must be adjusted in winter, but in winter and days with ice it is important to water the plants. When the sun shines, the plants evaporate water and if they are not watered they dry out.
GERHARD ZEMP

How do the plants survive the frost?

Welche Pflege ist für Rank- und Klettergewächse notwendig?

Die Pflege hängt von der Pflanze ab. Ein- bis zweimal pro Jahr ist ein Zuschnitt ratsam. Wer dies nicht selbst übernehmen will, sollte einen Pflegevertrag nach FLL-Richtlinien (Forschungsgesellschaft Landesentwicklung Landschaftsbau e. V.) mit einer Fachfirma abschließen; diese übernimmt auch die Wartung des Bewässerungssystems, die Kontrolle auf Schädlingsbefall sowie die möglicherweise notwendige Düngung.

Wie oft muss man die Pflanzen am Gebäude austauschen?

Die meisten Pflanzen haben eine sehr lange Lebensdauer. Gehölze und verholzende Kletterpflanzen können Jahrzehnte alt werden, ohne dass sie ausgetauscht werden müssen. Generell sind jedoch die Voraussetzungen, die den Pflanzen geboten werden, der begrenzende Faktor. Mit dem richtigen System und der optimalen Bepflanzung lassen sich Ausfälle von Beginn an reduzieren.

The care depends on the plant. Once or twice a year they need to be pruned. If you don't want to do this yourself, then it is advisable to sign an agreement in line with the FLL guidelines (Forschungsgesellschaft Landesentwicklung Landschaftsbau e.V. – non-profit research association on rural development and landscaping) with a specialist company that then handles all the maintenance of the irrigation system, checks for pests, and if necessary also adds fertilizer to the soil.

ALEXANDER HILDEBRAND

What care do vines and climbing plants need?

How often do the plants on the building need to be replaced?

Most plants have a very long lifespan. However, in general the limiting factor is the conditions under which plants are kept. Once the plants have grown, with good care and tending they can survive for decades. And with the right system and optimal planting, the chances of plants dying can be reduced from the outset.

ALEXANDER HILDEBRAND

Horizontales Grün

Horizontal greenery

Worin liegt der Unterschied zwischen einer intensiven und einer extensiven Dachbegrünung? Wann entscheide ich mich wofür?

Die extensiven Gründächer zeichnen sich durch eine geringe Aufbauhöhe (circa 8–15 cm), geringes Gewicht (circa 80–170 kg/m²) und eine trockenheitsverträgliche Vegetation aus; sie sind nährstoffarm. Auf Substraten mit geringem Humusanteil werden meist kleinwüchsige Pflanzenarten ausgesät, die auf humusreichen Böden nicht konkurrenzfähig wären. Je nach Dicke und Zusammensetzung des Substrats entwickelt sich eine pflegeleichte Pflanzengemeinschaft, die sich selbst reguliert.

Dagegen sind Intensivbegrünungen erweiterte Wohnräume (Dachgärten), auf denen ähnliche Pflanzen wachsen wie im ebenerdigen Garten. Dementsprechend ist der Gründachaufbau höher (ab circa 25 cm) und schwerer (ab circa 300 kg/m²). Die Pflege gestaltet sich je nach Pflanzenauswahl mehr oder weniger aufwendig. Intensiv begrünte Dächer gibt es in der Regel nur auf Flachdächern, dagegen können Extensivbegrünungen auf Flach- und Schrägdächern zum Einsatz kommen. Wenn man das Dach regelmäßig begehen und nutzen möchte wie einen ebenerdigen Garten, wäre das eine Intensivbegrünung.

The extensively greened roofs stand out for their low additional heights (approx. 8–15 cm), low weight (approx. 80–170 kg/m²) and vegetation that can endure heat; they require few nutrients. Usually, small plant types that would not be able to compete on humus-heavy soil are sown on substrates featuring a low ratio of humus. Depending on the substrate's thickness and composition, a group of plants grows that is easy to care for and regulates itself.

By contrast, intensive greenery comprises extended living space (roof gardens), on which similar plants grow to those in a ground-level garden. The superstructure on the roof is therefore accordingly higher (from approx. 25 cm) and heavier (from about 300 kg/m²). Depending on the choice of plants, more or less tending is required. Intensively greened roofs are, as a rule, only to be found on flat roofs, while extensive greenery can be planted on flat or sloping roofs. If I frequent the roof regularly and use it like a ground-level garden, then it is considered intensive greenery.

GUNTER MANN

What is the difference between intensive and extensive roof greening? When do I decide on which?

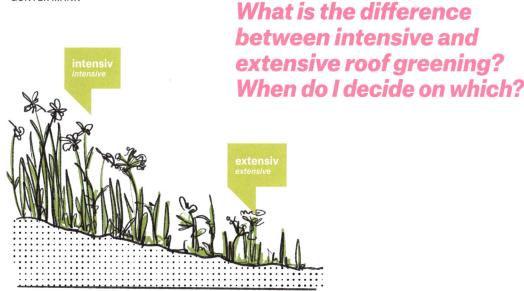

intensiv
intensive

extensiv
extensive

INTENSIVE DACHBEGRÜNUNG
INTENSIVE ROOF GREENERY

Höhere Substratschicht
Speicherung von Nährstoffen und Wasser
Mehr Wurzelraum
▸ **Pflanzen wachsen höher und dichter**

Thicker layer of substrate
Storage of nutrients and water
More space for roots
▸ *Plants grow higher and more densely*

EXTENSIVE DACHBEGRÜNUNG
EXTENSIVE ROOF GREENERY

Niedrige Substratschicht
Rasches Austrocknen
Geringer Wurzelraum
▸ **Pflanzen wachsen niedriger und weniger dicht**

Thinner layer of substrate
Swiftly dries out
Less space for roots
▸ *Plants do not grow as high and as densely*

Illustration nach/*Illustration after*
Stadt Zürich/*City of Zurich* 2018

Simple extensive roof greenery can perhaps best be referred to as a protective ecological layer, acting as a shield and thus extending the roof seal's service life – as well as offering the overall ecological advantages of roof greenery, of course. In the case of intensive roof greenery, the emphasis is on the added benefit of being able to use the roof as additional living space. In fact, essentially it can be used for anything that you could do with a ground-level garden.

What arguments speak in favor of intensive roof greenery and which in favor of extensive greenery?

Welche Argumente sprechen für eine intensive Dachbegrünung, welche für eine extensive?

Eine einfache Extensivbegrünung könnte man auch als ökologischen Schutzbelag bezeichnen: als Schutz und damit Verlängerung der Lebensdauer der Dachabdichtung, dies natürlich mit den gesamten ökologischen Vorteilen einer Dachbegrünung. Bei einer intensiven Dachbegrünung steht außerdem die Nutzung des Daches als zusätzlicher Lebensraum im Vordergrund. Mit ihr ist im Prinzip fast alles möglich, was auch in einem Garten auf ebener Erde realisiert werden kann.

JOACHIM STROH

Extensive Dachbegrünung/*Extensive roof greenery*
Photo: Gunter Mann, BuGG

Wie ist eine Dachbegrünung aufgebaut?

Wichtige Voraussetzungen sind
- eine wurzelfeste Dachabdichtung: Vliese, die Nährstoffe
  zurückhalten und den Wasserabfluss beeinflussen
- eine Substratschicht als Pflanzboden und
- eine Regulierung des Regenwassers.

Retentionsdächer sind Dachsysteme, bei denen das Regen-wasser aktiv im Substrat gestaut oder über spezielle Drainageelemente aus Kunststoff gesammelt wird. Das Regenwasser verdunstet zugleich über die bepflanzten Flächen, und Überschusswasser kann gesammelt oder zeitverzögert der Kanalisation zugeführt werden. Offene Wasserrückhaltsflächen können außerdem Vögeln als Wasserquelle dienen und zusätzliche Kühleffekte durch die Verdunstungskühlung bewirken.

Einschichtbegrünungen ohne Drainage funktionieren auch; aber nur, wenn ausreichend Gefälle vorhanden ist, da ansonsten eine Vernässung des Wurzelraums ein-treten kann. Ferner darf die Substratschicht nicht zu gering sein, da sonst kein dauerhaftes Pflanzenwachstum gegeben ist. Vom Systemaufbau und der Art der Wasser-speicherung ist die Pflanzenwahl abhängig – von feuchtig-keitsliebenden Pflanzen bis zu Gräsern oder Dickblatt-gewächsen.

Unterkonstruktion
Substructure

Dachabdichtung
Roof seal

Wurzelresistentes
Speichervlies
*Root-resistant storage,
nonwoven*

Drainage/*Drainage*

Filterschicht/*Filter layer*

Substrat/*Substrate*

What is the structure of roof greenery?

The key prerequisites are:
- *a roof seal that withstands roots: non-wovens that retain nutrients and influence water drainage*
- *a layer of substrate consisting of planting soil, and*
- *regulation of the rainwater flow.*

Retention roofs are roof systems where the rainwater is actively stored in the substrate or collected using special plastic drainage elements. The rainwater immediately evaporates over the planted areas and surplus water can be collected and released later into the drainage. Open water retention basins can also serve as a source of water for the birds and additionally cool the building through evaporative cooling.

Single-layer greenery without drainage systems can also work; but only if there is enough of a slope, as otherwise the roots may remain wet and rot. Moreover, the layer of substrate must not be too thin, as otherwise no durable plant growth will ensue. The choice of plants depends on the structure chosen and the kind of water storage system, and ranges from plants that love moisture to grasses or stonecrops.

GUNTER MANN / JOACHIM STROH

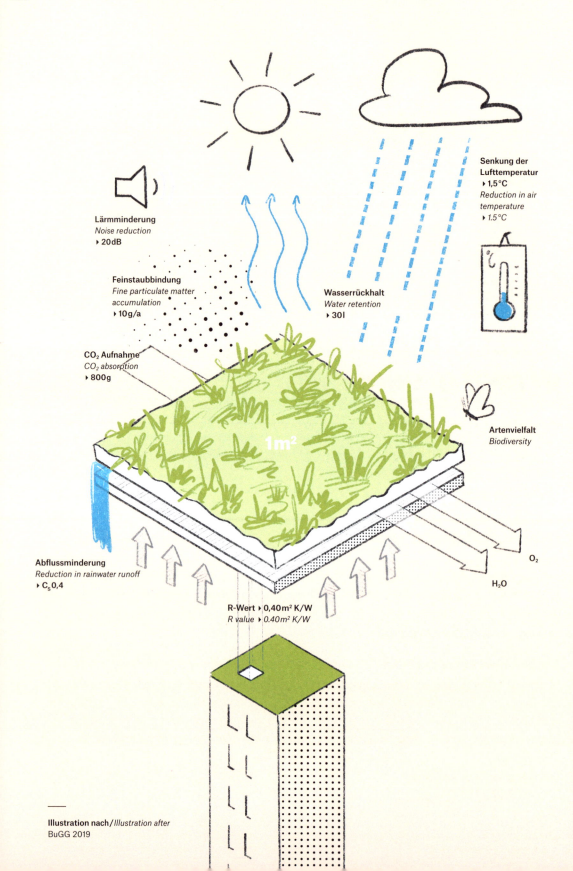

Lärmminderung
Noise reduction
‣ 20 dB

Feinstaubbindung
Fine particulate matter accumulation
‣ 10 g/a

CO₂ Aufnahme
CO₂ absorption
‣ 800 g

Senkung der Lufttemperatur
‣ 1,5 °C
Reduction in air temperature
‣ 1.5 °C

Wasserrückhalt
Water retention
‣ 30 l

Artenvielfalt
Biodiversity

1m²

O₂

H₂O

Abflussminderung
Reduction in rainwater runoff
‣ Cₛ 0,4

R-Wert ‣ 0,40 m² K/W
R value ‣ 0.40 m² K/W

Illustration nach/*Illustration after*
BuGG 2019

Was kann extensive Dachbegrünung klimatisch für Gebäude und Umwelt leisten?

Die positiven Effekte bestehen in Wasserrückhalt und Verdunstung. Die Verdunstung wiederum bewirkt Kühleffekte und Luftbefeuchtung. Der Gründachaufbau ist natürliche Wärmedämmung und schützt vor Frost und sommerlicher Hitzeeinstrahlung.[18]

What can extensive roof greenery contribute to the climate of the building and the surroundings?

The positive effects are water retention and evaporation. The evaporation in turn causes cooling and air moisture. The green superstructure on the roof provides natural heat insulation and protects against frost and summery heat irradiation.[18]

---

18   BuGG Bundesverband GebäudeGrün e.V., Fachinformation Positive Wirkungen von Gebäudebegrünungen: www.gebaeudegruen.info (1.12.2020)

Das Gegenteil ist der Fall. Durch die Kombination ergeben sich sogar Synergieeffekte. Photovoltaikmodule bringen ihre beste Leistung bei einer Umgebungstemperatur von 25°C. Durch die Verdunstungsleistung der Begrünung erzielt die Photovoltaikanlage an heißen Tagen damit eine höhere Leistung.

Besonders vorteilhaft sind auflastgehaltene Modulträgersysteme, bei denen der Gründachaufbau mit seinem Gewicht die PV-Anlage auf dem Dach fixiert. Dann muss auch nicht in die Dachabdichtung eingegriffen werden.[19] Allerdings stehen „Dachgärten", also Intensivbegrünungen, in Konkurrenz mit Photovoltaikanlagen.

Stehen Dachbegrünung und Photovoltaik in Konkurrenz zueinander?

19 BuGG Bundesverband GebäudeGrün e.V., Fachinformation Solar-Gründach: www.gebaeudegruen.info (1.12.2020).

The opposite is the case. The combination of the two actually offers synergies. Photovoltaic modules perform best if the ambient temperature is 25 °C. The evaporation effect of the greening means that the photovoltaic plant has a higher output on hot days.

Especially advantageous are modular frame systems held in place by weight as the roof greening superstructure can be used to firmly fix the photovoltaic system on the roof. Moreover, no alterations then need be made to the roof seal.[19] However, "roof gardens", meaning intensive greenery, compete with photovoltaic plants.

GUNTER MANN / JOACHIM STROH

Do roof greening and photovoltaic systems compete with each other?

1   **Aufgeständerte Photovoltaik-Paneele mit mindestens 30 cm Abstand zur Substratoberfläche an der tiefsten Stelle**
Raised photovoltaic panels with a distance of at least 30 cm from the surface of the substrate at the lowest point

2   **Ausreichender Abstand zwischen den Photovoltaik-Paneelen (mindestens 50 cm)**
Sufficient distance between the photovoltaic panels (at least 50 cm)

3   **Geringe Substratschicht für niederwüchsige Pflanzen**
Low substrate layer for plants of a low height

4   **Hohe Substratschicht für höhere und schattenverträgliche Vegetation**
High substrate layer for higher plants and those that grow well in shade

5   **Durch die Verdunstungskühlung der Pflanzen sinkt die Umgebungstemperatur der PV-Paneele. Diese wird dadurch an heißen Tagen leistungsstärker.**
The ambient temperature of the PV panels is lowered by the evaporation cooling of the plants, meaning their yield increases on hot days.

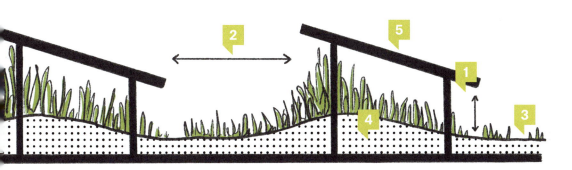

Illustration nach/*Illustration after*
Stadt Zürich/*City of Zurich* 2018

Muss eine intensive Dachwiese gemäht werden? Wie?

Wer eine Dachwiese als englischen Rasen versteht, muss natürlich mähen – wie zu ebener Erde sinnvollerweise mit einem Rasenmäher. Egal welche Form von Wiese oder Rasen auf dem Dach im Rahmen einer Intensivbegrünung realisiert werden soll, es gelten die gleichen Eckdaten wie zu ebener Erde.

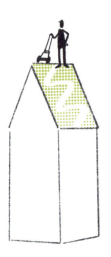

Do you need to mow an intensive roof lawn? If so, how?

Anyone who thinks a roof lawn should be like an English lawn will of course have to mow it the way they would if it were on the ground – preferably with a lawnmower. The same parameters apply as they do at ground level, irrespective of the form of lawn or grass to be planted on the roof as part of intensive greenery.

JOACHIM STROH

Roof gardens are all the rage, but who is it who will tend them? What effort will be required in future years?

Intensive roof greenery = intensive tending = the same effort as with a ground-level garden.

Extensive roof greenery = extensive care. As a rule, one or two checks a year to ensure the drains etc. are functioning and, if necessary, to remove unwanted plants that have popped up, e.g., owing to airborne seeds. A small birch tree, for example, is certainly an unwelcome addition to extensive greenery.
JOACHIM STROH

Dachgärten stehen hoch im Kurs. Doch wer soll sie dann pflegen? Welcher Aufwand entsteht in den Folgejahren?

Intensive Dachbegrünung = intensive Pflege = Pflegeaufwand wie zu ebener Erde.

Extensive Dachbegrünung = extensive Pflege. In der Regel reichen ein bis zwei Kontrollgänge pro Jahr, um die Funktion der Abläufe zu prüfen und gegebenenfalls Fremdbewuchs durch Flugbesamung zu entfernen. Denn eine kleine Birke hat nichts auf einer Extensivbegrünung zu suchen.

Ist eine Dachbegrünung genehmigungs- pflichtig?

Nutz- und begehbare Dachbegrünungen sind bei Bestands- und Neubauten genehmigungspflichtig, da sie gegebenenfalls Grenzabstände zum Nachbarn betreffen. Extensivbegrünungen sind in der Regel hinsichtlich von Bestandsgebäuden nicht genehmigungspflichtig, für Neubauten schon. Zu empfehlen ist in jedem Fall eine Kontaktaufnahme mit dem zuständigen Bauamt. Wenn das Gebäude unter Denkmalschutz steht, ist eine Absprache mit dem zuständigen Denkmalamt notwendig.

Wie steil darf mein Dach für eine Dachbegrünung sein?

Bis maximal 45 Grad Dachneigungen können Fachbetriebe mit geeigneten Gründachsystemen Dächer begrünen. In der Regel liegen Dachbegrünungen bei 0–30 Grad Dachneigung. Ab etwa 10–15 Grad Dachneigung ist eine Rutschsicherung vorzusehen.

Roof greenery that you use and can walk through needs planning permission, both if retrofitted on existing buildings and for new buildings, as it potentially affects the distance to be maintained from neighbors. As a rule, extensive greenery does not require planning permission if being retrofitted, but does for new builds. At any rate, it bears contacting your local building department. If the building is a heritage-listed property, then you will also need to consult the heritage office responsible.

GUNTER MANN / LARA-MARIA MOHR

Do you need official permission to green a roof?

How steep can the roof slope be if I want to green it?

Specialized tradesmen can attach suitable roof greening systems to roofs with a slope of a max. 45 degrees. As a rule, roof greenery is deployed on slopes of 0–30 degrees. From a slope of about 10–15 degrees upwards you will need to secure the greenery against slippage.

JOACHIM STROH

PROJEKT
„LEBENDIGE DÄCHER",
BOTANISCHER GARTEN

PROJECT "LIVING ROOFS",
BOTANICAL GARDENS

FRANKFURT

Lebensraum Dach-begrünung – da geht noch mehr!

Dachbegrünungen haben vielfältige positive Wirkungen und bieten neben Rückhaltung von Niederschlagswasser, Verbesserung des Stadtklimas, Bindung von Feinstaub auch Pflanzen und Tieren einen Lebensraum. Dachbegrünungen können daher einen wertvollen Beitrag für den Naturschutz leisten und eine Möglichkeit bieten, dem globalen Artensterben entgegenzuwirken.

Aktuell werden die meisten Dachbegrünungen nur als „einfache Extensivbegrünung" mit meist sehr eingeschränktem Artenspektrum angelegt. So werden in der Praxis meist Extensiv-Dachsubstrate mit geringer Schichtdicke von oft nur 6–8cm Höhe auf den Dächern gleichmäßig verteilt und mit einer Mischung aus Sprossstücken von Dickblattgewächsen begrünt. Bei dieser Form der Anlage wird das ökologische Potenzial von Dachflächen als Lebensraum für Pflanzen und Tiere nicht hinreichend ausgeschöpft.

Eine große Standort- und Strukturvielfalt ist neben einer artenreichen Begrünung elementare Voraussetzung für die Entwicklung biologischer Vielfalt. Auch auf Dächern lässt sich diese herstellen, ohne in Konflikt mit den notwendigen baulichen und sicherheitsrelevanten Aspekten wie Dichtigkeit, Dachlast, Wasserableitung und Verwehungssicherheit zu geraten.

Greening roofs has many favorable effects and not only enables the retention of rainwater, improves the urban climate, and binds fine particulate matter, but also creates a habitat for plants and animals. Greened roofs can therefore make an invaluable contribution to nature conservation and offer an opportunity to counteract global species extinction.

At present, most greened roofs simply entail "extensive greenery" with a very limited number of different plants. In practice, most extensively greened roofs have a low substrate layer of often only 6–8cm spread evenly across the roof and featuring a mixture of rootstock for plants from the stonecrop family. This type of system does not sufficiently exhaust the ecological potential roof areas afford as habitats for plants and animals.

Alongside greening with a broad range of different plants, elementary to the emergence of biological diversity is a pronounced variety of locations and structures. This can also be achieved on roofs and need not come into conflict with the necessary structural and safety-related aspects such as leak-proofing, roof loads, drainage of water and prevention of drift.

With biodiversity components, such as different substrate depths and composition (mounds of

Mit Biodiversitätsbausteinen wie unterschiedlichen Substrathöhen, unterschiedlichen Substratzusammensetzungen (Anhügelungen bis 40 cm, Sand- und Lehmflächen) oder einem insgesamt höheren Substrataufbau (mindestens 10 cm, besser 15 cm) mit verbessertem Wasserspeichervolumen (mehr Ton- und Kompostanteile) lassen sich Standort- und Strukturvielfalt erhöhen und Mikrohabitate als Lebensraum für Pflanzen und Tiere schaffen. Aufbringen von Totholz und Steinen als Haufen oder Einzelstrukturen sowie spezielle Nisthilfen für Insekten sind Elemente zur Förderung der Biodiversität auf Dächern, ebenso wie die Anlage von Wasserflächen von kleinen „Pfützen" bis hin zu Teichen. Wichtig ist die Auswahl von an die „extremen" Standortbedingungen angepassten Pflanzenarten. Dachflächen können seltenen und bedrohten Pflanzenarten neuen Lebensraum bieten, Insekten und Vögeln können sie Futterpflanzen liefern. Biodiversitätsdächer können helfen, die Auswirkungen des Klimawandels zu mildern.

up to 40cm, areas of sand/loam) or a higher layer of substrate overall (minimum 10cm, better is 15cm) with an improved water retention volume (higher proportion of clay and compost), the variety of locations and structures can be enhanced and micro-habitats created for plants and animals. The inclusion of dead wood and stones as piles or individual structures as well as special nesting boxes for insects are items that promote biodiversity on roofs, as does the installation of surfaces of water ranging from small "puddles" to actual ponds. It is important to select plant types adapted to "extreme" local

Roof greenery as a habitat – more is definitely possible!

Bepflanzung des „Biodiversitätsdaches" in der Schautischanlage im Botanischen Garten Frankfurt/Main (5.6.2020)
Planting the "Biodiversity Roof" in the demonstration facility at Frankfurt's Botanical Gardens (June 5, 2020)
Photo: Team „Lebendige Dächer"

Aufwertungsmaßnahme durch Saatfenster, Nachsaat,
Stauden- und Zwiebelpflanzung auf einem Partnerdach
(Schule Konradsdorf, Wetteraukreis) (2.11.2020)
Upgrading a roof using seeding windows, second seedings,
shrubs and bulbous plants on a partner project roof (school in
Konradsdorf, Wetteraukreis) (Nov. 2, 2020)
Photo: Team „Lebendige Dächer"

Gründächer sind Extremlebensräume. Große Hitze und lang anhaltende Trockenheit, wie sie in den letzten Jahren verstärkt auftreten, sowie komplettes Durchfrieren des Substrats im Winter, sind eine erhebliche Belastung für die Dachvegetation. Selbst den Spezialisten unter den Pflanzenarten bereiten diese Bedingungen Schwierigkeiten, und nur wenige Pflanzenarten sind diesen Extrembedingungen gewachsen. Eine Möglichkeit, dem Wassermangel zu begegnen, ist es, die Substrathöhe zu vergrößern und die Wasserspeicherfähigkeit des Substrats zu erhöhen.

Das am Botanischen Garten der Stadt Frankfurt angesiedelte und durch die KfW Stiftung geförderte Projekt läuft noch bis Mitte 2024. Das Team setzt sich aus Biologen, Gärtnern und Dachgärtnern zusammen. Neben der Strategieentwicklung in Bezug auf Fördermöglichkeiten für mehr Biodiversität auf Dachflächen sowie Bestandserfassungen von Pflanzenarten auf bereits bestehenden Dachflächen stehen die Öffentlichkeitsarbeit und die Suche nach neuen, für Dächer geeigneten Pflanzenarten im Vordergrund. Anhand von beispielhaften Aufwertungsmaßnahmen auf Partnerdächern wird die Wirksamkeit von Biodiversitätsbausteinen erprobt und veranschaulicht.

Das Projekt „Lebendige Dächer" soll zu einem Paradigmenwechsel der Dachbegrünung und Dachpflege beitragen. Dazu gehört, dass bestehende „einfache" Dachbegrünungen mit den verschiedenen oben genannten Biodiversitätsbausteinen ein „ökologisches Upgrade" erfahren. Gebietsheimische, darunter auch seltene und in ihrem Vorkommen zurückgehende Pflanzenarten, können auf Dachflächen einen neuen Lebensraum finden. Neue Dachbegrünung sollten stets als Bio-

conditions. Rare and threatened plant species can be given new habitats on roofs and provide food for insects and birds. Biodiversity roofs can help to mitigate the impact of climate change.

Green roofs are extreme habitats! Intense heat and protracted dry periods such as have occurred increasingly in recent years, as well as the complete freezing of substrates in winter, pose a considerable strain on roof vegetation. Even the specialists among the plant types find such conditions difficult and only a few types of plant can endure such extreme conditions! One way of countering water shortages is to opt for deeper substrates and increase their water retention ability.

The project underway at the City of Frankfurt Botanical Gardens and supported by the KfW Stiftung runs until mid-2024. The team is made up of biologists, gardeners and roof gardeners. Alongside the development of strategies for promoting greater biodiversity on roofs and monitoring of the number of different plant types on existing roofs, the emphasis is on PR work and the search for new types of plants suitable for roofs. By means of specimen measures to enhance partner roofs, the efficacy of biodiversity modules is being tested and visualized.

The "Living Roofs" project is intended to help bring about a paradigm shift in roof greenery

diversitätsbegrünung ausgeführt und damit zum selbstverständlichen Baustandard werden. Die Dachpflege sollte auf eine Steigerung der biologischen Vielfalt hinwirken.

Die Einrichtung von Biodiversitätsgründächern und die biodiversitätsfördernde Pflege sollten bereits in Bebauungsplänen für geeignete Gebäude festgeschrieben werden. Das Ziel ist es, für mehr Biodiversitätsdächer zu werben und an Städte- und Landschaftsplaner, Architekten und Bauherren sowie Entscheidungsträger zu appellieren, sich für die Anlage von Biodiversitätsdächern einzusetzen nach der Maxime: „Mehr Natur im Wohnumfeld wagen!".

Auch hinsichtlich der Betreuung und Pflege von Gründächern sollte es zu einem Paradigmenwechsel kommen: Nicht mehr allein die Pflege der oftmals nicht heimischen Dickblattgewächse (Sedum-Arten) und die Entfernung von „Fremd"-Bewuchs sollten im Vordergrund stehen, sondern vielmehr die Entwicklung hin zu einem möglichst vielfältigen Biodiversitätsgründach. Verbesserung der Ausstattung mit Biotopstrukturelementen, Nachpflanzungen und Nachsaaten mit Kräutern und Zwiebelgewächsen könnten zur Hauptaufgabe der Dachgärtner werden.

and roof care. This includes existing "simple" roof greenery being ecologically upgraded by means of the various biodiversity elements mentioned above. Native types of plants including rare varieties or those whose numbers are dwindling can find a new habitat on roofs. New roof greenery should always be realized as biodiversity greening and thus become the obvious building standard. Caring for roofs should lead to enhanced biological diversity.

Establishing biodiversity-greened roofs and care that promotes biodiversity should be a firm element of land-use plans for suitable buildings. The goal is to promote more biodiversity roofs and to appeal to urban and landscape planners, architects, and developers to advocate the adoption of biodiversity roofs in line with the adage: "Go for more nature in residential settings!"

There must be a paradigm shift as regards maintaining and caring for greened roofs, too: The emphasis should no longer only be on caring for often not native stonecrop plants (types of sedum) and removing "outside" plants, but rather developing as varied a biodiversity-greened roof as possible. Boosting the inclusion of biotope structural elements, follow-up planting and sowing with herbs and bulbous plants could become roof gardeners' main mission.

Das Ende des Jahres 2019 gestartete Projekt „Lebendige Dächer" am Botanischen Garten der Stadt Frankfurt beschäftigt sich mit der Frage, wie das Potenzial von Dachbegrünungen als Lebensraum für Pflanzen und Tiere besser ausgeschöpft werden kann. Das Projektteam besteht aus Andreas König (Diplom-Biologe und stellvertretender Technischer Leiter des Botanischen Gartens), Uwe Barth (Diplom-Biologe), Ralf Kremser (Gärtnermeister und Revierleiter im Botanischen Garten), Beate Alberternst (Diplom-Agrarbiologin), Stefan Nawrath (Diplom-Biologe) und Horst Ewerling (Diplom-Biologe und Dachgärtner), der das Team zu technischen und ökologischen Aspekten berät. Sie testen bedrohte heimische Pflanzenarten auf ihre Eignung für Gründächer, leisten Vermittlungsarbeit zur Verbreitung von Biodiversitätsgründächern und erproben Verfahren zur Aufwertung von artenarmen Dachbegrünungen.

The "Living Roofs" project launched at the end of 2019 at the City of Frankfurt Botanical Gardens addresses the question of how the potential for roof greenery can be better exploited as a habitat for plants and animals. The project team consists of Andreas König (graduate biologist and deputy technical director of the Botanical Gardens), Uwe Barth (graduate biologist), Ralf Kremser (master gardener and head groundsman at the Botanical Gardens), Beate Alberternst (graduate biologist), Stefan Nawrath (graduate biologist)and Horst Ewerling (graduate biologist and roof gardener), who advises the team on technical and ecological aspects of roof greenery. The team tests local plant species that are under threat to assess their suitability for greened roofs, do educational work to spread the message on biodiversity-greened roofs, and trial procedures to upgrade greened roofs that have only a limited number of different plants.

Informationen zum Projekt unter:
For details on the project please visit:

www.botanischergarten-frankfurt.de/der-garten/
projekte/lebendige-daecher-zusammen-
mit-der-kfw-stiftung/

Was darf ich und was wird gefördert – oder gefordert? Welche Rolle spielt die Politik?

What's allowed, what are the requirements, and for what are there grants? What role does politics play?

Gehsteige oder städtische Flächen sollen Grünpflanzen weichen? Wie geht das und was ist zu beachten?

Eine Fassadenbegrünung, die aus dem öffentlichen Gehweg herauswachsen soll, benötigt die Genehmigung der Kommune. Wichtig ist, dass der verbleibende Gehweg breit genug ist und die Pflanze nicht im Weg hängt, also gut gepflegt ist. Manchmal gibt es auch die Vorgabe, dass die Pflanze nicht giftig sein und keine Stacheln haben sollte. Außerdem muss geprüft werden, ob die Pflanzlöcher über oder in der Nähe von unterirdischen Leitungen gesetzt werden, die durch die Bauarbeiten oder durch die Pflanzenwurzeln beschädigt werden könnten.

In Frankfurt läuft die Antragstellung im Rahmen von „Frankfurt frischt auf" über das Umweltamt an das Amt für Straßenbau und Erschließung (ASE). Wenn noch mindestens 1,5m Gehwegbreite übrig bleibt und das Pflanzloch in Handschachtung ausgehoben wird (also ohne Bagger), ist eine Begrünung prinzipiell genehmigungsfähig. In anderen Kommunen weichen die Regelungen möglicherweise ab. Die Kosten für den Genehmigungsvorgang trägt der Antragsteller – und er muss auch die Pflanze betreuen. Es kann sein, dass man eine entsprechende Pflegeverpflichtung unterschreiben muss.

So the idea is for sidewalks or urban areas to make way for green plants? How do we approach this and what should we look out for?

Façade greening that is supposed to grow from a public sidewalk/footpath first requires local authority approval. The key is that the remainder of the sidewalk/footpath must be wide enough and the plant does not hang over it, meaning it is well tended. Sometimes there is also a stipulation that the plant must not be poisonous or have thorns. Moreover, you need to check whether the plant holes are above or close to underground cables/pipes that might be damaged by construction work or plant roots.

In Frankfurt, applications should be filed in the framework of the "Refreshing Frankfurt/Frankfurt frischt auf" program through the Environment Agency to the Agency of Roads and Access (ASE). If at least a footpath width of 1.5m remains and the hole for the plant is dug by hand (i.e., without a dozer), then in principle approval for the greening can be granted. Regulations may possibly be different in other local authorities. The applicant bears the costs for the approval process and must also care for the plants. It may be that the applicant has to sign a corresponding plant care commitment.

LARA-MARIA MOHR

*Whose approval
is needed for greening
a façade?*

Wessen Zustimmung ist für eine Begrünung der Fassade nötig?

Auf dem eigenen Grundstück ist nur die Zustimmung des Hauseigentümers nötig, keine behördliche Bewilligung. Für massive und größere Rankgerüste (mind. 15 cm über die Fassade und die Grundstücksgrenze hinausragend) ist eine Baubewilligung erforderlich. Wenn die Begrünung auf dem eigenen Grundstück, aber nahe am Nachbargrundstück geplant ist, müssen gegebenenfalls auch die Nachbarn um Einverständnis gebeten werden. In beiden Fällen ist die zuständige Bauaufsicht zu konsultieren.

On your own grounds, you only need the house owner to agree and no official approvals are required. For massive or larger climbing frames for vines (protruding min. 15 cm from the façade and the limits of the grounds), you need building permission. If the greening is planned for your own grounds but is close to the neighbor's plot, the neighbor's consent may be required. In both cases, the relevant building authorities should be consulted.

LARA-MARIA MOHR

Warum sind Dachbegrünungen im Baurecht vorgesehen, werden aber nicht ausgeführt, wie z. B. in Gewerbegebieten?

Viele unbegrünte Dächer sind älter als der dazugehörige Bebauungsplan. Für diese Gebäude gilt Bestandsschutz. Sollte an ihnen größere Veränderungen vorgenommen werden, muss dies entsprechend dem Bebauungsplan genehmigt werden. Oft ist allerdings, insbesondere bei Gewerbehallen, die Tragwerkskonstruktion nicht ausgelegt auf eine zusätzliche Dachlast. In diesem Fall wird dann von einer aufwendigen statischen Umrüstung abgesehen. Gänzlich neue Gebäude müssen die Auflagen erfüllen, wenn keine besonderen Gründe dagegen sprechen (z. B. die Entscheidung für eine Solaranlage, wobei auch beides kombiniert umsetzbar wäre).

Many ungreened roofs are older than the relevant development plans. Such buildings are protected as existing structures, so if a major aspect is to be changed then this has to receive approval under the respective development plan. However, often in the case of commercial halls in particular, the load-bearing structure is insufficient to take the additional roof load. In such cases, a major load-bearing retrofit is usually not considered. Completely new buildings must meet the stipulations and if no special reasons speak against it (e.g., if a solar system is being installed on the roof – whereby this is usually possible in combination with greenery), then they need to be greened.

LARA-MARIA MOHR

Why is roof greenery envisaged in German building law but then not realized, for example in business parks?

Welche Rahmenbedingungen müssen für Bauherren und Architekten geschaffen werden, damit Gebäudegrün vermehrt Einsatz findet?

What overall conditions need to be put in place for developers and architects to prompt the greater use of greenery on buildings?

Es bedarf der Regulierung in Bebauungsplänen durch die Politik, vergleichbar mit Vorgaben, wie sie z.B. für Wärmedämmung gemacht wurden. Aber auch Schulungen oder die Schaffung von Verständnis in der Architekturausbildung sind wichtige Faktoren. Darüber hinaus muss man dem Bauherrn über Simulationen aufzeigen, welche Effekte mit Fassadenbegrünung erzielt werden können und wie viel Technik erforderlich ist, um vergleichbare Qualitäten durch den Betrieb technischer Geräte zu erzielen. Durch eine Berechnung der Kosten für die technischen Geräte und für deren Unterhalt kann man schnell sehen, ob die Fassadenbegrünung und deren Betrieb effektiver ist. Darüber hinaus hat ein „grünes Image" für den Wert einer Immobilie große Vorteile und bietet gegebenenfalls bei einer Zertifizierung zusätzliche Vorteile.

We need policymakers to regulate this in building planning permission, comparably to the stipulation made, for example, on heat insulation. Training sessions and fostering an understanding for the topic on architectural curricula are also key factors. Furthermore, developers can be shown in simulations what effects façade greenery has and what technology is required to achieve comparable qualities through operation of technical appliances. By comparing the costs for operating and maintaining the technical apparatus with the greenery and tending it, you soon see which option is more effective. Indeed, a "green image" is of great benefit to the value of a property and potentially offers advantages for certification.

RUDI SCHEUERMANN

Wie wirkungsvoll ist ein durch politische Vorgaben gesteuerter Einsatz von Gebäude- grün? Fordern und/oder fördern?

In Deutschland ist die Gebäudebegrünung nicht in der Bauverordnung verankert. Die Gebäude- begrünung unterliegt im Rahmen der kommunalen Bauleitplanung politischen Abwägungsoptionen. In Stuttgart gilt zum Beispiel seit 2020 die Vorgabe, 30 Prozent der städtischen Gebäude zu begrünen. Um Initiativen von Unternehmen und privaten Bau- herren und Eigentümern anzukurbeln, konzentrieren sich vor allem die Großstädte auf unterschiedliche Förderprogramme.

In Germany, greenery on the outer shells of buildings is not anchored in building regulations. Within the framework of communal urban land use planning, the greening of buildings is subject to political consider- ation options. Authorities in Stuttgart, for example, introduced a stipulation for 30 percent of urban buildings to be greened from 2020. In order to foster initiatives among companies, private developers and property owners alike, big cities are focusing primarily on various funding programs.

HILDE STROBL

How effective is building greenery dictated by official policy? Obligation and/or incentive?

STÄDTISCHE FÖRDERPROGRAMME
FÜR GEBÄUDEGRÜN

*MUNICIPAL FUNDING PROGRAMS
FOR BUILDING GREENERY*

Stadt / *City*	Förderprogramm/*Funding program*	Rahmenbedingungen/*Basic condition*
Berlin	„GründachPlus" Dachbegrünung / *Roof greening*	Zuschuss/*Subsidy of 75%*, max. 60€/m² Max. pro Maßnahme/*max. per project* 60.000€
Hamburg	„Auf die Dächer – fertig – grün!" Dachbegrünung *Roof greening*	Zuschuss/*Subsidy of 40%*, 14–56€/m² Max. pro Maßnahme/*max. per project* 50.000€
München *Munich*	„Grün in der Stadt" Umfassendes Begrünungsprogramm für Dächer, Fassaden, Höfe *Extensive greening program for roofs, façades, courtyards*	Zuschuss/*Subsidy of 50%*, max. 25€/m² Anwendbar auf verschiedene Flächen *Applicable for various surfaces*
Köln *Cologne*	„GRÜN hoch 3" Dächer, Fassaden, Höfe *Roofs, façades, courtyards*	Zuschuss/*Subsidy of 50%*, 40€/m² Max. pro Maßnahme/*max. per project* 20.000€
Frankfurt	„Frankfurt frischt auf" Dächer, Fassaden, Höfe *Roofs, façades, courtyards*	Zuschuss/*Subsidy of 50%* Max. pro Maßnahme / *max. per project* 50.000€
Stuttgart	„Kommunales Förderprogramm" Dächer, Fassaden, Höfe *Roofs, façades, courtyards*	Zuschuss/*Subsidy of 50%*, 60€/m² Max. pro Maßnahme/*max. per project* 10.000€
Düsseldorf	„Förderprogramm Dach-, Fassaden-, Innenhofbegrünung (DAFIB)" Dächer, Fassaden, Höfe *Roofs, façades, courtyards*	Zuschuss/*Subsidy of 50%*, 40€/m² Max. pro Maßnahme/*max. per project* 20.000€
Dortmund	„Dachbegrünung in Dortmund" Dachbegrünung/*Roof greening*	Zuschuss/*Subsidy of 50%*, 30€/m²
Essen	„Hof- und Fassadenprogramm" Dächer, Fassaden, Höfe *Roofs, façades, courtyards*	Zuschuss/*Subsidy of 50%*, 30€/m²

Umfrage des BuGG, 2019
BuGG survey, 2019

Forderungen für Fassadenbegrünungen für ein „smarteres" Wien?

Die Stadt Wien schreibt in der Bauordnung Fassadenbegrünung im gesamten Stadtgebiet vor.[20] Eine entsprechende Bestimmung gilt seit 2018 bei jeder neuen Festsetzung oder Abänderung eines Flächenwidmungs- und Bebauungsplans. Dabei wird nicht zwischen Bestand und neuen Stadtentwicklungsgebieten unterschieden. Die Forderung richtet sich an Mehrgeschossbauten mit Gebäudehöhen über 7,5 und bis 26 Metern (aus Gründen des Brandschutzes) und zielt auf mindestens ein Fünftel der betreffenden Fassaden. Die Abteilung Stadt Wien – Umweltschutz (MA 22) fördert straßenseitige Fassadenbegrünungen und Grünfassaden zum Innenhof unterschiedlich (max. 5.200/3.200€).[21] Die eingeforderte Begrünung wird nach Zustand und Dichte der Fassadenbegrünung in Abhängigkeit von den Standortfaktoren und der Begrünungstechnik bemessen. Die Abnahmekriterien sind durch die FFL-Fassadenbegrünungsrichtlinie (Forschungsgesellschaft Landschaftsentwicklung Landschaftsbau e.V.) definiert. Das Umweltamt der Stadt war von Anfang an selbst initiativ und Vorreiter: Vor zehn Jahren wurde die Straßenfassade des Amtsgebäudes MA 48 begrünt und 2016 ein weiteres Gebäude, das MA 31. Die verschiedenen Systeme und Anwendungen werden durch Forschung und ein durchgehendes Monitoring begleitet.

20 Planungsgrundlagen zur Bebauungsbestimmung Begrünung der Fassaden der Stadt Wien/*Planning principles for the building regulations Greening of façades of the city of Vienna*: www.wien.gv.at/stadtentwicklung/strategien/pdf/planungsgrundlagen-bebauungsbestimmung-fassadenbegruenung.pdf (9.11.2020).
21 www.wien.gv.at/umweltschutz/raum/gruene-waende.html#foerderung (9.11.2020).

Requirements for façade greening – for a "smarter" Vienna

Fassadenbegrünung, MA 31, Wien, Österreich
Façade greening, MA 31, Vienna, Austria
Photo: Stadt Wien / *City of Vienna*

The City of Vienna has incorporated façade greening into its building regulations throughout the city.[20] Since 2018, there has also been a corresponding provision for each new designation or modification of zoning and construction plans. No distinction is made here between existing buildings and new urban development areas. The requirement is aimed at multi-story buildings of a height between 7.5 and 26 meters (for reasons of fire prevention) with a target of at least one fifth of the relevant façades. The City of Vienna's environmental protection department (MA 22) promotes roadside façade greening and rear-facing green façades in different ways (max. €5,200/€3,200).[21] The greening required is measured based on the condition and density of the façade greening in relation to the location factors and the greening technique, and the acceptance criteria are outlined in the façade greening directive of the Research Society for Landscape Development and Landscaping (Forschungsgesellschaft Landschaftsentwicklung Landschaftsbau e.V. – FFL). The city's Environment Agency has been the driving force and pioneer from the outset: Ten years ago, the roadside façade of the MA 48 office building was greened, and the MA 31 building followed suit in 2016. The various systems and applications are subject to research and ongoing monitoring.

HILDE STROBL

Gemüsegarten auf dem Dach der Opéra Bastille, Paris, Frankreich
Vegetable garden on the roof of the Opéra Bastille, Paris, France
Photo: © Sarah Langinieux – Cityside

Paris und die Charta „Objectif 100 ha"

Paris and the "Objectif 100 ha" charter

Als 2013 in Nantes der World Green Infrastructure Congress (WGIC) ausgerichtet wurde, verkündete die Stadt Paris, sie werde 40.000 m² Gebäudegrün schaffen. Mit der neuen Bürgermeisterin Anne Hidalgo wurde 2014 die Zahl auf 100.000 m² erhöht. Das ambitionierte Ziel sollte bis 2020 umgesetzt sein und jeweils zu einem Drittel Fassaden, Dachgärten und landwirtschaftliche Flächen auf Dächern (agriculture urbaine) umfassen. Zwei Jahre später unterzeichneten 33 Bauherren, die Stadt Paris, öffentliche Einrichtungen und Unternehmen die Charta „Objectif 100 ha" – eine Verpflichtung, Grünflächen zu konkretisieren. Die Stadt Paris begleitet die Bauherren, bewirbt die Projekte auf einer Website und veranstaltet Konferenzen, um die Bevölkerung zu sensibilisieren und zu motivieren. Im Rahmen des Programms „Parisculteurs" wurden Firmen und Vereine dazu aufgerufen, Projektvorschläge für die 33 vorgeschlagenen Standorte einzureichen. Die Idee: Partnerschaften zwischen den Inhabern von Gebäudeflächen und Betreibern der Flächen zu bilden, die die neuen Dachgärten auch wirtschaftlich nutzen können, um dort z.B. Gemüse- und Obstanbau zu betreiben. So sind 14.000 m² landwirtschaftliche Anbaufläche und Urban-Gardening-Initiativen auf den Dächern des Messegeländes Paris Expo Porte de Versailles geplant, von denen ein großer Teil bereits verwirklicht ist. Das Konzept zielt auf eine Begrünung der Stadt und zugleich auf kürzere Transportwege der Nahrungsversorgung.

When the World Green Infrastructure Congress (WGIC) was established in Nantes back in 2013, the City of Paris announced that it would create 40,000m² of building greenery. Its new mayor Anne Hidalgo increased the figure to 100,000m² in 2014. The ambitious goal was to be implemented by 2020 and would involve the three equal components of façades, roof gardens and rooftop cultivation (agriculture urbaine). Two years later, 33 developers, the City of Paris, public institutions and businesses signed the "Objectif 100ha" charter – a commitment to making green spaces a reality. The City of Paris supports developers, publicizes projects on a website and organizes conferences to raise awareness and boost motivation among the population. As part of the "Parisculteurs" program, businesses and associations are called upon to submit project proposals for the 33 proposed locations. The idea is to form partnerships between the owners of building surfaces and operators of the spaces, which can then use the new roof gardens commercially too for the purposes of fruit and vegetable cultivation, for example. Hence, 14,000m² of cultivated agricultural space and urban gardening initiatives were planned for the roofs of the Paris Expo Porte de Versailles exhibition site, of which a large proportion has already been implemented. The concept is aimed at greening the city and also at shorter transport routes for food supplies.

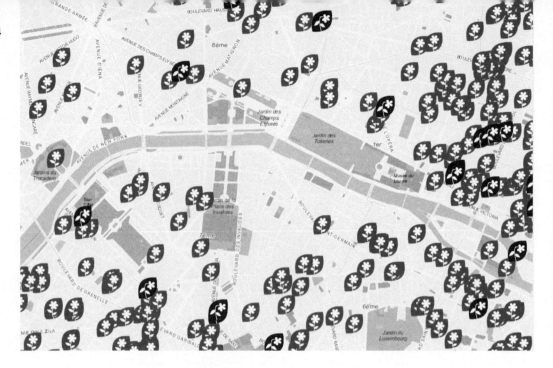

2017 startete „Parisculteurs 2" mit dem Fokus auf Privateigentümer. Die finanzielle Unterstützung durch die Stadt Paris richtet sich vor allem auf den sozialen Wohnungsbau. Darüber hinaus ist seit 2016 im Stadtentwicklungsplan vorgegeben, dass jedes Dach über 200m² im Neubau begrünt werden muss. Ein weiteres Programm richtet sich an die Begrünung von 1.000 Bestandsgebäuden.[22]

The year 2017 saw the launch of "Parisculteurs 2" with a focus on private ownership. Financial support from the City of Paris was aimed primarily at social housing. In addition to this, there has been an urban development plan in place since 2016, according to which each new-build roof must incorporate more than 200m² of greening. Another program targets greening of 1,000 existing buildings.[22]

HILDE STROBL

Website der Stadt Paris zu „Végétalisons Paris" mit einer Karte der verwirklichten Projekte:
Website of the city of Paris on "Végétalisons Paris" with a map of the implemented projects:
www.paris.fr/pages/vegetalisons-la-ville-2459

---

22 François Lassalle, Pariser Vorgehen für die Gebäudebegrünung. Konkretisierung eines politischen Willens, WGIC 2017: www.gebaeudegruen.info/fileadmin/website/downloads/wgic_vortraege/Lassalle_Francois.pdf (9.11.2020); Website der Stadt Paris zu „Végétalisons Paris" mit einer Karte der verwirklichten Projekte/*Website of the city of Paris on "Végétalisons Paris" with a map of the implemented projects:* www.paris.fr/pages/vegetalisons-la-ville-2459 (9.11.2020).

Fordern und zugleich Anreize schaffen? Ein Blick nach Singapur

Allen voran geht die hochverdichtete Megacity Singapur. Hier bestimmt die Urban Redevelopment Authority (URA) im Programm Landscaping for Urban Spaces and High-Rises (LUSH) eine Green Plot Ratio, eine Grünflächen-GFZ, die im Bebauungsplan festgelegt wird. LUSH läuft seit 2004 und wird regelmäßig überarbeitet und angepasst. Die Green Plot Ratio unterscheidet sich analog zum Dichtedruck des jeweiligen Stadtgebiets. Auch wenn grundsätzlich 100 Prozent landschaftlicher Rückgewinn der bebauten Fläche gefordert wird, gibt es gleichzeitig Anreize für weitere Grünmaßnahmen, so beispielsweise Steuerermäßigungen oder eine Erhöhung der Geschossflächenzahl. Je höher die Grundstückspreise sind, desto attraktiver sind Nutzungsintensivierungen, da hierdurch die Rentabilität steigt. Das Regulierungssystem ist wirksam und hat bei Bauherren ebenso wie bei der Bevölkerung eine grundsätzliche Akzeptanz gefunden, sodass Singapur zu den Vorreiterstädten im Bereich Gebäudegrün zählt.

Setting requirements and creating incentives at the same time? A look at Singapore

Leading the way in this area is the densely developed megacity of Singapore. Here, the Urban Redevelopment Authority (URA) runs a program called Landscaping for Urban Spaces and High-Rises (LUSH), whereby a green plot ratio is stipulated in the development plan. LUSH has been running since 2004 and is regularly revised and amended. The green plot ratio varies in line with the density of development in the relevant district. Although there is basically a requirement for 100 percent recovery of space for cultivation on developed sites, there are also incentives for further greening measures, such as tax reductions or an increase in the floor-space index. The higher the prices of the plots, the more appealing it is to intensify usage, which in turn increases profitability. The system of regulations is effective and has been largely accepted by developers and the population alike, meaning Singapore is now a pioneer in the area of building greenery.

HILDE STROBL

Was ist zu tun, um eine Förderung für Begrünung in Frankfurt abzurufen? Was genau wird gefördert?

What do I need to do to lock into funding for greening my building in Frankfurt? What exactly is required?

„Frankfurt frisch auf" heißt das Programm der Stadt Frankfurt, über das ein „Klimabonus" vergeben wird. Haben Sie daran Interesse, nehmen Sie mittels des Beratungsfragebogens Kontakt mit dem Umweltamt Frankfurt auf. Sie bekommen einen Termin für eine kostenlose und unverbindliche Vor-Ort-Beratung. Anschließend planen Sie Ihr Vorhaben und reichen die Planungs-unterlagen beim Umweltamt ein. Wenn Ihnen ein Bescheid zugegangen ist, können Sie loslegen. Nach Fertigstellung der Maßnahme reichen Sie die Rechnungen ein und bekommen dann die Fördermittel erstattet.

Die Hälfte der Kosten einer Maßnahme kann durch den Klimabonus gefördert werden. Bis zu 50.000 € werden pro Liegenschaft erstattet. Dabei können auch mehrere Maßnahmen pro Liegenschaft beantragt und umgesetzt werden, wie z.B. die Dachbegrünung als eine Maßnahme, die Fassadenbegrünung als eine weitere, und dann noch die Hofbegrünung. Die Stadt Frankfurt stellt hier-für jährlich (bis inkl. 2021) 2 Millionen € zur Verfügung.[23]

"Refreshing Frankfurt/Frankfurt frisch auf" is the name of the City of Frankfurt program under the terms of which a "climate bonus" can be awarded. If you are interested, use the advice form to contact the Frankfurt Environment Agency. You will be granted a date for on-site advice that is free of charge and not binding on you. You can then plan what you want to do and submit the planning documents to the Environment Agency, and you can start once you have received official approval. On commissioning the measure, you then submit your invoices and receive the grant.

Half of the costs of a measure can be covered by the Climate Bonus grant, up to a sum of € 50,000 per property. In this context, an application can be filed to realize several measures per property, such as roof greenery as one measure, façade greenery as another, and greenery for an inner courtyard as a third. The City of Frankfurt is making € 2 million available each year through 2021 for this purpose.[23]

LARA-MARIA MOHR

---

23 Antragsformulare und weitere Informationen unter: www.frankfurt.de/klimabonus
For the application forms and further information click: www.frankfurt.de/klimabonus

IM GESPRÄCH MIT
IN CONVERSATION WITH

SCHIRIN TARAZ

Learning from Singapore?

Grün als Greenwashing oder echte Chance?

ST   Grüne Fassaden sind immer wieder der Frage ausgesetzt, ob es sich um „echtes Grün" handle und es „etwas bringt". Doch wir verstehen Pflanzen zunächst einmal als ein Material der weiten architektonischen Palette wie Holz, Stahl, Beton und Stein! Daher ist es auch nicht weiter verwerflich, Grün als dekoratives und ästhetisches Material einzusetzen. Gleichwohl lässt sich darüber hinaus viel mehr erreichen und die Nachhaltigkeit von Gebäuden erhöhen – auch wenn diese nicht per se durch den Einsatz von Pflanzen gegeben ist.

Gebäudegrün fordern oder fördern? Worauf zielen Regulierungssysteme in Singapur?

ST   Sobald Rahmenbedingungen festgelegt sind, stehen sie auf der Agenda für den Planungsprozess, und die Grünplanung wird zu einem Werkzeug unter vielen anderen Bauvorschriften. Je stärker messbar und bezifferbar, desto effektiver. Im dicht bebauten Singapur bestimmt die Urban Redevelopment Authority (URA) im Programm Landscaping for Urban Spaces and High-Rises (LUSH) eine Green Plot Ratio, eine Grünflächen-GFZ, die im Bebauungsplan fest-

Green as greenwashing or as a real chance?

ST   *Greened façades seem to always raise the question of whether it is "real green" and "is it worth it". That said, we initially view plants as a material in the broad architectural range that includes wood, steel, concrete, and stone, which is why it is not objectionable in any way to use green as a decorative and aesthetic material. Moreover, one can achieve much more with it, too, and enhance a building's sustainability – even if this is not per se solely because plants are used.*

Should one call for and subsidize building greenery? What is the case with the system of regulations in Singapore?

ST   *As soon as the basic conditions have been defined, they are placed on the agenda for the planning process, and the green planning becomes one tool among many other building regulations. The more you can measure things, put figures on them, the more regulations are effective. In densely built Singapore, it is the Urban Redevelopment Authority (URA) with its Landscaping for Urban Spaces and High-Rises*

WOHA Architects,
Newton Suites, Singapur / *Singapore*
Photo: Patrick Bingham-Hall

gelegt wird.[24] Diese unterscheidet sich entsprechend dem Dichtedruck des jeweiligen Stadtgebiets. Das Regulierungssystem ist wirksam und hat bei Bauherren ebenso wie bei der Bevölkerung eine grundsätzliche Akzeptanz gefunden.

(LUSH) program that sets a Green Plot Ratio that is a firm part of the land-use plan.[24] It varies in line with the density of the respective part of town. The system of regulations is effective and has fundamentally been accepted by developers and inhabitants alike.

Bringt Gebäudegrün grundsätzlich eine Budgeterhöhung mit sich?

Does building greenery per se spell a higher budget?

ST   Mit klugen und kreativen Strategien nicht unbedingt. Vielfach ist es eher eine Frage danach, wofür und an welcher Stelle Kosten eingespart oder auf der anderen Seite finanzielle Mittel investiert werden. Das Ziel sollte ja grundsätzlich ein Mehrwert für den Nutzer sein, eine Verbesserung der Raumqualität. Die Umverteilung von Kosten zeigte sich als wirksame Methode bei der Planung eines Wohnhochhauses, das WOHA in Singapur gebaut hat. Bei Hochhäusern wird die Zahl der Liftsysteme entsprechend der akzeptablen Wartezeit berechnet. Und Liftsysteme sind sehr teuer. Wenn aber die Liftlobby ein angenehmer, heller und gut belüfteter Grünbereich mit hoher Aufenthaltsqualität ist, kann man von einer längeren zumutbaren Wartezeit ausgehen und weniger Lifte einplanen. Das sind natürlich sehr subjektive Aspekte, die aber dennoch Kriterien für die Qualität eines Bauwerks sein können und dafür, wofür Geld ausgegeben wird – für Grünbereiche oder mehr Lifte. Bislang haben sich die Bewohner noch nicht beschwert, dass die Liftwartezeit zu lang wäre. Ähnlich verhält es sich mit begrünten Dachgärten, die den Nutzern zusätzliche Wohn- und Aufenthaltsbereiche bieten und dadurch den Mehrwert eines Gebäudes steigern.

ST   With smart and creative strategies, that is not necessarily the case. Often it is more a question of for what and at what juncture costs get saved or, on the other hand, what financial resources are invested. In principle, the goal should be to achieve value added for the user, to improve the quality of the space. A redistribution of costs proved to be an effective method during planning of a residential high-rise WOHA designed in Singapore. In the case of high-rises, the number of elevator systems is calculated in line with the acceptable waiting time. And elevator systems are very expensive. Hence, if an elevator lobby is a more pleasant, brighter and well-ventilated greened zone where one can more willingly spend time, then waiting times can be longer and fewer elevators can be incorporated in the planning. Those are subjective aspects, of course, that nevertheless can be criteria for the quality of a building and for what one spends money on – for green zones or for more elevators. To date, the inhabitants have not complained that the waiting time for the elevators is too long. Things are similar when it comes to greened roofs that create additional living and leisure space for the users and thus enhance a building's added value.

24 Aktuell gilt LUSH 3.0 aus dem Jahr 2017 / Currently LUSH 3.0 as enacted in 2017 applies: www.ura.gov.sg/Corporate/Guidelines/Circulars/dc17-06 (3.11.2020)

Sind die Grünkonzepte aus Singapur übertragbar?

Can the Singaporean green concepts be used elsewhere?

ST   Das ist eher eine Frage des Standorts. Wenn man auf einer Alm sitzt und von Grün umgeben ist, erscheint es wenig sinnvoll, an die Bepflanzung der Gebäudeflächen zu denken. Grünprogramme sind ein Thema für hochverdichtete Ballungsgebiete weltweit, egal ob in Deutschland oder Singapur. Die Herausforderungen sind identisch, auch wenn natürlich die klimatischen Unterschiede groß sind. Ein angenehmer Aufenthaltsbereich in tropischen Gegenden muss schattig und gut durchlüftet sein, in Deutschland würde dagegen aufgrund anderer Klimaverhältnisse dieselbe Raumkonstitution nicht funktionieren. Auch der ortsspezifische bauliche Kontext im Hinblick auf die Höhe von mehrgeschossigen Gebäuden oder Hochhäusern spielt eine Rolle und die Windlast, mit der die Pflanzsysteme konfrontiert werden. In Singapur gibt es zum Beispiel weniger Wind, in Taipeh sieht die Situation wieder ganz anders aus. Und natürlich unterscheiden sich die Vegetation und ihre Anforderungen.

ST   That is more a question of location. If the site is a meadow in the mountains and is surrounded by green, then it does not seem particularly sensible to think of plants on areas of buildings. Green programs are an issue for very densely built-up areas worldwide, irrespective of whether you're in Germany or Singapore. The challenges are identical, even if the climatic conditions are of course very different. A pleasant leisure-time zone in the Tropics needs to be shady and well-ventilated; in Germany, by contrast, this form of space would not work because of the climate. Furthermore, the local built context as regards the height of multi-story buildings or high-rises plays a role, as does the wind load the plant systems have to withstand. In Singapore, for example, there is less wind, whereas things are quite different in Taipei. And, of course, the vegetation and the plants' requirements differ, too.

Die größte Herausforderung ist das klimagerechte Bauen. Gerade im tropischen Gürtel sind die Wachstumsraten der neuen Megastädte am höchsten. Zugleich gibt es noch sehr wenige geeignete Typologien für das Bauen in den Tropen, da die meisten Hochhaustypologien im Westen entwickelt wurden. Die westlichen Modelle zielen auf möglichst kompaktes Bauen und hermetisches Abriegeln – und das ist in Bezug auf klimagerechtes Bauen in den Tropen genau falsch.

The greatest challenge is to build in line with the climate. In the Tropics in particular, the growth rates of the new mega-cities are the fastest. At the same time, there are very few suitable typologies for building in the Tropics, as most high-rise typologies were developed in the West. The Western models focus on being as compact as possible and creating hermetically sealed environments – and that is precisely what you don't want when it comes to building in line with the climate in the Tropics.

SCHIRIN TARAZ

studierte Architektur an der RWTH Aachen und der ETH Zürich und arbeitet seit 2005 bei WOHA in Singapur. Sie wurde 2017 zum Direktor ernannt und arbeitet seither als Chief Operating Officer bei WOHA.

studied architecture at RWTH Aachen and ETH Zurich and has been with WOHA since 2005. She was made a director of the firm in December 2017 and has been working as WOHA's chief operating officer ever since.

Ein Blick in die Geschichte

A glance back through time

Gab es historisch gesehen Hochphasen der Auseinandersetzung mit Grün an der Gebäudehülle?

Das Interesse an Begrünungen steigt derzeit. Wenn wir zurückblicken, zeichnen sich einzelne Hochphasen im Lauf der Geschichte ab – gekoppelt an äußere Ereignisse. Vom Anfang bis zur Mitte des 19. Jahrhunderts zeigt sich ein überwiegendes Interesse an den Themenfeldern „Botanik" und „Anwendung/Planung". Bei einer natürlichen Volatilität mit häufiger Überschneidung der Themenfelder Anwendung, Forschung und Botanik verharrt dieser Zustand beständig bis zum Jahr 1978 („Club of Rome"), in welchem zunächst die Botanik, dann dicht folgend weitere Themenfelder zu einem Interessenhöhenflug ansetzten, mit Spitzenwerten ab 1984 („Öko-Bewegung"). Von 1992 bis 1998 stieg die Kurve vor allem in der Auseinandersetzung mit vertikalen Gärten erneut – was auch auf die Initiativen durch Patrick Blanc zurückzuführen ist. Seit 2006, bis heute anhaltend, zeichnen sich Spitzenwerte ab (Brisanz des Klimawandels, Zielsetzung Ressourcenschutz, Problemkreis Stadt).

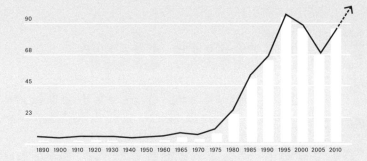

Anzahl der Veröffentlichungen zur Fassadenbegrünung. Die Auswertung bezieht sich auf alle Themenfelder.
The development in publications on façade greenery. The evaluation covers all fields of the topic. [25]

Have there been high points in history when it comes to greenery on the outer shells of buildings?

Currently the interest in greenery is growing. If we look back, we can discern individual high points in the course of history that are coupled with external events. From the beginning to the middle of the 19th century, the interest was predominantly in the topics of "botany" and "applications/planning". This situation persisted with the natural volatility of frequent overlaps among the topics of application, research and botany until the year 1978 ("Club of Rome"), when first botany and then the other topics really took off in quick succession, reaching a new heyday from 1984 onwards (the "Eco Movement"). From 1992 to 1998 the curve headed skywards again, above all with the critical focus on vertical gardens – something attributable to the initiatives started by Patrick Blanc. Since 2006 and still today, the topics continue to attract great attention (the explosive impact of climate change, the new objective of sparing resources, and the questions relating to urbanity).

NICOLE PFOSER

---

25 Grundlage der Auswertung/*Basis of the evaluation.* Manfred Köhler, Veröffentlichungen zu Fassadenbegrünungen, 2011. **Grafik nach**/*graphic after:* Pfoser 2018.

Die Idee der „grünen Haube" zum Schutz von Gebäuden ist nicht neu. Nein!

The idea of a "green hood" to protect buildings is far from new. Far from it!

Jahrtausende alt? Woher kommt sie?

Thousands of years old? Where does it come from?

Bodegas in Baltanás, Spanien/*Spain*
Photo: Carmen García Fdez, 2016

Die „grüne Haube" schützt die Behausung, die Wohnhöhle und Erdhäuser. Diese unterscheiden sich von herkömmlichen Häusern in erster Linie dadurch, dass sie nicht einem aufbauenden und additiven Prinzip folgen – kein Stein wird auf den anderen gelegt –, sondern durch ein subtraktives Verfahren gebildet werden: Meist werden die Aushöhlungen in Berge oder hügeliges Gelände eingegraben. In der Antike entstanden so die Stadt Petra (Jordanien, 300 v. Chr.), in frühchristlicher Zeit ganze Siedlungen in den kappadokischen Bergen (Türkei), in Matera (Italien) und in Baltanás (Spanien). Die Wohnhöhlen und Erdhäuser, die in ihrer terrassierten Siedlung immer wieder aus dem Berg vorkragen, sind von wiesen- oder baumbekrönten Grünbereichen durchzogen. Durch Gestein, Erdreich und Pflanzen klimatisch vor Hitze und Kälte geschützt, überdauerten die Höhlen Jahrtausende.

Altstadt von Matera, Italien
Old city of Matera, Italy
Photo: Georgie Knaggs, 2017

The "green hood" protects dwellings, inhabited caves and earth houses. These differ from customary houses primarily by the fact that they do not obey some stacking and additive principle – no stone or brick is laid one on top of the other – but are created by a subtractive process: Usually the cavities are dug into mountain sides or hilly terrain. In ancient times, the city of Petra (Jordan, 300 BCE) arose in this way, in early Christian times entire settlements in the mountains of Cappadocia (Turkey), in Matera (Italy) and in Baltanás (Spain). The inhabited caves and earth houses that in the terraced settlements repeatedly protruded out of the mountain side are interrupted by green areas with meadows or trees. Climatically protected by rocks, earth and plants against the heat and cold, these caves endured for centuries.

Erdhäuser
in Skogár, Island
*Earth houses
in Skogár, Iceland*
Photo:
Einar Páll Svavarsson,
2016

Grassodenhäuser entstanden in Island ab dem 18. Jahrhundert. Für den Hausbau wurden vor allem von Zuwanderern in den Moorkolonien gestochene Grassoden (Grasnarbenstücke) oder Plaggen von Torf (Torfstücke) gestapelt. Sie dienten als Füllmaterial von Hauskonstruktion aus Holz – dort, wo kein anderes Baumaterial vorhanden war. Auch die Dächer aus Holz wurden damit belegt. Die Grasnarbe und der neue Bewuchs waren zugleich Dämmung und Schutz des Gebäudes.

Grass-covered barrow houses arose in Iceland from the 18th century onwards. To build the houses, cuts of turf dug above all by immigrants in the moors or slabs of peat were stacked or served as filler material for the wooden house structure wherever no other building material was available. The peat or grass was also used to cover the wooden roofs. The grass cover and the new plant growth were both insulation and protection of the building.

Peter Vetsch
Erdhäuser in Dietikon, Schweiz, 1974
Earth houses in Dietikon, Switzerland, 1974
Photo: Archi0780, 2007

Der „Treibhauseffekt" und eine sich entwickelnde Ökologie- und Klimadiskussion bildete in den 1970er- und 1980er-Jahren für eine geringe Schar an Architekten die Motivation, unkonventionelle Bauweisen zu erproben, Dächer zu begrünen und naturverweisende, hügel- und wellenbildende Formensprachen anzuwenden.

The "greenhouse effect" and the nascent ecology and climate discussion in the 1970s to 1980s was the motivation for a small number of architects to try out unconventional forms of buildings, to green roofs and apply formal languages that reference nature and form hills and waves.

Johannes Peter Hölzinger
Evangelisches Gemeindezentrum in Friedberg-West, „Wellenhaus", 1980
Protestant community center in Friedberg-West, "Wellenhaus", 1980
Photo: Norbert Miguletz, 2012

Diller Scofidio + Renfro + FXFOWL
Hypar Pavilion, New York, USA
Photo: Iwan Baan, 2010

Die Idee des „Einhausens" durch Grün verharrte nicht in der Pionierphase des entstehenden Umweltbewusstseins. Das Revival der Initiativen nach der Jahrtausendwende ging einher mit dem Umstand, dass sich nun Umweltschutz als grundlegende Selbstverständlichkeit etablierte. Verändert haben sich dadurch die Größendimensionen sowie die Position im Stadtraum: von den privaten Einzelobjekten an den Stadträndern zu den öffentlichen Bauten in den Stadtzentren. Die Spannweite reicht von New York über Vancouver bis Frankfurt. Überdeckt werden Sporthallen, Bibliotheken, Ausstellungsräume und Restaurants. In der Regel werden sie als erweiterter öffentlicher Grünraum positiv angenommen.

The idea of "enclosures" through green did not remain lodged in the pioneer phase of the emerging environmental consciousness. The revival of such initiatives after the turn of the new millennium relied instead on a renewed awareness of environmental protection. As a result, the scale of projects changed, as did their position in the urban space: from private single properties on the city limits to public buildings downtown. The spectrum ranges from New York via Vancouver to Frankfurt. Sports halls, libraries, exhibition spaces and restaurants all have grass covers. As a rule they are favorably received as an expansion of the public green spaces.

HILDE STROBL

Der Baum und das Haus – ein uraltes Verhältnis?

The tree and the house – an ancient relationship?

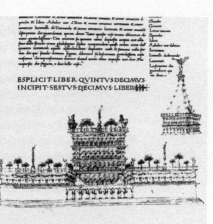

Antonio Averlino (Filarete), Filarete
Gartenpalast / *Garden palace*
in: Trattato di architettura, 1464

Wenn Dieter Wieland im Film „Der Hausbaum" (BRD, 1983) den Hausbaum als „die Krone eines Hauses" beschreibt, bezieht er sich auf das enge Verhältnis von Baum und Haus auf dem Land: „Häuser ohne Bäume waren früher so wenig denkbar wie Männer ohne Bart." Doch Häuser bekrönende Bäume finden sich tatsächlich in historischen Beispielen wie der Torre Guinigi in Lucca aus dem 14. Jahrhundert. Auch der Architekt Antonio Averlino, genannt Filarete, beschreibt in seinem „Trattato di architettura" im 15. Buch (1464) einen Gartenpalast in der Idealstadt Sforzinda. Diesen fünfgeschossigen Palast inmitten eines Gartens bezeichnet der Architekt als „Giardino e palazzo" – als Garten und Palast zugleich. Terrassen und Dach beschreibt und illustriert Filarete als mit Bäumen bepflanzt.

When in the film "Der Hausbaum" (Germany, 1983) Dieter Wieland refers to the "house tree" as the "crown of a house" he is referring to the close relationship between tree and house in rural areas: "Houses without trees were once as inconceivable as men without beards." However, there are in fact historical examples of trees crowning houses, such as the 14th-century Torre Guinigi in Lucca, Italy. Architect Antonio Averlino, known as Filarete, likewise described a garden palace in the ideal city of Sforzinda in the 15th book of his "Trattato di architettura" (1464). Filarete termed this five-story palace in the middle of a garden a "Giardino e palazzo" – a garden and palace in one. He also described the terraces and roofs as covered with trees.

Torre Guinigi, Lucca
Italien, 14. Jahrhundert
Italy, 14th century
Photo: Lucarelli, 2009

Friedensreich Hundertwasser räumte Bäumen sogar ein Teilhaberecht an Wohnungen ein und prägte den Begriff des „Baummieters" – neben dem „Menschenmieter". Bäume, so Hundertwasser, „sind ein Geschenk des Hauses an die Außenwelt, für die Menschen, die am Haus vorbeigehen. Der Mensch gibt freiwillig von seinem Wohnbereich kleine Territorien an die Natur zurück, von den großen Gebieten, die wir ihr widerrechtlich genommen haben" (1985).[26] Die „Miete" zahlt der Baummieter nach Hundertwasser mit „wahren Werten" zurück, so produziert der Baum Sauerstoff, mildert den Lärm und schluckt den Feinstaub.[27]

Friedensreich Hundertwasser actually granted trees co-ownership rights to apartments and coined the term "tree tenants" – alongside "human tenants". Trees, or so Hundertwasser felt, "are a gift of the house to the outside world, to the people passing by. Humans voluntarily give small territories from their residential spaces back to nature, small pieces of the large territories that we have illegally taken from it" (1985).[26] The tree tenant repays the "rent" Hundertwasser suggested in the form of "true assets", as the tree produces oxygen, reduces noise, and absorbs fine particulate matter.[27]

26 www.hundertwasser-haus.info/blog/2011/07/18/die-baummieter (4.11.2020).
27 Friedensreich Hundertwasser, Baummieter sind Botschafter des freien Waldes in der Stadt, in: Christoph Goritz, Auseinandersetzung mit einer Wechselbeziehung, Leipzig 2002, S./*p.* 43.

WALD AUF DEM DACH
FLACHWURZLER

MENSCHMIETER

REGENWASSER ZULEITUNG
ZUM BAUMMIETER

MIETER MENSCH MIETER

LAUBWERK

BEFESTIGUNG

BAUM MIETER

KEIN FENSTER
KEIN GLAS
IMMER OFFEN

SCHICHT
WASSERDICHTE

TORF + HUMUS

LECCA ODER BIMSTEIN

SCHAUMSTOFF
DAZWISCHEN

ÜBERLAUF ABFLUSS

MENSCH MIETER

STÜTZPFEILER

REINES
WASSER!

links / *left*
„Baummieter Wien", 1976,
Hundertwasser Gemeinnützige Privatstiftung
ARCH 22/I 766

oben / *top*
Triennale Mailand 1973, Italien / *Milan Triennale 1973, Italy*
Hundertwasser Gemeinnützige Privatstiftung
ARCH 22

rechts / *right*
„Hochhaus Architektur-Heilvorschlag",
1971/72, Sammlung Peter Schamoni,
München, Deutschland / *Munich, Germany*
Hundertwasser Gemeinnützige Privatstiftung
ARCH 20/II 713/II

Im Rahmen der Mailänder Triennale 1973 verpflanzte Hundertwasser in einer Aktion 15 Bäume in Wohnungen an der Via Mazoni in Mailand. In einer im Presseclub Concordia in Wien gehaltene Rede „Los von Loos – Gesetz für individuelle Bauveränderungen oder Architektur-Boykott-Manifest" (1968) forderte der Künstler: „Das Erdstück, das beim Hausbau zugedeckt und umgebracht wird, muss auf das Dach verlegt werden. Eine dicke Erdschicht, dass auf den Dächern 100-jährige Bäume, riesige Bäume, wachsen können." Er war der festen Überzeugung, dass Architektur durch Pflanzen „geheilt" werden könne und übertrug die Idee auch auf bestehende Wohnhochhäuser.

In the context of the 1973 Milan Triennale in an action Hundertwasser planted 15 trees in apartments along Via Mazoni in Milan. In a speech he gave at the Concordia Press Club in Vienna entitled "Away from Loos – Law for Individual Changes to Buildings or Architecture Boycott Manifesto" (1968) Hundertwasser demanded: "The piece of earth that gets covered over and is killed when building a house must be transposed onto the roof. A thick layer of earth that can enable 100-year-old trees, huge trees, to grow on the roofs." He was firmly convinced that architecture could be "healed" by plants and transposed the idea onto existing residential towers.

Der italienische Architekt Luciano Pia ging noch einen Schritt weiter und entwarf ein Haus mit Trägern aus Cortenstahl in Baumformen, Lärchenholzverkleidung und 150 Bäumen, die in großen Trögen in die Fassadenstruktur eingebunden sind. Das Condomino Verde 25 überträgt die Idee des Baumhauses in die Stadt, inmitten eines Industriegebiets in Turin.

Italian architect Luciano Pia went even further and designed a house with load-bearing columns made of Corten steel but shaped like trees, with larch wood panels and 150 trees that are incorporated into the façade structure in large planters. "Condomino Verde 25" transposes the idea of a tree house into the city, in this case the very middle of an industrial zone in Turin.

HILDE STROBL

Ein Blick zurück: Was haben Balkon-, Terrassen- und Dachgärten mit den „Hängenden Gärten der Semiramis" im antiken Babylon gemeinsam?

Die berühmten „Hängenden Gärten der Semiramis" im antiken Babylon, die zu den sieben Weltwundern zählen, sind nur durch schriftliche Quellen überliefert. Die bildlichen Rekonstruktionsversuche reichen von Athanasius Kircher im Barock über Gottfried Semper im 19. Jahrhundert bis Robert Koldewey in der 1930er-Jahren.[28] Allen gemein ist eine Vorstellung von einer auf quadratischem Grundriss überbauten Fläche mit horizontaler Gebäudebegrünung auf verschiedenen Ebenen – um Garten mit Architektur zu verweben und den Garten „in das Haus zu holen". Die Rekonstruktionen unterscheiden sich deutlich in der Art der Technik der Substruktion, des Erdreichaufwands, der Bewässerung und der Bepflanzung. Die bildlichen Darstellungen geben aber immer auch die zeittypische Vorstellung eines idealen Gartens wieder – vom geordneten Park mit niedrigem Bewuchs im Barock bis zu den künstlich geschaffenen wilden Naturszenarien späterer Jahrhunderte.

---

28 Stefan Schweizer, Die hängenden Gärten von Babylon. Vom Weltwunder zur grünen Architektur, Berlin 2020.

Looking back: What do balcony, patio, and roof gardens have in common with the "Hanging Gardens of Babylon"?

All that remains of the famous "Hanging Gardens of Babylon" are written descriptions of what were considered one of the Seven Wonders of the World in their day. Visual attempts to reconstruct them range from Athanasius Kircher in Baroque times and Gottfried Semper in the 19th century to Robert Koldewey in the 1930s.[28] What all sketches share is the idea of a square footprint with an area built upwards with horizontal lines of greenery on different levels – in order to bond architecture and garden and bring the garden 'into the house'. The reconstructions differ clearly in terms of the technology used for the substructure, the amount of soil deployed, the irrigation, and the plants. However, the visual representations always reveal the notion of an ideal garden typical at the time, from the orderly Baroque park with its low bushes to the artificially created expanses of natural wild preferred in later centuries.

Lieven Cruyl, Coenraet Decker
Hängende Gärten der Semiramis/
Hanging Gardens of the Semiramis,
Aus/*From*: Athanasius Kircher,
Turris Babel, 1679
© Bayerische Staatsbibliothek München

Gottfried Semper
Die Hängenden Gärten
von Babylon, um 1860
*The Hanging Gardens
of Babylon, approx. 1860*
© gta-Archiv ETH Zürich

In der Renaissance wurde der Begriff des „Hortus conclusus" geprägt, des kontemplativen Raums, der der christlichen Vorstellung eines „Paradies-gärtleins" folgte. Daraus entwickelten sich in den architektonischen Konzepten der italienischen Renaissance-Palazzi Dachgärten, wie sie in Urbino oder Pesaro verwirklicht wurden. Die geschaffenen Grünräume waren auf den privaten Gebrauch reduziert.

Auf die Erweiterung des Privatraums durch die Nutzung und Begrünung von Dächern zielte Le Corbusier in seiner Schrift „Fünf Punkte zu einer neuen Architektur" im Jahr 1927. Doch Le Corbusier ging über den privaten Vorteil hinaus einen Schritt weiter und betonte den Aspekt der Reproduktion der verbauten Fläche durch den Dachgarten aus stadtplanerischer Perspektive: „Allgemein bedeu-ten Dachgärten für die Stadt die Wiedergewinnung der gesamten verbauten Fläche."[29] Ein heute in den verdichteten Großstädten verstärkt formulier-ter Ansatz, der auf ökologische und klimatische Argumente baut.

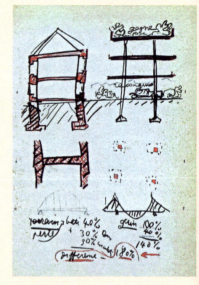

Le Corbusier
Feststellungen zu Architektur und Städtebau,
1929, S. 51
*Precisions on the present state of architecture
and urbanism, 1929, p. 51*

During the Renaissance a concept evolved of the "hortus conclusus", a contem-plative space that followed the Christian view of a "small Garden of Paradise". This led in architectural concepts for Italian Renaissance palazzi to the inclusion of roof gardens such as were then realized in Urbino or Pesaro. The green spaces thus created were exclusively for private use.

In his "Five Points of Architecture" published in 1927, Le Corbusier set out to extend private space by using and greening roofs. That said, Le Corbusier goes far beyond the private benefits and emphasizes the aspect of reproducing the built space in the form of roof gardens from the point of view of urban planning: "In general, roof terraces mean regaining for the city the entire space that has been built over."[29] – it is an approach being brought to bear in our densely built-up cities today on the basis of ecological and climatic arguments.

29 Le Corbusier, Fünf Punkte zu einer neuen Architektur, in: Die Form. Zeitschrift für gestaltende Arbeit, 2/1927, S./*p.* 272; Frank Maier-Solgk, Von den Hängenden Gärten zur zeitgenössischen Hortitecture, in: Stefan Schweizer, Die hängenden Gärten von Babylon. Vom Weltwunder zur grünen Architektur, Berlin 2020, S./*p.* 161–192, hier/*here* S./*p.* 170–171.

Fritz Stucky
Terrassenhaus in Zug, Schweiz, 1951
Terraced house in Zug, Switzerland, 1951
Photo: Christian Schwager, 2006

Kleine private Paradiese in Form von Terrassengärten in vorfabrizierten Beton-
fertigteilen waren ab den 1960er-Jahren eine willkommene Alternative. Sie
versprachen ein Leben in mehrgeschossigen Wohnanlagen in der Stadt und
gleichzeitig dennoch grüne Inseln vor der Haustüre.

Die durch die Schaffung von Dachgärten erweiterte Fläche nicht nur wenigen
Privilegierten zugänglich zu machen, sondern diese gemeinschaftlich zu
nutzen, ist einer der Grundsätze, die sich vor allem in genossenschaftlichen
Wohnprojekten abbilden, die in den letzten Jahren realisiert wurden.

*Small private paradises in the form of terraced gardens made of prefabricated
concrete parts were a welcome alternative that appeared on the scene from the
1960s onwards. They promised a life in multi-story residential blocks downtown
where you could still enjoy having an island of green on your doorstep.*

*One of the principles to be observed above all in cooperative housing projects is
to create areas extended to include roof gardens that are not just the privilege
of a few but are open to common use.*

HILDE STROBL

Pflanzen an Fassaden gab es schon immer? Nur Pflanzenarten und Anliegen wandeln sich...

So there have always been plants on façades? It is only the species of plants and concerns that have changed...

Am weitesten geht die Geschichte der Bepflanzung von Fassaden zurück. Schon in der Antike zierten Efeu und Weinstöcke die Fassaden – nicht zuletzt um die Wärme der Wand für die Reifung der Trauben zu nutzen. Seit der Renaissance wurden an den europäischen Höfen, Klosterbauten und in den Städten vielfach Weinreiben in waagrecht geführten Kordonen an Fassaden gezogen. Lange vor den heute in der Gebäudebegrünung üblichen Systemen mit Drahtseilen wurde schon im Barock der Wuchs von Spalierobst an Drähten gelenkt.[30]

The history of the cultivation of plants on façades goes back a very long way. Even way back in Ancient Greece, façades were decorated with ivy and vines – not least to take advantage of the warmth generated by the walls to ripen the grapes. Since the Renaissance, grapevines have often been grown in horizontally cultivated cordons on façades, at the European courts, on monastery buildings and in the towns. And in the Baroque era, long before the systems currently in use for greening buildings on wire cables, fruit was grown on espaliers and guided along wires.[30]

Waagerecht-Kordon in Königsbrück, 1835
Horizontal cordons in Königsbrück, 1835

---

30 www.fassadengruen.de/uw/weinreben/uw/weinstock/uw/kordon/kordon.html (10.11.2020)

Durch den seit der Frühen Neuzeit einsetzenden weltweiten Handel und die Entdeckungsreisen der Europäer verbreiteten sich immer mehr Pflanzenarten – zunächst aus Nordamerika (z.B. Wilder Wein oder Pfeifenwinde) und im 19. Jahrhundert aus Ostasien (z.B. Blauregen, Clematis oder Knöterich). Viele der Pflanzenarten kamen über England nach Deutschland.

In der Romantik bedienten wuchernde, unbändige Kletterpflanzen an Hausfassaden die Vorstellung der Macht einer wilden Natur, die die Grenzen der Architektur (Ratio und Wissenschaft) übertrifft. Ende des 19. Jahrhunderts erreichten die Kletterpflanzen in ihrer Artenvielfalt als „Bekleidungspflanzen" ihren Höhepunkt.[31] Die kultivierten Importarten fanden vor allem während der Reformbewegung großen Anklang, sodass bepflanzte Hausfronten das Bild zahlreicher Gartenstädte prägten. Architekten wie Hermann Muthesius, Theodor Fischer oder Richard Riemerschmid setzten Rankgerüste und Zierspaliere als dezidierte Elemente der Fassadengestaltung ein. Auch Gartenarchitekten Leberecht Migge stellt in seiner „Gartenkultur des 20. Jahrhunderts" (1913) verschiedene Verwendungsmöglichkeiten von Kletterpflanzen und Spalierobst für die Stadt vor.

With the dawn of global trade in early modern times and the expeditions by Europeans, more and more species of plants became widespread – initially those from North America (e.g. Virginia creeper and Dutchman's pipe) and then, in the 19th century, from the Far East (e.g. wisteria, clematis and knotweed). Many of these plant species came to Germany via England.

In Romanticism, rampant, untamable climbing plants on the façades of houses serviced the notion of the power of a wild nature overstepping the limits of architecture (rationality and science). At the end of the 19th century, the biodiversity of climbing plants as covering plants reached a climax.[31] The cultivated, imported species met with their greatest approval during the Reform movement at the beginning of the 20th century, meaning that greened façades adorned the houses in numerous garden cities. Architects such as Hermann Muthesius, Theodor Fischer and Richard Riemerschmid used trellises and ornamental latticework as accentuating features of façade design. In his "Gartenkultur des 20. Jahrhunderts" (20th-Century Horticulture, 1913), landscape architect Leberecht Migge also presents various uses for climbing plants and espalier fruit in cities.

---

31   Rudi Baumann, Begrünte Architektur. Bauen und Gestalten mit Kletterpflanzen, München 1983, S./*p.* 20–23.

Goethes Gartenhaus in Weimar
Goethe's summer house in Weimar,
in: Paul Schmitthenner,
Das deutsche Wohnhaus,
Stuttgart 1932, S./*p.* 9.

Das Gartenhaus Goethes in Weimar, das der Schriftsteller 1776 erwarb, stand für viele Architekten wie Theodor Fischer oder Paul Schmitthenner als Inbegriff einer geistigen Baukunst. Der Spalierbewuchs des Gartenhauses geht auf Goethe selbst zurück und ist Teil seines Gartenkonzepts. Er ließ an allen vier Hausseiten Rankgerüste anbringen und an den West- und Nordseiten Rosen, an der Ostseite Geißblatt und an der Südseite Weinreben anpflanzen.[32]

For many architects such as Theodor Fischer and Paul Schmitthenner, the summer house in Weimar which was acquired by Goethe in 1776 represented the epitome of an intellectual approach to architecture. The espalier plants that covered it were selected by the famous author himself and were part of his garden concept. He had trellises erected on all four sides of the house, growing roses on the west and north-facing sides, honeysuckle on the east-facing side and vines on the south-facing side.[32]

O. M. Ungers, Fassadengestaltungen für
Kaufhaus Woolworth, Berlin-Wedding 1980,
façade design for the Woolworth store in
Wedding, Berlin, 1979,
aus/*from*: db 10/1979, S./*p.* 43.

---

32 Dorothee Ahrendt, Gertraud Aepfler, Goethes Gärten in Weimar, Leipzig 2009, S./*p.* 21.

Oswald Mathias Ungers verbildlicht die Herleitung der grünen Fassade in einem Wettbewerbsbeitrag für das Kaufhaus Woolworth in Berlin-Wedding, indem er den barocken Park buchstäblich über die Fassade legt. Die architektonische Großform des Kaufhauses, das nach innen „funktionell-kommerziellen Funktionen" dient, zeigt sich nach außen als „öffentliches Grünelement", so Ungers. Der Architekt bezieht sich auf die Tradition der dreidimensionalen Grünelemente, die im 19. Jahrhundert auf Uferbefestigungen und ehemaligen Befestigungsanalgen angelegt wurden. Über die mit Basaltlava verkleidete, terrassierte Fassade stülpen sich Rank- und Hängegewächse und Bäume.[33]

Oswald Mathias Ungers visualized the basis for the green façade in his competition entry for the Woolworth store in Berlin's Wedding by quite literally spreading the Baroque park across the façade. The large architectural shape of the department store which serves "functional-commercial functions" on the inside dons a "public green element" on the outside, so Ungers. The architect draws on the tradition of three-dimensional green elements that were aligned in the 19th century to embankments and former fortifications. Across the terraced façade clad in the basalt lava run the climbing and hanging plants and trees.[33]

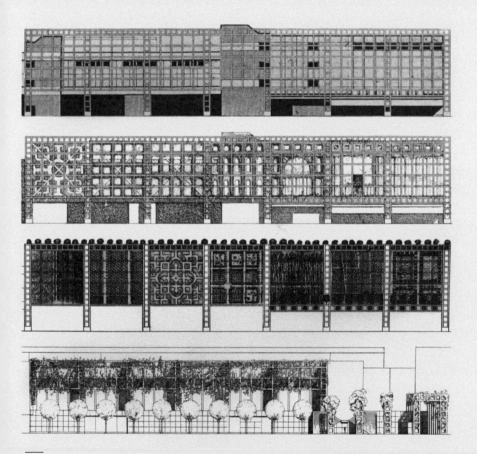

33   O.M. Ungers, „Fassadengestaltung Kaufhaus Woolworth in Berlin-Wedding", in: db 10/1979, S./*p.* 42–47.

Patrick Blanc, Caixa Forum,
Madrid, Spanien/*Spain*, 2008
Photo: © Patrick Blanc

Der Pariser Botaniker Patrick Blanc wird zu Recht als der Vater der Fassadenbegrünung bezeichnet. Beginnend mit seinen ersten Projekten in den
1980er-Jahren etablierte er eine neue Dimension in der Fassadengestaltung,
die „Murs végétaux". Blanc schafft durch die Anordnung der verschiedenen
Pflanzen abstrakte Wandbilder.

Zu den in Europa bekanntesten Projekten von Blanc zählt das 600 m² umfassenden Wandprojekt mit circa 2.500 Pflanzen an der Brandmauer des
benachbarten Wohnhauses am Paseo del Prado, das er im Zuge des Umbaus
des Caixa Forums durch Herzog & de Meuron realisierte. Der Forscher und
Spezialist für Tropenpflanzen hatte ein System für Wandbepflanzungen
entwickelt, das er sich 1988 patentieren ließ. Blanc arbeitet mit einem dop-
pelt gelegten Kunststoffvlies, in das Taschen eingeschnitten werden, die
dünnste Substratschichten tragen und die Wurzeln der Pflanzen aufnehmen.
Ein Metallgerüst, das einen Abstand zum Mauerwerk gewährleistet, damit
dahinter Luft zirkulieren kann, dient als Unterkonstruktion für die Bepflanzung.

Die Methode machte Schule und wurde von vielen Herstellern übernommen. Der anfänglichen Kritik zu wenig ökologisch basiert und ausschließlich ästhetisch motiviert zu handeln, setzte Blanc früh Argumente entgegen, die heute von den Befürwortern der Fassadenbegrünung geteilt werden.

Niemand hat so viele Fassaden weltweit im Innen- und Außenbereich in den verschiedensten Techniken bepflanzt wie Patrick Blanc. Allein in Paris lassen sich über 50 Projekte zählen, darunter auch die Neugestaltung des Museé du Quai Branly. In Zusammenarbeit mit dem Architekten Jean Nouvel entstanden Projekte wie One Central Park in Sydney oder die „Le Nouvel"-Türme in Kuala Lumpur.[34]

Parisian botanist Patrick Blanc is rightly known as the father of façade greening. Starting with his initial projects in the 1980s, he has opened up a new dimension in façade design, something known as "murs végétaux". Blanc creates abstract murals with his arrangements of various plants.

One of Blanc's best-known projects in Europe is his 600 m² wall-based greening project on Paseo del Prado, on the fireproof wall of a neighboring residential building using approximately 2,500 plants, something he realized as part of the conversion of the Caixa Forum by Herzog & de Meuron. The researcher and expert in tropical plants came up with a system of wall planting which he had patented in 1988. Blanc works with a double layer of plastic nonwovens into which pockets containing the thinnest of layers of substrate are cut; these hold the roots of the plants. A special metal frame which maintains a distance from the masonry so that air can circulate behind it serves as a substructure to the plantings. The method caught on and was adopted by a large number of manufacturers. Today, the kind of arguments that Blanc supplied at an early stage to refute initial criticisms that the system did not really have a basis in ecology but was exclusively aesthetically motivated, are now shared by other advocates of façade greening.

Nobody else anywhere in the world has used so many different techniques to include plants on façades both inside and outside buildings as has Patrick Blanc. In Paris alone there have been more than 50 projects, including redesigning the Musée du Quai Branly. Projects such as One Central Park in Sidney and the "Le Nouvel" towers in Kuala Lumpur represent collaborations with the architect Jean Nouvel.[34]

HILDE STROBL

34 Patrick Blanc, Vertikale Gärten. Die Natur in der Stadt, Stuttgart 2009; Beate Taudte-Repp, Die Vertikalen Gärten von Patrick Blanc, in: Annette Becker, Peter Cachola Schmal, Stadtgrün. Europäische Landschaftsarchitektur für das 21. Jahrhundert, Basel 2010, S./p. 26–31.

Wie steht es um die „Zimmerpflanze" oder grüne Inseln im Inneren der Gebäude?

Eigentlich gibt es keine „Zimmerpflanzen", denn hierbei handelt es sich um Pflanzen aus tropischen oder subtropischen Gegenden, die sich aufgrund ihrer genetischen Eigenschaften für das Raumklima eignen.

Der Wunsch des Menschen, ein Stück Natur im Innenraum zu erleben und damit wieder mit der Natur verbunden zu sein, besteht seit Jahrhunderten, und es gibt viele Beispiele dafür (Palmgärten, Orangerien, Wintergärten, Gewächshäuser, Pflanzenfensterbänder usw.). Pflanzen beeinflussen die Akustik und Luftfeuchtigkeit von Räumen. Dass Pflanzen eine Anziehungskraft ausüben, das Raumklima verändern und die Aufenthaltsqualität steigern – und den Aufenthalt bisweilen auch verlängern –, zeigen einzelne Studien. Diese Wirkungen werden nicht nur in der Arbeits- und Konsumwelt gezielt eingesetzt, sondern auch vielfach in öffentlichen Einrichtungen.

Actually there are no "indoor plants", as the latter are simply plants from tropical or subtropical regions which are suitable for indoor life in our country thanks to their genetic properties.

People's wish to experience a bit of nature indoors and thus to remain bonded to nature has existed for centuries and there are many examples of it (palm houses, orangeries, conservatories, green-houses, window boxes, etc.). There is agreement that plants change the ambient climate and enhance the quality of the room, and often help to reduce stress levels. For many people, indoor plants are a substitute for not having a garden.
ALEXANDER HILDEBRAND / GERHARD ZEMP

What is the status of "house plants" or green islands inside buildings?

BEGRÜNT EUCH! REALISIERTE GRÜNBAUTEN

GET GREENED! EXISTING GREENED BUILDINGS

Dakpark

Buro Sant en Co
Rotterdam, Niederlande
Netherlands

Photo: Stijn Brakkee

Der Dakpark auf einem ehemaligen Hafenareal in Rotterdam gelegen kombiniert verschiedene Bedürfnisse unter einem grünen Dach. Er ist zugleich Stadtteilpark, Einkaufszentrum, Parkhaus und Deich. Zum Wohnviertel Bospolder-Tussendijken hin fällt der Park als Flutschutz steil ab und bildet zum Hafen eine Plattform unter der sich Einzelhandelsgeschäfte befinden. Zugleich nimmt er in seinem Inneren sowohl die ehemaligen Rangiergleise der Hafenbahn auf als auch neue Parkmöglichkeiten. Strukturiert werden die weitläufigen Rasenflächen von diagonal verlaufenden Fußwegen, steinernen Treppenläufen, einem Wasserspiel, drei Themengärten, einem Gewächshaus mit integriertem Restaurant sowie Spielplätzen für Kinder. Die Anwohner des angrenzenden Stadtteils wurden nicht nur bei der Planung des Parks mit einbezogenen, sie werden auch weiterhin in die Verwaltung und Bewirtschaftung der Grünanlagen eingebunden.

Dakpark is located in a former area of the port in Rotterdam and combines different usages under a single, green roof. It is a district park, shopping center, carpark and dyke all in one. On the side facing the Bospolder-Tussendijken residential quarter, the park drops steeply to function as flood protection and on the port side forms a platform beneath which the retail outlets are to be found. At the same time, its interior includes the erstwhile shunting yard for the port railway and new parking spaces. The spacious areas of grass are lent structure by diagonal footpaths, a fountain, three themed gardens, a greenhouse with an integrated restaurant and playgrounds for children. Local inhabitants from the district nearby were involved not only in planning the park but will continue to be involved in the administration and operation of the green areas.

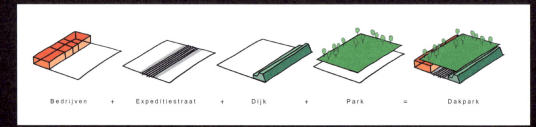

Bedrijven + Expeditiestraat + Dijk + Park = Dakpark

BAUTYP, NUTZUNG *TYPE OF BUILDING, USAGE*	**In einen Deich integrierte Parkanlage auf einem Dach mit Einkaufs-zentrum und öffentlichem Außengelände in einer multifunktionalen Deichumgebung** *Rooftop park incorporated into a dike with retail facility and a public outdoor area in a unique, multi-functional dike setting*
FERTIGSTELLUNG *COMPLETION*	**2015**
ARCHITEKTEN & GRÜN-PLANUNG / *ARCHITECTS & GREENERY PLANNERS*	**Buro Sant en Co**
BAUHERR / *BUILDER*	**Stadt Rotterdam /** *City of Rotterdam*
ART DER BEGRÜNUNG, METHODE *TYPE OF GREENERY, METHOD*	**Intensive Dachbegrünung** *Intensive roof greening*
FLÄCHE DER BEGRÜNUNG *AREA GREENED*	**Circa 80.000 m², die Parkanlage ist 1.200 m lang und 85 m breit** *Circa 80,000 m², the park is 1,200 m long and 85 m wide*
TECHNIK *TECHNIQUE*	**Gewächshaus, Deich, Wasserspiele** *greenhouse, dike, water stairs*
PFLANZEN *PLANTS*	**Der Park besteht vorwiegend aus Rasenflächen mit Bäumen entlang der Hauptgehwege. Bei den Bäumen handelt es sich um verschiedene Ahorn-arten – kombiniert mit Kirschbäumen und Magnolien. Beinahe alle Bäume sind mehrstämmig oder großwüchsig. Die vielfältige Bepflanzung gewähr-leistet eine farbenreiche Vegetation durch alle Jahreszeiten hindurch. Auch für die Ränder des Parks wurde eine farbenfrohe Bepflanzung gewählt mit Arten wie Sanddorn, Schafskopfhortensien und Perückensträucher.** *The park consists mainly of lawn with trees along the main walkways. The trees vary from various species of maple combined with cherry and magno-lia. Almost all trees are multi-stemmed with a number of monumental speci-mens. Varied planting has been chosen so that the park looks colorful in all seasons. The edges of the park also have colorful planting. Fire buckthorn, wig tree and plume hydrangea are some examples of colorful plants that come to the eaves.*
AUFWAND DER PFLEGE *OUTLAYS FOR CARING FOR THE PLANTS*	**2-5 Schafe grasen auf dem Rasen und halten ihn kurz.** *2-5 sheeps graze on the lawn and keep it short.*
KLIMAERGEBNIS, KLIMA-KONZEPT, KLIMAZIELE *CLIMATIC IMPACT, CLIMATE CONCEPT, CLIMATE GOALS*	**Das Projekt ist Teil von Rotterdams Strategieplan zum Klimawandel. Das Konzept des Dakpark zielt auf eine innerstädtische räumliche Erneue-rung als Reaktion auf die sich wandelnden klimatischen Voraussetz-ungen wie Trockenheit, Hitzebelastung und Überflutungen. Ein bislang versiegelter Bodenbereich wurde beispielsweise in eine grüne Lunge verwandelt – mit kühlendem Effekt für die Stadt. Zudem wurde in den Dakpark ein Hafendamm als wesentliche Maßnahme gegen Überflut-ungen integriert. Eine spezielle Schicht des Aufbaus gewährleistet eine Wasseraufnahme von 100 bis 200 Litern pro Quadratmeter und stellt den verzögerten Rückfluss von Wasser zur Stadt sicher.** *The project is part of Rotterdam's Climate Change Adaptation Strategy. The park is an example of spatial renewal that responds to changing climate, with effects such as drought, heat stress, flooding and flooding. For example, a stony area has been transformed into a green lung, which has a cooling effect on the city. A working seawall has been integrated into the Dakpark, which plays an essential role against flooding. The design provides for the*

construction of a layer that guarantees a water buffering capacity of around 100 to 200 litres per square metre. This also ensures the delayed return of water to the city.

Der grüne Park umfasst drei spezielle Bereiche: einen mediterranen Garten, Spielplätze und Nachbarschaftsgärten. Im Mittelpunkt des Dachgartens stehen eine Orangerie und eine Wassertreppe. Die Haupteingänge im Osten und Westen öffnen sich zu den völlig unterschiedlichen Funktionsräumen: Auf der östlichen Seite wurde in der Sockelzone des Walls ein städtischer Bereich mit Geschäften eingerichtet, flankiert von Hecken und hohen Bäumen. Auf der Westseite, Richtung Wohnviertel, stuft sich das Gelände mit weiten Grünflächen ab und variiert mit verschiedenen Themengärten an den Haupteingängen.

It is a green park with three special places: the Mediterranean garden, the playground and the neighborhood garden. The central heart of the roof park is formed by an Orangery with a water staircase. Here are also the main entrances. The east and west sides of the roof park are completely different in character. The east side has a metropolitan character with a plinth of businesses on which the park manifests itself through hedges and tall trees. The west side is facing the district and has a very green character, a buckled ground level with themed gardens at the main entrances.

Größter öffentlicher Dachpark in Europa
Largest public roof park in Europe

Perspektive/*Perspective:* @ Buro Sant en Co

Der Park verfügt über mehrere schöne (Gemüse-)Gärten. Die Schafe des städtischen Schäfers Martin Oosthoek grasen im Park. Bei windigem Wetter kann man sich im Wärmeraum zurückziehen, einem ummauerten Garten mit mediterranen Pflanzen. Im Sommer gibt es in der Regel einen Kiosk, an dem hausgemachte Erfrischungen angeboten werden. Außerdem werden verschiedene Aktivitäten von Yoga bis Bootcamps angeboten. Die Anwohner waren am gesamten Gestaltungsprozess beteiligt und sind auch in die Verwaltung des Parks eingebunden. Nachbarschaftsbetreuer öffnen den Park früh am Morgen und stellen auch die Überwachung tagsüber sicher.

The park also has several beautiful (vegetable) gardens. The sheep of city shepherd Martin Oosthoek graze in the park. If the wind blows, you can retreat to the Warmth Room, a walled garden with Mediterranean plants. In the summer, there is often a kiosk selling home-made refreshments, and all kinds of activities take place, from yoga to bootcamp. Residents participated throughout the design process and now have a role in management. Neighbourhood parents open the park early in the morning and supervise during the day.

Photo: Edwin Santhagens

BIG Bjarke Ingels Group
SLA
Kopenhagen, Dänemark
Copenhagen, Denmark

CopenHill

Photo: Rasmus Hjortshøj

Das Amager Ressource Center – eine moderne Müllverbrennungsanlage – im industriellen Hafengebiet Kopenhagens, ist so gestaltet, dass die Dachfläche des 41.000 m² großen Gebäudes zu einem künstlichen Berg im ansonsten flachen Dänemark wird. Anknüpfend an Sportarten wie Wakeboard und Go-Kart fahren, die in der Umgebung ausgeübt werden, erstreckt sich oberhalb des Energiegewinnungskomplexes eine Berglandschaft für ursprünglich nicht-städtische Sportarten: zum Skifahren (ohne Schnee) und Wandern lädt eine gräserner Skipiste, ein Lift und Wanderpfade ein. Über nachhaltig, ökologische Aspekte hinaus, wurde so ein in Stadtnähe wenig beliebter Ort (Müllverbrennung) – begleitet durch eine im Vorfeld langfristig angelegte Werbekampagne – positiv umgewidmet. Das Gras auf der Skipiste wird mit einem Netz aus Kunststoffmatten geschützt, damit die Grasnarben geschont werden. An den Rändern der Pisten wuchern Gräser, Büsche und Bäume. Im Bauch des Berges werden jährlich 440.000 Tonnen Abfall in Energie für 150.000 Haushalte umgewandelt.

The Amager Ressource Center, a modern waste incineration plant, is located in the industrial harbor in Copenhagen. It is designed such that the roof area of the building, which has a footprint of 41,000 m², becomes an artificial mountain in what is otherwise flat Denmark. Emulating sports such as Wakeboarding and Go-Karting, both of which are popular in the vicinity, the roof of the energy reclamation complex boasts a mountain world for originally non-urban types of sports: The grass ski slope encourages visitors to ski (without snow) or go hiking. In addition to the sustainable ecological aspects, in this way a hardly popular location close to the city center (a waste incineration plant) – and accompanied by a long-term ad campaign that is launched well in advance – was given a new positive image. The grass on the ski slope if protected by a net made of plastic mats that ensure the swards are spared. At the edges of the slope, grass, bushes and trees grow at random. And beneath the slope each year 440,000 tons of waste are converted in energy for 150,000 households.

BAUTYP, NUTZUNG *TYPE OF BUILDING, USAGE*	**Müllheizkraftwerk** *Waste-to-energy plant*
FERTIGSTELLUNG *COMPLETION*	**2019**
ARCHITEKTEN / *ARCHITECTS*	**BIG Bjarke Ingels Group**
GRÜNPLANUNG *GREENERY PLANNERS*	**SLA**
BAUHERR / *BUILDER*	**Amagar Resscourcecenter ARC**
ART DER BEGRÜNUNG, METHODE *TYPE OF GREENERY, METHOD*	**Intensive Dachbegrünung** *Intensive roof greening*
FLÄCHE DER BEGRÜNUNG *AREA GREENED*	**35.000 m² Landschaftspark, 41.000 m² Gebäude** *35,000 m² nature park and landscape, 41,000 m² building*
PFLANZEN *PLANTS*	**Die wilde und üppige Berglandschaft umfasst Pflanzen (Gräser, Kräuter, Stauden), 7.000 Sträucher und 300 Kiefern und Weidenbäume. Die Bepflanzung wurde auf die spezifische Umgebung und die Windverhältnisse abgestimmt, um ein optimales Mikroklima zu schaffen.** *The wild and sensuous mountain nature includes plants (grasses, herbs, perennials), 7,000 bushes and, 300 pine and willow trees. The planting is specially chosen to meet the challenging living conditions and create optimal micro climate and wind condition.*
BEWÄSSERUNG *WATERING SYSTEM*	**Tropfbewässerungsleitungen** *Drip-line irrigation*

212

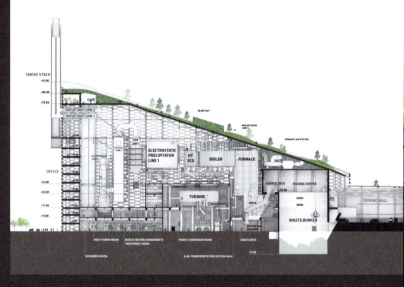

Schnitt/*Section:*
© BIG Bjarke Ingels Group

AUFWAND DER PFLEGE
OUTLAYS FOR CARING FOR
THE PLANTS

Wichtig ist, dass das Gras auf der Piste regelmäßig gemäht wird, sodass die Skifahrer auf ihrem Weg nach unten nicht ausgebremst werden.
The only requirement is that the grass that is growing through is mowed regularly so that the downhill skiers won't be slowed down.

BESCHREIBUNG
DESCRIPTION

CopenHill ist eine ganz neue Form von Müllheizkraftwerk. Ausgestattet mit Skipiste, Wanderweg und Kletterwand verkörpert CopenHill eine Art hedonistische Nachhaltigkeit. Zugleich bringt das Projekt die Stadt Kopenhagen dem Ziel näher, bis 2025 auch die erste kohlenstoffneutrale Stadt der Welt zu sein.
CopenHill opens as a new breed of waste-to-energy plant topped with a ski slope, hiking trail and climbing wall, embodying the notion of hedonistic sustainability while aligning with Copenhagen's goal of becoming the world's first carbon-neutral city by 2025.

FÜR DEN FALL: FAUNA
IN THE CASE: FAUNA

Auf dem Copenhill können Vögel, Bienen, Schmetterlinge und Blumen heimisch werden. Es entstehen eine lebendige grüne Oase und ein völlig neues urbanes Ökosystem für die Stadt Kopenhagen.
Copenhill becomes the home for birds, bees, butterflies and flowers, creating a vibrant green pocket and forming a completely new urban ecosystem for the city of Copenhagen.

WAS ICH ERWÄHNEN MÖCHTE ...
WHAT I WANT TO MENTION ...

Auf Amager Bakkes natürlichem Dachpark mit Wanderweg können Bürger der Stadt und Besucher auf dem Dach eines der weltweit saubersten Müllheizkraftwerke eine Berglandschaft mit ihren Pflanzen erkunden. Überdies wird durch CopenHill und seine weitläufige Grünfläche das angrenzende Industriegebiet enorm aufgewertet.
Amager Bakke's nature roof park and hiking trail invites locals and visitors to traverse a mountainous landscape of plants and rockscapes atop the world's cleanest waste-to-energy plant. It also acts as a generous 'green gift' that will radically green-up the adjacent industrial area.

Dachplan / *Roof plan*
© SLA Architects

Baumhaus

Ot Hoffmann
Darmstadt, Deutschland
Germany

Das Baumhaus in Darmstadt steht unter Denkmalschutz. Der Architekt Ot Hoffmann war Vorreiter einer ökologisch motivierten Bewegung der 1970er-Jahre. Kompromisslos experimentierte er mit Bepflanzungsmethoden und den technischen und baustofflichen Herausforderungen am eigenen Haus. Er integrierte darüber hinaus das Baumhaus in ein städtebauliches Konzept, das unter seiner Federführung entwickelt wurde und vorsah, die Innenstadt Darmstadts umzugestalten und Verkehrs- in Fußgängerstraßen umzuwandeln. Die Fußgängerzone sollte mit dem Herrngarten verbunden werden und das Baumhaus eine Art Brückenkopfbau bilden. Eine Fußgängerbrücke über die Zeughausstraße sollte über das Vordach des Baumhauses im ersten Obergeschoss führen. Das Vordach ist das Relikt des mutigen Vorhabens.

Entgegen gegenwärtiger Tendenzen streng vorgeplanter und versorgter Gebäudebegrünungen ging Ot Hoffmann dezidiert von einer Gestaltung durch die Nutzer oder den Kreislauf der Natur selbst aus. Der Architekt schafft lediglich die Rahmenbedingungen.[35]

The Baumhaus in Darmstadt is heritage-listed. The architect Ot Hoffmann was a pioneer of an ecologically motivated movement during the 1970s. He was uncompromising in his experimentation with greening methods and with the technical and material challenges of his own designs. On top of this, he integrated the Baumhaus into an urban development concept that was crafted under his leadership and provided for a transformation of Darmstadt's city center including the conversion of roads into pedestrian streets. The pedestrian zone was to be linked to the Herrngarten park, with the Baumhaus forming a kind of bridgehead structure. A footbridge over Zeughausstrasse was to lead over the porch roof of the Baumhaus on the first floor, hence the protruding roof is the relic of this bold plan.

Bucking the trend towards rigidly pre-planted and maintained building greenery prevalent at the time, Ot Hoffmann opted decisively for a design inspired by users or by the cycle of nature itself. The architect merely created the basic conditions.[35]

35 Ot Hoffmann, Handbuch für begrünte und genutzte Dächer. Konstruktion - Gestaltung - Bauökologie für flache und geneigte begehbare, befahrbare begrünte Dächer, Stuttgart 1987; Alexander Heinigk, Erich Roethele, Besonders ökologisch, 9.11.2008: www.p-stadtkultur.de/besonders-darmstadt-7 (11.11.2020); Nachruf von/*Obituary from* Dirk Junklewitz, 1.7.2017: biotope-city.com/de/2019/07/01/ein-pionier-interview-mit-ot-hofmann (11.11.2020).

Ot Hoffmann und / and Peter Cachola Schmal,
Dachgarten / Roof garden Baumhaus
Photo: Oliver Elser, 2009

BAUTYP, NUTZUNG *TYPE OF BUILDING, USAGE*	**Mischnutzung: Büros, Atelier und Gewerberaum** *Mixed usage: Offices, studio and commercial space*
FERTIGSTELLUNG *COMPLETION*	**1972**
ARCHITEKTEN, GRÜN-PLANUNG UND BAUHERR *ARCHITECTS, GREENERY PLANNERS & BUILDER*	**Ot Hoffmann**
ART DER BEGRÜNUNG, METHODE *TYPE OF GREENERY, METHOD*	**Extensive Dachbegrünung (Erdschüttung auf der obersten Dachterrasse sowie Pflanztröge mit 30 bis 80cm Höhe auf dem unteren Dachgarten); einzelne Pflanzbehälter (zweckentfremdete Betonfertigteile) auf den Terrassen und dem Vorbau; Wintergarten** *Extensive roof greening (earth-fill on the uppermost roof terrace plus plant troughs of 30 to 80cm in height in the lower roof garden); individual plant containers (repurposed precast concrete components) on the terraces and the porch; winter garden*
FLÄCHE DER BEGRÜNUNG *AREA GREENED*	**Die Bepflanzung konzentriert sich auf die Ostseite des Gebäudes.** *The greening is concentrated on the east side of the building.*
TECHNIK *TECHNIQUE*	**Hoffmann konnte auf keine bewährten Techniken zurückgreifen. Er setzte auf den Dächern und Terrassen wasserundurchlässigen WU-Beton ein, ohne weitere Abdichtungen, und verwendete einen entsprechenden Aufbau mit Filterschicht, Vlies für den Wurzelschutz und Erdreich. Aus Kanalrohren wurden Rankhilfen und Pergolen gebaut.** *Hoffmann was unable to draw on the expertise of experienced engineers. On the roofs and terraces he used watertight concrete without further sealing and used a corresponding additional structure with a filter layer, felt to protect the roots, and soil. Sewage pipes were used for construction of climbing supports and pergolas.*
PFLANZEN *PLANTS*	**Die obersten Ebenen bekrönten 24 Kiefern. Diese werden aktuell durch Bäume ersetzt (Steineichen/Felsenbirne), die den sich verändernden klimatischen Bedingungen besser gewachsen sind. Neben Bambus und Efeu wurden Orangen-, Pfirsich und Aprikosenbäume und Feigen gepflanzt. Ot Hoffmann setzte die Selbstaussaat weiterer Pflanzen und damit unkalkulierbare Vegetation voraus.** *The uppermost levels were crowned by 24 pines, which are currently being replaced by trees (holly oaks/juneberries) that are better adapted to the changing climatic conditions. Alongside bamboo, ivy, orange, pear, apricot and fig trees were also planted. Ot Hoffmann assumed other plants would self-seed and that there would therefore be incalculable vegetation.*
BEWÄSSERUNG *WATERING SYSTEM*	**Die automatische Bewässerung nutzt Regen- und Grauwasser sowie zusätzlich Brauchwasser. Das Regenwasser wird in Sammelbecken gefangen, ebenso das Überschusswasser, das jeweils auf die darunter liegenden Terrassen abgeleitet wird.** *The automatic irrigation makes use of rain and grey water as well as additional process water. The rainwater is collected in collecting tanks as is the excess water drawn from each of the terraces below.*

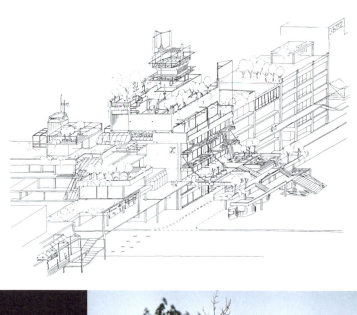

AUFWAND DER PFLEGE *OUTLAYS FOR CARING FOR THE PLANTS*	**Einmal im Jahr werden die Pflanzen beschnitten.** *Once a year the plants are pruned.*

KLIMAERGEBNIS, KLIMA-KONZEPT, KLIMAZIELE
CLIMATIC IMPACT, CLIMATE CONCEPT, CLIMATE GOALS

Die Pflanzen an der Ostseite wirken als Kühlfilter für das Gebäude und erzeugen eine hohe Luftfeuchtigkeit durch die Bewässerung. Allerdings ist das Gebäude durch den verwendeten Baustoff aus den 1970er Jahren schlecht gedämmt und die Südseite erhitzt sich stark. Diese ist nicht begrünt. Auf dem Dach befand sich eine Windanlage zur Strom-erzeugung.

The plants on the east side act like a cooling filter for the building and gene-rate a high level of humidity through their watering. Nevertheless, the 1970s construction materials used mean that the building is poorly insulated, and the south side heats up considerably. This side is not greened. On the roof there was a wind turbine to generate electricity.

BESCHREIBUNG
DESCRIPTION

Hoffmanns Baumhaus sollte zeigen, dass Gebäudebegrünung mit relativ einfachen Mitteln und dem Einsatz herkömmlicher Baustoffe und Bau-elemente ohne Bauschäden möglich ist. Die Verbindung von Natur und Technik setzte der Architekt als selbstverständlich und notwendig vor-aus. Mehr als die bebaute Fläche wird in Dach- und Terrassengärten re-kultiviert.

Hoffman's Baumhaus aims to show that building greenery can be implemented with relatively simple means and with use of conventional construction materials and structural elements, without causing damage to the building. The architect viewed the connection between nature and technology as necessary and a matter of course. The greenery on the roof and terraces more than recultivates the land used for the building.

BESONDERHEIT
SPECIALTY

Das Baumhaus steht inklusive Grünkonzept unter Denkmalschutz und wird aktuell saniert – auch die Bepflanzung. Es war Teil und Wegmarke städtebaulicher Planungen einer Fußgängerbrückenverbindung über die Zeughausstraße zur Innenstadt, die schließlich nicht zur Ausführung kamen. Der Architekt nutzte das Baumhaus als Büro und Atelier, entwi-ckelte mobile und zusammenklappbare Möbelsysteme, zu denen auch ein Bett zählte, das sich an die Decke ziehen ließ. Erdgeschoss und weitere Büroräume werden vermietet.

The Baumhaus with its greening concept is heritage-listed and is currently undergoing renovation – which includes the greenery. It formed a landmark and part of the urban planning of a footbridge link across Zeughausstrasse to the city center, which was ultimately never realized. The architect used the Baumhaus as an office and studio, where he developed mobile and folding furniture systems, including a bed that could be hoisted to the ceiling. The ground floor and other office spaces are rented.

FÜR DEN FALL: FAUNA
IN THE CASE: FAUNA

Das Baumhaus zieht viele Singvögel an, auch durch die vielen Pfützen, die durch die Bewässerung entstehen. Gegen eine Taubenplage werden Netze angebracht.

The Baumhaus enjoys frequent visits from songbirds, partly thanks to the many puddles that result from the watering. Nets are used to deter flocks of pigeons.

WAS ICH ERWÄHNEN MÖCHTE ...
WHAT I WANT TO MENTION ...

Die Nutzer des Gebäudes bestätigen eine hohe Mieterzufriedenheit und eine enge emotionale Bindung an das Gebäude.

The users of the building confirm the high level of tenant satisfaction and their close emotional bond to the building.

Isometrie / *Isometry*: Ot Hoffmann
Photos: Georg Dörr

Holland Creates Space

Expo-Pavillon

MVRDV
Hannover, Deutschland
Hanover, Germany

Der niederländische Pavillon auf der Expo 2000 in Hannover widmete sich in einem monumentalen, mehrgeschossigen Park dem Thema „Holland schafft Raum". Ohne Außenwände, und durch eine das Gebäude umschlingende Kaskadentreppe erschlossen, bildete der Pavillon eine offene Struktur. Auf acht Ebenen wurden die niederländischen Landschaftstypen präsentiert und das Verhältnis von Natur, Mensch und Technik thematisiert. In künstlich geschaffenen, stereotypischen Landschaften mit Tulpen, Windmühlen und Deichen wurde gezeigt, wie durch menschliche Eingriffe die Natur bereits kultiviert und verändert wurde. Wie kann unter dem Einsatz von Technologie eine „neue Natur" langfristig auf die globalen Herausforderungen wirken? Wie kann die Zunahme der Bevölkerung mit der Fragilität der Natur und dem Bedürfnis nach Lebensqualität in Einklang gebracht werden? Dominierendes Herzstück des Pavillons, der in sich ein geschlossenes Ökosystem bildete, war eine raumgreifende Waldinstallation aus gepflanzten Bäumen, Sträuchern und als Stützen positionierten Baumstämmen – eine optimistische und zukunftsweisende Geste an die Verbindung von Architektur und Pflanzen.

Nach Jahren des Verfalls wird der Pavillon von den Architekten in ein Co-Working und Bürogebäude umgewandelt. Der Wald wird beibehalten.[36]

In a monumental, multi-story park, the Dutch pavilion at Expo 2000 in Hanover was devoted to "Holland creates space". Without any outside walls and accessed by a cascading staircase that wrapped round the building, the pavilion boasted an open structure. The different types of Dutch countryside were presented across eight levels, highlighting the relationship between nature, technology and artificially created, stereotypical countryside with tulips, windmills and dykes, while visitors learned how human intervention cultivated and changes nature. How can the use of technology enable a "new nature" to respond long-term to the global challenges? How can the population increase be brought into harmony with the fragility of nature and the need for due quality of life? Pride of place in the pavilion, which formed a hermetic eco-system, was an extensive forest installation consisting of planted trees, bushes and tree trunks used as pillars – an optimistic and pioneering gesture on combining architecture and plants.

After falling into decay for years, architects are now converting the pavilion into a co-working und office space. The forest will be kept.[36]

Photo: Rob 't Hart

36   Catherine Slessor, Total Landscape, in: The Architectural Review, 1/2000, S./p. 64–67.; Andreas und Ilka Ruby (Hg.), MVRDV Buildings, Basel 2013, S./p. 94–105, Thomas Schröpfer, Dense+Green, „Innovation Building Types for Sustainable Urban Architecture", Basel 2016, S./p. 26.

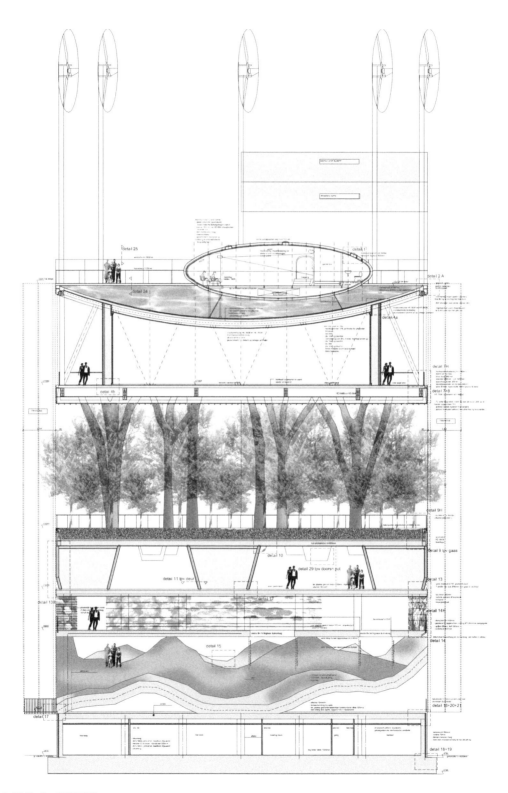

Schnitt/*Section:* © MVRDV
Photo: Joop van Reeken

BAUTYP, NUTZUNG *TYPE OF BUILDING, USAGE*	**Ausstellungspavillon** *Exhibition pavilion*
FERTIGSTELLUNG *COMPLETION*	**2000**
ARCHITEKTEN / *ARCHITECTS*	**MVRDV**
BAUHERR / *BUILDER*	**Foundation Holland World Fair,** **den Haag, Niederlande** / *Netherlands*
ART DER BEGRÜNUNG, **METHODE** *TYPE OF GREENERY, METHOD*	**Zwei Ebenen der sechs übereinander gestapelten Schichten wurden horizontal, intensiv bepflanzt: eine Ebene, die dem Wald als eines der zentralen Elemente des Ökosystems gewidmet war, und das oberste Level mit Dachterrasse.** *Two levels of six layers stacked on top of one another were given intensive horizontal greenery: one level that was devoted to the forest as one of the central elements of the eco-system, and the uppermost level with the roof gardens.*
TECHNIK *TECHNIQUE*	**Eichen mit Stahlelementen im Boden verankert, kleinere Bäume mit Wurzeln im Substrat eingepflanzt** *Oak with steel elements anchored in the ground, smaller trees with roots are planted in the substrate*
PFLANZEN *PLANTS*	**Eichenbäume, kleinere Bäume und Sträucher** *Oak trees, smaller trees and bushes*
BEWÄSSERUNG *WATERING SYSTEM*	**Bewässerungssystem, das das auf der obersten Ebene gesammelte Regenwasser auf die Waldebene leitet.** *Irigation system that directs the water collected on the top level to the forest level.*
KLIMAERGEBNIS, KLIMA- **KONZEPT, KLIMAZIELE** *CLIMATIC IMPACT, CLIMATE* *CONCEPT, CLIMATE GOALS*	**Der Pavillon wurde als ein autarkes Ökosystem konzipiert.** ‣ **Pflanzen produzieren Biomasse als alternativen Brennstoff, sie produzieren Nahrung und reinigen das Wasser.** ‣ **Warme Luft, die im Auditorium erzeugt wird, wird für die Fußbodenheizung verwendet.** ‣ **Natürliche Belüftung hilft, Temperatur, Geruch und Feuchtigkeit zu kontrollieren.** ‣ **Betonsanddünen reinigen Wasser und Windräder auf dem Dach versorgen das gesamte Gebäude mit Strom.** *The pavilion was developed as an independent eco-system.* ‣ *Plants produce biomass as an alternative fuel, they produce nutrients and purify the water.* ‣ *Warm air generated in the auditorium is used for the underfloor heating.* ‣ *Natural ventilation helps regulate the temperature, smell, and humidity.* ‣ *Sand dunes built with concrete purify the water, and windmills on the roof generate electricity for the entire building.*

Bosco Verticale

Stefano Boeri Architetti
Laura Gatti
Mailand, Italien
Milan, Italy

Die beiden Apartmenttürme sind Teil eines Revitalisierungsprojekts der Stadt Mailand, dem Programm „Metrobosco". Auf den unterschiedlich weit auskragenden Balkonen, die den Wohnraum über deckenhohe Schiebetüren hinaus ins Freie erweitern, wachsen in großen Pflanztrögen Bäume, Stauden, Sträucher und Bodendecker. Sie bilden zusammen einen Hektar Wald, einen „Bosco Verticale." Dem Pionierprojekt ging intensive Grundlagenforschung in Bereichen wie Botanik, Statik, Bewässerung, Brandschutz und Windlast voraus. Nun, sechs Jahre nach der Fertigstellung, hat sich nicht nur die Fassadenhülle durch den erfolgreichen Bewuchs erweitert und verdichtet, auch die Begrünungstechnik hat sich etabliert und die Hochhaustürme avancierten zur Ikone der Fassadenbegrünung in Europa. Den kritischen Stimmen, Stefano Boeris Vision sei ästhetische Spielerei und Kosmetik für ein zahlungskräftiges Klientel, konnten Architekt und Grünplanerin Laura Gatti messbare Zahlen im Hinblick auf z.B. die Temperaturentwicklung im und am Gebäude entgegenhalten. Über das Mikroklima des Hochhauses hinaus wirkt der vertikale Wald aber vor allem auf das Stadtklima seiner Umgebung, das Quartier.

The two apartment blocks are part of a revitalization project in Milan known as the "Metrobosco" program. On the balconies, which project to differing degrees and take the living space out through floor-to-ceiling sliding doors into the open air, trees, shrubs, bushes and ground-cover plants all grow in large planters. Altogether, they constitute one hectare of forest, a "bosco verticale". This pioneering project was preceeded by intensive basic research into areas such as botany, structural engineering, irrigation, fire prevention and wind loads. Now, six years after it was finished, not only has the successful plant growth ensured the greenery is denser and more extensive, but the greening technique has also become established and the high-rise towers have advanced to become icons of façade greening in Europe. The architect and his greenery planner Laura Gatti have been able to silence the critical voices that claimed Stefano Boeri's vision was merely an aesthetic gimmick and a cosmetic touch for a high-paying clientele, and can cite measurable figures relating, for example, to the temperature development both in and on the building. Beyond the microclimate of the high-rise, however, the vertical wall primarily affects the urban climate of its surroundings, the district itself.

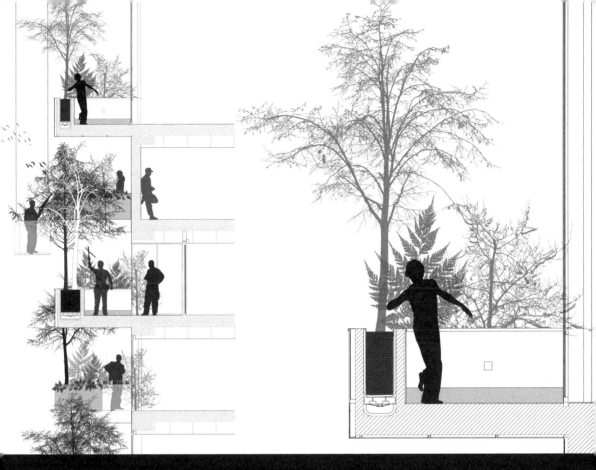

Fassadenschnitt / *Facade section:* © Stefano Boeri Architetti

2021 wird Boeris Sozialwohnungsanlage „Trudo Vertical Forest" in Eindhoven ebenfalls mit hochverdichteter Wandbepflanzung fertiggestellt. Der „Bosco Verticale" wird auf verschiedene historische Baum-Haus-Allianzen zurückgeführt. Stefano Boeri nennt als Inspiration seiner Idee hingegen Italo Calvinos Roman „Der Baron auf den Bäumen" (1957). Der junge Cosimo entschied, ausschließlich in Bäumen zu leben. Von Natur umgeben zu sein, brachte vor allem eines mit sich: einen Perspektivwechsel.

In 2021, Boeri's social housing project "Trudo Vertical Forest" in Eindhoven will likewise be completed with dense vertical greenery. The "Bosco Verticale" can be traced back to various historical building-tree alliances. As the inspiration behind his idea, Stefano Boeri cites Italo Calvino's novel "The Baron in the Trees" (1957), in which the young Cosimo decides to go and live exclusively in the trees. Being surrounded by nature brings one thing above all: a change of perspective.

BAUTYP, NUTZUNG *TYPE OF BUILDING, USAGE*	**Wohnhochhäuser, Zwillingstürme, Eigentumswohnungen** *Apartment blocks, twin towers, condominiums*
FERTIGSTELLUNG *COMPLETION*	2014
ARCHITEKTEN *ARCHITECTS*	**Entwurfsarchitekten/** *planning architects:* **Stefano Boeri Architetti, Gianandrea Barreca, Giovanni La Varra** **Tragwerksplanung/** *structural planning:* **Structural engineers Arup Italia Srl**
GRÜNPLANUNG *GREENERY PLANNERS*	**Laura Gatti, Beratung/** *consultant:* **Emanuela Borio**
BAUHERR / *BUILDER*	**Hines Italia SGR S.p.A.**
ART DER BEGRÜNUNG, METHODE *TYPE OF GREENERY, METHOD*	**Vertikaler Wald durch Balkonbegrünung** *Vertical wall with balcony greenery*
FLÄCHE DER BEGRÜNUNG *AREA GREENED*	**Die Türme sind 78 und 122m hoch und umfassen 18 bis 24 Etagen. Rundumlaufend wurden 10.000m² biologisches Habitat geschaffen, das entspricht einem Hektar Wald.** *The two towers are 78 and 122m in height and comprise 18 and 24 floors respectively. Surrounding them, a total of 10,000m² of biological habitat has been created, which corresponds to one hectare of forest.*
TECHNIK *TECHNIQUE*	**Um einen zentralen Gebäudekern angeordnete Stockwerksplatten kragen unregelmäßig über die Fassaden aus. Dort bilden sie über 3m tiefe Terrassen und Balkone aus, die an den Außenkanten mit Pflanzkästen mit einer Höhe von 1,30m begrenzt sind.** *Arranged around a central structural core, floor plates protrude irregularly beyond the façade. This way, they create terraces and balconies more than 3m deep, bordered at their outer edges with plant troughs measuring 1.30m in height.*
PFLANZEN *PLANTS*	**Die Bepflanzung beider Wohntürme umfasst insgesamt 900 Bäume in Höhen von 3 bis 9m. Zusätzlich wurden 5.000 Sträucher und 14.000 Bodendecker eingesetzt. Sie ergeben einen Pflanzenteppich an der Fassade und bilden damit die eigentliche äußere Hülle, die sich von Frühling bis Winter verändert. Die Pflanzen wurden entsprechend der Position an der Fassade ausgewählt: „Jede Fassade und jedes Stockwerk weist je nach Anforderungen der verschiedenen Arten und abhängig von den mikroklimatischen Bedingungen ein anderes Pflanzschema auf. So entstehen letztlich über 400 Gärten unterschiedlicher Größe und Pflanzenzusammenstellung. Zudem sind die Pflanzen so ausgewählt, dass sie für ein angenehmes Klima in den Wohnungen sorgen: immergrüne an der Süd- und Westseite, laubabwerfende an der Nord- und Ostseite." Die verschiedensten Pflanzen, so Laura Gatti, sollen die Hochhäuser zu einem „Biodiversitäts-Hotspot" in der Stadt machen. Die Pflanzen wurden in zweijähriger Vorkultur gezogen und speziell auf den windintensiven Standort vorbereitet. Zu den Pflanzen zählen Rotbuchen, Felsenbirnen, Kamellen, Baum-Haseln, Zieräpfel, Purpur-Weiden, Granatäpfel, Steineichen, Olivenbäume, Magnolien oder Jasmin.** *The greening of both residential towers incorporates a total of 900 trees at heights ranging from 3 to 9m, as well as 5,000 bushes and 14,000 ground-cover plants. These produce a carpet of plants across the façade and thus form the actual outer shell of the building, which varies from spring to winter. The plants were selected according to their position on the façade: "Each façade and each story boasts a different planting scheme according to the*

requirements of the various species and depending on the microclimatic conditions. The final result is more than 400 gardens of different sizes and plant compositions. In addition, the plants have been chosen to help ensure a pleasant climate in the apartments: evergreens on the south and west sides, deciduous trees on the north and east sides." The wide variety of plants, Laura Gatti explains, is intended to make the high-rises a "biodiversity hotspot" within the city. The plants were pre-cultivated over two years and specially prepared for this location with its high wind load. They include common beech, shadbush, chestnut, hazel, crabapple, basket willow, pomegranate, holly oak, olive, magnolia and jasmine.

BEWÄSSERUNG
WATERING SYSTEM

Nach den Verdunstungsberechnungen beträgt der gesamte Wasserbedarf für die Begrünung des kleineren Turms 2370 m³ und für die des höheren 4450 m³ pro Jahr. Das begrünte Dach recycelt das Brauchwasser des Gebäudes (unter anderem aus der mit Grundwasser gespeisten Klimaanlage). Das Bewässerungssystem ist auf den Wasserbedarf sowie auf die Verteilung der Pflanzen auf die Stockwerke und auf ihren Standort abgestimmt. Sensoren erfassen die jeweilige Feuchtigkeit und schalten die Bewässerung ein und aus.
According to the evaporation calculations, the total water requirements for the greenery of the small tower amount to 2,370 m³ per year, or 4,450 m³ in the case of the higher tower. The greened roof recycles the used water from the building (among other things, from the water-fed climate control system). The irrigation system is tailored to the water requirements, as well as to the distribution of plants on the different floors and their locations. Sensors capture the humidity levels in each case and activate and deactivate the irrigation accordingly.

KOSTEN DER EINRICHTUNG UND DER INSTANDHALTUNG
COSTS OF THE SYSTEM AND MAINTENANCE

5% Mehrkosten
Additional costs of 5%

Diagramm **Wasserversorgung und Vegetation** / *Water supply and vegetation diagram:*
© Stefano Boeri Architetti

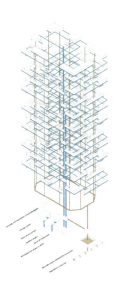
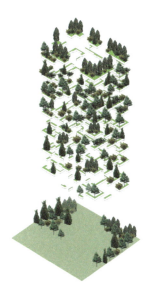

WATER SUPPLY SYSTEM   VEGETATION   VERTICAL FOREST

AUFWAND DER PFLEGE
OUTLAYS FOR CARING FOR THE PLANTS

Die Bepflanzung der Tröge geht mit dem Kauf der Eigentumswohnungen nicht in der Verantwortung der Bewohner über. Sie ist Teil des "Klimasystems Fassade" und darf daher auch nicht individuell verändert werden. Die Betreuung erfolgt über einen Wartungsvertrag mit einer Fachfirma. Die Gärtner seilen sich mithilfe eines Krans, der an der Dachkante geführt wird, mehrmals im Jahr ab und übernehmen die Pflege und den Schnitt.

The greenery in the planters does not become the residents' responsibility once an apartment has been purchased. It forms part of the "climate system façade" and cannot therefore be individually altered either. It is cared for by means of a maintenance contract with a specialist firm. Several times a year, the gardeners abseil down with the help of a crane positioned on the edge of the roof and thus take care of upkeep and pruning.

KLIMAERGEBNIS, KLIMAKONZEPT, KLIMAZIELE
CLIMATIC IMPACT, CLIMATE CONCEPT, CLIMATE GOALS

Die Pflanzenfassade ersetzt moderne Klimatechnik. Das Laub der Bäume schützt im Sommer vor der Sonne und im Winter ist durch das herabgefallene Laub dennoch Helligkeit gewährleistet. Die Pflanzenmasse des vertikalen Waldes produziert Sauerstoff, bindet Feinstaub und schützt vor Lärmbelastung. Damit unterstützt die Grünfassade die Verbesserung des Mikroklimas der Wohnungen und darüber hinaus die Klimabilanz der Umgebung.

Am Bosco Verticale in Mailand lässt sich an heißen Sommertagen an den durch Bäume beschatteten Fassaden eine Reduktion der Hitze von bis zu 30°C nachweisen (Laura Gatti), außerdem 20–40% höhere relative Luftfeuchtigkeit im Sommer und 2–8% im Winter.

The green façade replaces modern climate-control technology. The foliage of the trees provides protection from the sun in the summer and allows light to penetrate in the winter when the leaves have been shed. The plant mass of the vertical forest produces oxygen, captures particulate matter and provides noise insulation. Thus, the green façade helps to improve the microclimate of the apartments as well as the climate balance of the surrounding area.

At the Bosco Verticale in Milan, the shaded façades enjoy proven heat reduction of up to 30°C on hot summer days (Laura Gatti), as well as 20–40% greater relative humidity in summer and 2–8% in winter.

Diagramm Umwelteinflüsse und Bepflanzung / *Environmental impact and greening diagram:*
© Stefano Boeri Architetti

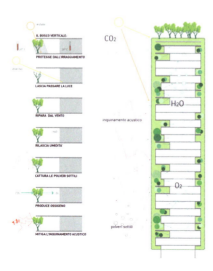
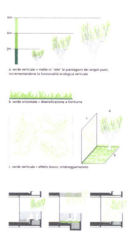

Photo: Dimitar Harizanov © Stefano Boeri Architetti

BESONDERHEIT
SPECIALTY

Der Entwurf basiert auf botanischen Analysen zur Pflege und Versorgung der Bäume sowie ihrem Windverhalten und der Stabilität. Es sollte verhindert werden, dass im Falle eines Sturms Äste oder Bäume von den Hochhäusern stürzen. Detaillierte Untersuchungen des Windklimas am Standort und Windkanal-Testkampagnen bildeten die Grundlage für ein neu entwickeltes System eines Wurzelballenankers, das das Anheben der Wurzelballen in den Pflanzgefäßen verhindert. Die Bäume werden zudem über Halterungen gegen Windbruch geschützt. Die Tests richteten sich auf die Langzeitwirkung der wachsenden Bäume und ihren Einfluss auf Gebäudestruktur und Baustatik.
Zudem gingen der Bepflanzung Forschungen zur notwendigen Größe der Pflanzgefäße voraus, zur Zusammenstellung des Erdreichs und der Verhinderung des Brandüberschlags.

The design is based on botanical analyses of the care and maintenance of trees, as well as their stability and behavior in the wind, since it was important to ensure that trees or branches wouldn't fall from the highrises in the case of a storm. Detailed investigation into the wind climate at the site and wind tunnel testing formed the basis for a newly developed system of a root-ball anchor that prevents the root balls in the plant pots from lifting up. The trees are also protected from any wind breakage by means of brackets. The tests aim to ensure the long-term effectiveness of the growing trees and their influence on the building structure and architectural statics.

In addition, the greening was preceeded by research into the necessary size of the plant pots, the composition of the soil and the prevention of fire flashover.

FÜR DEN FALL: FAUNA
IN THE CASE: FAUNA

Berechnet wird im Durchschnitt anhand der Anzahl an Pflanzen das Vorkommen von circa 20 Vögeln und Schmetterlinge pro Person. Nach dem Pflanzen der Bäume wurden rund 1.200 Marienkäfer freigelassen, um das Ökosystem des Standorts anzukurbeln.

This is calculated based on the number of plants, rendering an average of approx. 20 birds and butterflies per person. Once the trees were planted, around 1,200 ladybirds were released to spur on the ecosystem at the site.

Photo: Qingyan Zhu

1000 Trees

Heatherwick Studio
Urbis
Shanghai, China

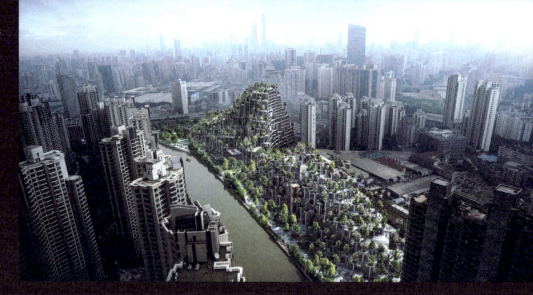

Mitten in einem ehemaligen Industriegebiet im Süden Shanghais, das sich seit der Jahrtausendwende als Kreativquartier M50 entwickelt, sollte eine Wohn- und Gewerbeeinheit mit einer Fläche von 300.000 m² entstehen. Heatherwick Studios Konzepte zielte darauf, inmitten der niedrigen Nachbarschaftsbebauung einen Hochhausturm zu vermeiden und entwickelte einen Raumplan, dessen Hülle sich nach außen wie ein von Bäumen gesäumter Berg in die Topographie am Fluss einbettet. In riesigen Pflanzschalen, die aus einzelnen Betonsäulen zu sprießen scheinen, wurden Bäume und Sträucher gepflanzt. Sie bekrönen die Silhouette des in Terrassen gestaffelten Neubaus wie ans Licht drängende Blüten. Die Bepflanzung setzt sich am Flussufer fort und mündet in einen bewaldeten Park. Der Neubau und die Bewaldung fassen die historischen Bestandsgebäude geschickt ein. Der erste „bewaldete Hausberg" ist fertiggestellt. Ein zweiter und höherer wird im Osten anschließen – zusammen bilden sie eine grüne Insel am Fluss.

The plan was to create a housing and commercial estate with a total area of 300,000 m² in the middle of a former industrial estate to the south of Shanghai that has since the turn of the millennium evolved into the M50 creative district. Heatherwick Studio's concept entailed avoiding a high-rise in the middle of the low buildings in the vicinity and instead hinged on a spatial configuration with an envelope that on the outside embeds itself into the riverside topography like a hill flanked by trees. Trees and bushes were placed in huge planters that seem to sprout from individual concrete columns. Like so many blossoms yearning for the light they crown the silhouette of the new build which rises upwards like a set of staggered terraces. The planting continues along the riverbank and culminates in a park with woods. The new build and the woods skillfully embrace the existing historical buildings. The first "wooded local hill" is now complete. A second, higher one will join it to the east and together they will form a green island on the river.

BAUTYP, NUTZUNG *TYPE OF BUILDING, USAGE*	**Mischnutzung: Wohnungen, Gewerbe, Hotel, Büros** *Mixed usage: Apartments, commercial premises, hotel, offices*
FERTIGSTELLUNG *COMPLETION*	**2020 (westlicher Berg); 2024 (Anschluss im Osten)** *2020 (western hill); 2024 (connection to the east)*
ARCHITEKTEN /*ARCHITECTS*	**Heatherwick Studio; MLA Architects (HK) Ltd**
GRÜNPLANUNG *GREENERY PLANNERS*	**Urbis**
BAUHERR /*BUILDER*	**Tian An China Investments Company Ltd**
ART DER BEGRÜNUNG *TYPE OF GREENERY*	**Pflanztröge, horizontale Begrünung** *Planters, horizontal greenery*
TECHNIK *TECHNIQUE*	**Hunderte von Betonsäulen, die sich nach oben kelchartig erweitern, tragen das Gewicht riesiger Pflanztröge. Sie wirken freistehend, sind aber mit dem Gebäude statisch verbunden. Die versetzten Geschosshöhen mit horizontalen Terrassen und die knapp darüber hinausragenden – fast schwebenden Pflanzgefäße – bilden die charakteristische Struktur der Gebäudehülle.** *Hundreds of concrete columns which toward the top expand outward like calyx and bear the weight of the huge plant tubs. They look as though they are free-standing but are actually connected to the building in structural terms. The staggered heights of the stories with their horizontal terraces and the planters that jut out over them, almost as if floating, form the characteristic structure of the building envelope.*

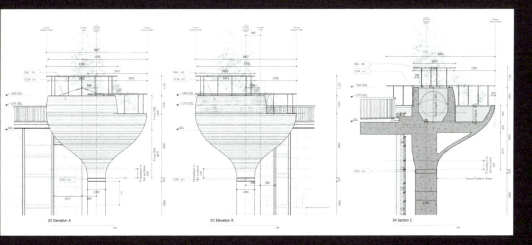

PFLANZEN *PLANTS*	**Die vorgezogenen Pflanzen stammen von der Shanghaier Insel Chongming, einem fruchtbaren Landstreifen im Delta des Jangtse-Flusses. Die weit über 1.000 Einzelpflanzen in 46 verschiedenen Pflanzenarten (Bäume, Stauden und Hängepflanzen) wurden nach Kriterien der Winterhärte und der Widerstandsfähigkeit gegen Wind ausgesucht. 60 % der Pflanzen sind immergrün.** *The plants chosen all come from the Shanghai island of Chongming, a fertile stretch of land in the Yangtze delta. A total of well over 1,000 plants covering 46 different plant species (trees, shrubs and hanging plants) were selected in line with winter hardiness and resilience to the wind, whereby 60% of them are evergreens.*

Rendering, Konstruktionszeichnungen /*Construction drawings:*
© Heatherwick Studio

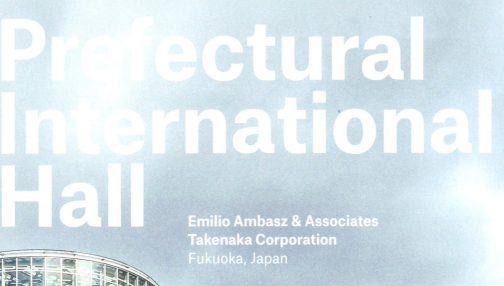

Prefectural International Hall

Emilio Ambasz & Associates
Takenaka Corporation
Fukuoka, Japan

Der argentinische Architekt und Vorreiter im Umdenken hinsichtlich der Verantwortung und Aufgabe des Bauens, Emilio Ambasz, verwirklichte vor 25 Jahren im Herzen der japanischen Stadt Fukuoka einen immensen Grünbau. Die Prefectural International Hall – oder auch ACROS (Asian Cross Roads Over the Sea) – sollte auf einem Teil des letzten großen Parks Fukuokas entstehen, was Ambasz dazu veranlasste, den Park durch 15 abgetreppte Terrassen auf dem Gebäude fortzuführen. So konnte die Grünfläche mit nahezu identischem Ausmaß beibehalten werden. Die weitläufige, vertikale Gartenlandschaft ist öffentlich zugänglich. Darunter befinden sich 100.000 m² Nutzfläche für öffentlichen Kultur- und Verwaltungseinrichtungen und Gewerbe.

Nach Emilio Ambasz ist die Vorstellung überholt, Natur in die Vororte zu verbannen. Im Gegenteil sei es die Aufgabe, Natur und Architektur zu verbinden: „Jedes Gebäude ist ein Eingriff in die Vegetation, es fordert die Natur heraus: Wir müssen uns eine Architektur vorstellen, die einen Akt der Versöhnung zwischen Natur und Gebäuden über das Eindringen in die Natur stellt. Wir müssen Gebäude entwerfen, die sich so mit der umgebenden Landschaft vereinen, dass man die Idee bekommt, dass sie genau das Gleiche sind."[37]

Emilio Ambasz, the Argentinian architect and a pioneer in rethinking the responsibilities and tasks of construction, created an immense green structure in the heart of the Japanese city of Fukuoka no less than 25 years ago. The Prefectural International Hall – or the ACROS (Asian Cross Roads Over the Sea) – was to take shape on part of Fukuoka's last big park, and this is what prompted Ambasz to continue the greenery of the park with 15 staggered terraces on the building. This way, it was possible to maintain the acreage of green space to an almost identical extent. The expansive, vertical garden landscape is open to the public, while beneath it lie 100,000 m² of usable space for public cultural and administrative institutions and enterprises.

Emilio Ambasz believes the idea of conjuring up nature in the suburbs is outdated. Rather, the challenge is to combine nature and architecture: "Each building constitutes an intrusion into the vegetation, it challenges nature: we have to devise an architecture that rises above the intrusion, that stands as an act of reconciliation between nature and buildings. We need to design buildings that are so intermingled with the surrounding landscape that one gets the idea that they are just the same thing."[37]

———
37 Emilio Ambasz, Nature and architecture. Emilio Ambasz and Fukuoka's ACROS centre 25 year later: www.ambasz.com/fukuoka-25th-anniversary (10.11.2020); Barry Bergdoll, Emilio Ambasz. Emerging Nature – Precursor of Architecture and Design, Zürich 2017, S./p. 88–102.

BAUTYP, NUTZUNG *TYPE OF BUILDING, USAGE*	**Öffentliches Gebäude: Museum, Theater, Konzerthalle, Verwaltung, Büros, Gewerbe** *Public building: museum, theater, concert hall, administration, offices, commercial spaces*
FERTIGSTELLUNG *COMPLETION*	**1995**
ARCHITEKTEN / *ARCHITECTS*	**Emilio Ambasz & Associates**
GRÜNPLANUNG *GREENERY PLANNERS*	**Takenaka Corporation**
BAUHERR / *BUILDER*	**Dai-ichi Seimei Insurance**
ART DER BEGRÜNUNG, METHODE *TYPE OF GREENERY, METHOD*	**Das Gebäude entstand in einen ehemaligen Park. Ambasz Anliegen zielte daher darauf, die komplette bebaute Fläche als bepflanzten Garten auf das Gebäude zu übertragen. Dafür wurden auf der Südseite 15 Terrassenebenen geschaffen. Wasserbecken und Wasserfälle haben nicht nur eine kühlende Funktion, sondern das Plätschern des Wassers wirkt auch atmosphärisch gegen den Stadtlärm.** *The site of the building is a former park, hence Ambasz's goal was to transfer the full scope of the site onto the structure itself in the form of a landscaped garden. To this end, 15 terraced levels were created on the south side. Ponds and waterfalls not only have a cooling function, but the sound of the water also helps atmospherically in countering the noise of the city.*
FLÄCHE DER BEGRÜNUNG *AREA GREENED*	**10.622 m² Grünfläche** *10,622 m² of green space*
TECHNIK *TECHNIQUE*	**Intensive Dach- und Terrassenbegrünung** *Intensive roof and terrace greening*

Photo: Hiromi Watanabe – Watanabe Studio

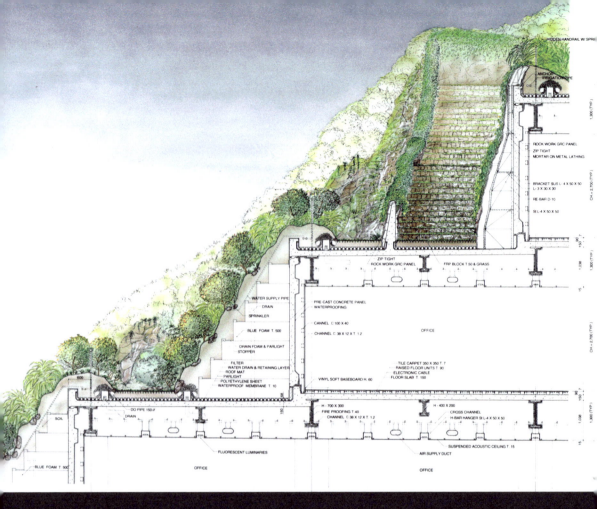

PFLANZEN *PLANTS*	Die 1995 eingesetzten 37.000 Einzelpflanzen aus 76 verschiedenen Pflanzenarten wurden im Laufe der Jahre aufgestockt. 2020 zählt der Grüngarten über 120 Arten und 50.000 Pflanzen. *The 37,000 individual plants from 76 different plant species used back in 1995 have been increased over the years. In 2020, the green garden boasts more than 120 species and 50,000 plants.*
BEWÄSSERUNG *WATERING SYSTEM*	Der vertikale Garten wird mit einem eigenen Bewässerungssystem aus Regen- und Brauchwasser versorgt. *The vertical garden is supplied with its own irrigation system that uses rain and process water.*
KLIMAERGEBNIS, KLIMA-KONZEPT, KLIMAZIELE *CLIMATIC IMPACT, CLIMATE CONCEPT, CLIMATE GOALS*	Inmitten eines dicht bebauten Finanzviertels mit fehlenden Grünflächen zeigt sich das ACROS mit seinem hohen Baumbewuchs und dem zugehörigen Tenjin Central Park als wichtiges innerstädtisches Element im Hinblick auf die CO_2-Produktion, die Feinstaubbindung und die Reduzierung des Stadtlärms. Der vertikale Garten wirkt nicht nur dem heat island effect entgegen (es werden 15 °C geringere Lufttemperaturen in der Umgebung gemessen), sondern auch die Betriebskosten des Gebäudes werden erheblich gesenkt, da sowohl zum Heizen als auch zum Kühlen weniger Energie verbraucht wird. *In the middle of a densely developed financial district with a lack of green spaces, the ACROS with its high level of vegetation and the adjoining Tenjin Central Park emerge as an important downtown element as regards absorbing CO_2 emissions, capturing of particulate matter and reduction of urban*

noise. The vertical garden not only counters the heat island effect (air temperatures up to 15 °C lower have been measured in the surrounding area), but the operating costs of the building are also reduced considerably because less energy is required, both for heating and for cooling.

BESCHREIBUNG
DESCRIPTION

Die Terrassen sind für die Öffentlichkeit zugänglich. Durch die entwickelten Grünflächen und die zugleich intensive Raumausnutzung des Geländes (das Gebäude reicht vier Stockwerke unter die Erde, außerdem schiebt sich ein V-förmiger Keil in die Terrassen, um im Inneren eine höhere Raumausnutzung zu erhalten) schafft das ACROS zwei Faktoren zu kombinieren: den Wunsch des Entwicklers nach profitabler Nutzung und den Bedarf der Öffentlichkeit an nutzbaren Grünflächen.

The terraces are open to the public. Thanks to the green spaces that have developed and the simultaneous intensive use of the space on the site (the building stretches four stories underground and there is a V-shaped wedge in the terraces to ensure greater usage of the inside space), the ACROS manages to combine two factors: the developer's desire for profitable usage and the general public's need for usable green spaces.

Schnitt / *Section*: © Emilio Ambasz
Photo: Hiromi Watanabe – Watanabe Studio

Maison Edouard François
Patrick Blanc
Paris, Frankreich
France

Flower Tower

Die Architekten Maison Edouard François haben im 17. Pariser Arrondissement in Paris einen Pflanzenturm über neun Stockwerke geschaffen, bestückt mit 380 Balkontöpfen, aus denen hohe Bambuspflanzen wachsen. Die Sichtbetonwände der Fassade verschwinden hinter einem grünen Vorhang. Das robuste und schnell wachsende Grün bietet den Bewohnern Schatten, Sichtschutz und lässt die Wohnungen in den heißen Sommermonaten nicht so stark aufheizen. Hinter dem im ersten Moment etwas skurrilen Erscheinungsbild verbirgt sich ein sozialer Wohnungsbau – und ein kostengünstiges Grünkonzept, von dem nicht nur die Bewohner profitieren. Mit dem angrenzenden Park bildet das Gebäude eine grüne Insel in der Stadt.

In Paris' 17th arrondissement, architects Maison Edouard François have created a tower of plants incorporating nine stories, adorned with 380 balcony pots from which sprout high bamboos. Thus, the exposed concrete wall of the façade disappears behind a green curtain. The robust, rapidly growing vegetation provides residents with shade and privacy and helps prevent the apartments from heating up too much in the hot summer months. Behind what initially appears to be a somewhat quirky exterior hides a social housing project – and a low-cost greening concept that benefits more than just the residents. With the adjoining park, the building represents a green island in the city.

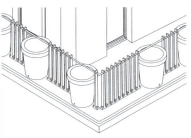

Plan: © Maison Edouard François
Photo: Paul Raftery

BAUTYP, NUTZUNG *TYPE OF BUILDING, USAGE*	Sozialer Wohnungsbau *Social housing project*
FERTIGSTELLUNG *COMPLETION*	2004
ARCHITEKTEN / *ARCHITECTS*	Maison Edouard François
GRÜNPLANUNG *GREENERY PLANNERS*	Patrick Blanc
BAUHERR / *BUILDER*	Opac de Paris
ART DER BEGRÜNUNG, **METHODE** *TYPE OF GREENERY, METHOD*	Fassadenbegrünung durch einzelne Pflanztröge *Façade greening using individual plant troughs*
FLÄCHE DER BEGRÜNUNG *AREA GREENED*	An drei Fassadenseiten komplett begrünt mit 380 1,20 m hohen Pflanztrögen *Entirely greened on three sides of the façade with 380 plant troughs measuring 1.20 m in height*
TECHNIK *TECHNIQUE*	Für die Pflanztröge und Fassadenelemente wurde Ultrahochleistungs-beton (UHPC) eingesetzt. Die Pflanztröge sind in den Boden der umlau-fenden Balkone eingepasst und bilden zusammen mit einem Geländer die Balkonbrüstung. *FFor the plant troughs and façade elements, ultra-high-performance concrete*

PFLANZEN *PLANTS*	**Es wurden ausschließlich Bambuspflanzen verwendet – mit dem Vorteil, dass Bambus schnell und hoch wächst.** *Bamboo plants are used exclusively – with the advantage being that bamboos grown high and quickly.*
BEWÄSSERUNG *WATERING SYSTEM*	**Die Töpfe sind an ein Bewässerungssystem angeschlossen, das im Terrassengeländer verläuft. Genutzt wird aufbereitetes Regenwasser. Zugleich werden die Pflanzen über einen separaten Düngertank automatisch mit Nährstoffen versorgt.** *The pots are attached to a watering system that runs around the rails of the balconies, which uses collected rainwater. At the same time, the plants are supplied with nutrients automatically via a separate fertilizer tank.*
AUFWAND DER PFLEGE *OUTLAYS FOR CARING FOR THE PLANTS*	**Aufgrund der Widerstandfähigkeit der Bambuspflanzen und der automatischen Bewässerung und Düngerversorgung ist der Pflegeaufwand sehr gering.** *Thanks to the resilience of the bamboo plants and the automated watering and fertilizer system, care costs are very low.*
KLIMAERGEBNIS, KLIMA- KONZEPT, KLIMAZIELE *CLIMATIC IMPACT, CLIMATE CONCEPT, CLIMATE GOALS*	**Die Bepflanzung verbessert die thermischen Eigenschaften und die Energieleistung des Gebäudes. Die Kübelpflanzen wirken als natürlicher Sonnenschutz für die Fassade. Die Verdunstung der Pflanzen trägt zudem zum Kühleffekt bei. An der Südseite konnten folgende Temperaturunterschiede gemessen werden (August 2011): Bei einer Umgebungstemperatur von 36°C wurden an der äußeren Betonoberfläche 45°C festgestellt. Die durch die Pflanzen verschattete Wandfläche waren mit 31°C deutlich kühler. An den Pflanzen selbst wurden 33°C festgestellt. Auch die Luftfeuchtigkeit war in der Nähe der Pflanzen 12% höher als in der Umgebung.[1]** *The greenery improves the thermal properties and the energy performance of the building. The trough plants act as natural sun protection for the façade, and plant evaporation also contributes to the cooling effect. On the south side, the following temperature differences were measured (August 2011): With an ambient temperature of 36°C, a temperature of 45°C was measured on the outer concrete surface. The wall surfaces shaded by the plants, meanwhile, were considerably cooler at just 31°C. On the plants themselves, a temperature of 33°C was recorded. The humidity level close to the plants was also 12% higher than in the surrounding area.[1]*
BESCHREIBUNG *DESCRIPTION*	**Am Flower Tower wird die Tradition der verschiedensten Topfpflanzen auf den Pariser Balkonen radikal formalisiert – und die Pflanztröge werden als Module fester Bestandteil der Fassadengestaltung.** *At the Flower Tower, the tradition of widely varying pot plants on Paris balconies has been given a radical formal structure – and the plant troughs as modules become firm components of the façade design.*
BESONDERHEIT *SPECIALTY*	**Der Flower Tower ist ein sozialer Wohnungsbau. Eine einfache, unkonventionelle und kostengünstige Lösung ermöglichte eine intensive Begrünung der Gebäudefassaden. Ein positiver Nebeneffekt der Bambusbepflanzung ist über den Schutz vor Stadtlärm hinaus das angenehme Rascheln der Bambusruten im Wind.** *The Flower Tower is a social housing project. A simple, unconventional and low-cost solution permits intensive greening of the building façade. A positive side-effect of bamboo planting, aside from insulation from the noise of the city, is the pleasant rustling of the plants in the wind.*

Kö-Bogen II

ingenhoven architects
Düsseldorf, Deutschland
Germany

IM GESPRÄCH MIT
IN CONVERSATION WITH

MARTIN REUTER

The new heart of Düsseldorf is green and sets new climate standards

Die neue Mitte in Düsseldorf ist grün und setzt neue Klimastandards

Warum bepflanzte Fassaden und Dächer am Einkaufszentrum Kö-Bogen II?

Why the planted façades and roofs at the Kö-Bogen II shopping mall?

MR   Die spezifische Aufgabe war, ein Retailgebäude mit Schaufensterflächen und Eingängen zur Schadowstraße, der Einkaufsstraße, zu erstellen. Die Rückseite richtet sich zum Gustav-Gründgens-Platz mit dem Schauspielhaus von Bernhard Pfau, zum Dreischeibenhochhaus und dahinterliegend, nach Norden, zum Hofgarten – drei sehr bedeutende Elemente im städtischen Zusammenhang Düsseldorfs. Unser Wettbewerbsbeitrag Kö-Bogen II hat mit dem V-förmigen Taleinschnitt eine Blickachse Richtung Schauspielhaus und damit einen städtisch belebten Raum geschaffen.
Die Bauaufgabe eines Retailgebäudes richtet sich an die Schaffung eines großen Volumens mit verhältnismäßig – z.B. im Vergleich zu Wohnbauten – geringen Belichtungsflächen und unterliegt dadurch anderen Anforderungen an die Fassadengestaltung. In Anknüpfung an den Hofgarten drängte sich schnell die Idee auf, den Park auf dieses Gebäude zu spiegeln. Die Entscheidung für Grünflächen, in Form der Hecken und der begehbaren Rasenfläche, versteht sich nicht als Aussage einer Nichtarchitektur, sondern als Reaktion auf die städtebauliche Situation

MR   *The specific task was to design a retail building with shop-window frontage and entrances on Schadowstrasse, the shopping street. The rear of the building faces the Gustav-Gründgens plaza with the theater designed by Bernhard Pfau, the Dreischeibenhochhaus and behind it to the North the Hofgarten – three very significant elements in the Düsseldorf urban fabric. Our competition entry for Kö-Bogen II relied on a V-shaped insert into the slope to create a line of vision toward the theater and thus provided a vibrant urban space. The task involved in designing a retail building is to create a large volume that requires few illuminated surfaces and thus involves quite different requirements than designing façade surfaces for housing, for example. Taking our cue from the Hofgarten, we swiftly had the idea of reflecting the park on the building. The decision in favor of greenery in the form of hedges and lawns you can walk on was not meant as a statement on non-architecture, but as a response to the urban situation – and as our response to contemporary construction. The architectural gesture is more one of insertion than an attempt to form a new sculptural icon or one that stands out for especially gleaming materials.*

Photo: HGEsch © ingenhoven architects

und unsere Antwort auf zeitgemäßes Bauen. Die architektonische Geste fügt sich mehr ein, als dass sie den Anspruch erhebt, eine neue skulpturale oder sich durch besonders glänzende Materialen herausstechende Ikone zu sein. Wir beschäftigen uns seit vielen Jahren mit ökologisch, sozial und energetisch nachhaltigem Bauen. Dabei geht es nicht nur um die minimiert negative Wirkung auf die Umwelt – z.B. durch die Passivhausbauweise, sondern um einen darüber hinaus gehenden positiven Beitrag. Die Fassaden, als Schnittstelle zwischen Haus, Stadt und Umwelt, wirken insofern auf den Stadtraum, da sie die Luft verbessern, den Staub binden und Kühle produzieren. Letzterer Aspekt hat zudem einen positiven Effekt auf den Energieverbrauch der Lüftungsanlage des Hauses, da die Luft, die durch die Kühlgeräte auf dem Dach eingesaugt wird, durch die großflächige Dachbepflanzung bereits niedriger temperiert ist. Auch die immer wieder benannte Biophilie (Erich Fromm) spielt eine wesentliche Rolle – eine lebendige Fassade mit dem Wechsel durch die Jahreszeiten erzeugt eine völlig andere Bindung und Sensibilisierung der Menschen als eine Granitoberfläche es leisten könnte.

Erfordert das Entwerfen mit Pflanzen eine besondere Herangehensweise?

MR   Wir haben mit vielen beteiligten Fachplanern – wie Baumschulen und Spezialisten für Bewässerung und Botanik während

For many years, we have been concerning ourselves with ecological and social buildings that have sustainable energy consumption levels. The focus here is not only to minimize the impact on the environment, as with passivhaus structures, but also to make a positive contribution. The façades as the interfaces between the building, the city and the environment thus impact on the urban space in so far as they improve the air quality, bind dust, and produce cooler air. The latter aspect also has a positive impact on energy consumption by the building's ventilation system, as the air that is sucked in by the air conditioning units on the roof is already cooler thanks to the extensive roof greenery. A not inconsiderable role is also played by what Erich Fromm termed biophilia, and which is cited so often nowadays – A living façade that changes with the seasons creates a completely different bond and sensitizes people in a very different way than would a granite surface, for example.

Does designing with plants require a special approach?

MR   During the entire process we work with many specialist planners such as experts from nurseries, watering experts or botanists. You need to assess the plants' growth patterns, the size of the planters or the fire load, for example. In some test series we examined how the plants, in our case hawthorn hedges, responded to vandalism or confrontation with fireworks during Carnival or New Year's Eve. To exclude further risks, scientific analyses had to be undertaken to check the plants' robustness, resilience to pests, how they dealt with cold,

des gesamten Prozesses zusammengearbeitet. Das Wachstumsverhalten der Pflanzen, die Größen der Pflanzbehälter sowie die Brandlast mussten analysiert und bewertet werden. In einigen Testreihen wurde geprüft wie die Pflanzen, in unserem Fall die Hainbuchenhecken, auf Vandalismus oder auf Konfrontation mit Knallkörpern beim Karneval oder Silvesterraketen reagieren. Um weitere Risiken auszuschließen wurde in wissenschaftlichen Analysen ihre Widerstandsfähigkeit untersucht, die Anfälligkeit für Schädlinge, das Verhalten bei Kälte, Trockenheit und starkem Wind. Der Aspekt der Pflege beinhaltete Überlegungen über einfache Zugänglichkeit und ein wenig wartungsintensives System, damit Gärtner die Hecke regelmäßig beschneiden können und der Beschnitt effizient entsorgt werden kann.

Argumente von Entwerfern gegen das Bauen mit Pflanzen ist deren Unberechenbarkeit. Der Kö-Bogen II umfasst acht Kilometer Hainbuchenhecken. Sind diese berechenbar?

MR Pflanzen, als lebendige Organismen, folgen ihrem eigenen Wachstumsverhalten. Trotz aller wissenschaftlichen und ingenieurstechnischen Forschungen, Vorab-Überlegungen und getroffenen Maßnahmen zur ihrer Versorgung, besteht stets ein Rest Unberechenbarkeit. In der Gartenbaukunst der landschaftsplanenden Kollegen wird gezielt mit diesen Faktoren als Mittel der Gestaltung gearbeitet: der wilde Garten oder der kultivierte französische Park. Das sind Fragen des Gestaltungsprinzips und der Haltung: die prozesshafte Entwicklung und Entfaltung eines Gartens gegenüber der Setzung einer finalen Form. Der Kö-Bogen II zeigt, dass funktional ökologische und aktiv klimaverbessernde Aspekte sich mit einer klaren Gestaltung der Gebäudehülle durchaus vereinen lassen.

dryness and strong winds. As regards care, we needed to consider ease of access and a low-maintenance system so that the gardeners can prune the hedges regularly and dispose of the cuttings efficiently.

One argument architects voice against building with plants is their unpredictability. The Kö-Bogen II features eight kilometers of hawthorn hedges. Are they predictable?

MR *Plants as organisms follow their own growth logic. For all the scientific and engineering research, prior deliberations and measures taken to supply the plants with nutrients and water, there is always an element of unpredictability. Landscape planners and architects consciously rely on these factors as an additional design medium, as examples such as the conscious creation of wild gardens or French landscaped gardens show. These are questions of taste and mindset, whether you want a garden to gradually evolve or wish to define its definitive shape from the outset. Kö-Bogen II shows that functional ecological aspects and active climate-improving features can evidently be combined with the clear design of a building's outer shell.*

MARTIN REUTER

Nach seinem Abschluss an der RWTH Aachen ist Martin Reuter bereits seit über 20 Jahren bei ingenhoven architects tätig. Als Managing Director ist er für die Architektursprache des Büros mitverantwortlich. Er hat bereits die Realisierung von vielen großen internationalen Projekten geleitet, bei denen der supergreen® Aspekt, für den sich das Büro ingenhoven architects im Besonderen einsetzt, prägend für Entwurfskonzept und Umsetzung ist und war. Martin Reuter engagiert sich zudem im Rahmen von Fachkonferenzen und Workshops an der Weiterentwicklung des ganzheitlichen Konzeptes einer aktiv zu Umwelt und Gesellschaft positiv beitragenden Architektur.

After graduating from RWTH Aachen, Martin Reuter has worked for ingenhoven architects for over 20 years. As Managing Director, he is one of those responsible for the practice's architectural style. He has lead-managed the realization of many major international projects where the supergreen® aspect that ingenhoven architects so champions has played a key part in the design concept and the realization. At specialist conferences and workshops, Martin Reuter advocates advancing a holistic concept of architecture that actively contributes positively to the environment and society.

Schnitt / *Section*:
© ingenhoven architects

BAUTYP, NUTZUNG *TYPE OF BUILDING, USAGE*	Mischnutzung: Einzelhandel, Gastronomie, Büros, Tiefgarage *Mixed usage: Retail and hospitality outlets, offices, underground carpark*
FERTIGSTELLUNG *COMPLETION*	2020
ARCHITEKTEN / *ARCHITECTS*	ingenhoven architects
GRÜNPLANUNG *GREENERY PLANNERS*	ingenhoven architects
BAUHERR *BUILDER*	Düsseldorf Schadowstraße 50/52 GmbH & Co. KG; CENTRUM Projekt-entwicklung GmbH, Düsseldorf; B&L Gruppe, Hamburg
ART DER BEGRÜNUNG, METHODE *TYPE OF GREENERY, METHOD*	Grünfassaden und Gründächer *Green façades and green roofs*
FLÄCHE DER BEGRÜNUNG *AREA GREENED*	An zwei Fassaden und auf dem Dach mehr als 8km Heckenlänge. Das entspricht etwa 30.000m² Laubfläche. *On two façades and on the roof hedges more than 8km in length. This amounts to about 30,000m² surface area of foliage.*
TECHNIK *TECHNIQUE*	Auf dem Dach wachsen Hainbuchen in Pflanzbeeten und an den Schräg-fassaden in terrassierter Abstufung in Pflanzgefäßen, die wiederum in Tragbehältern aus Metall eingesetzt wurden. *Hornbeam bushes grow in flowerbeds on the roof and on the angled façades in terraced sequences in planters which are in turn installed in metal tubs.*
PFLANZEN *PLANTS*	Das Einkaufszentrum wurde mit 35.000 Hainbuchen bepflanzt, die in einer Höhe von 1,30m beschnitten werden. Das Hainbuchenlaub wech-selt seine Farbigkeit von Hell- und Dunkelgrün im Frühjahr und Sommer, über Gelb bis Braun im Herbst und Winter. Es wurden Pflanzen ausge-wählt, deren Laub in den Wintermonaten besonders lange haften bleibt. Auf der begehbaren großen Schrägfläche des gegenüberliegenden Bau-körpers wurde Rasen angelegt. *The shopping center boasts 35,000 hornbeams which are pruned at a height of 1.30m. The hornbeam foliage changes color from light to dark green in spring and summer, via yellow to brown in autumn and winter. Plants were chosen that retain their foliage as long as possible in the winter months. Grass was planted on the big sloped section of the building opposite, which can be walked on.*

Photo: HGEsch
© ingenhoven architects

BEWÄSSERUNG
WATERING SYSTEM

Die Bewässerung erfolgt über den Regen und über ein komplexes Bewässerungssystem in rund 160 Kreisen, das über einen Computer gesteuert wird.
Water is supplied by the rain and via a complex watering system in roughly 160 loops that are controlled by a computer.

KOSTEN DER EINRICHTUNG
UND DER INSTANDHALTUNG
COSTS OF THE SYSTEM AND
MAINTENANCE

Die Pflege ist auf 99 Jahre vertraglich garantiert.
Care has been contractually arranged for 99 years.

AUFWAND DER PFLEGE
OUTLAYS FOR CARING FOR
THE PLANTS

Ein ausgefeiltes Pflegekonzept soll Aufwand und Kosten so gering wie möglich halten. Die Hecken werden zwei bis dreimal jährlich beschnitten und sind über sog. Catwalks oder eine handbetriebene Fassadenbefahranlage erreichbar. In einem Monitoring werden Messwerte für Wasserverbrauch und Nährstoffversorgung dokumentiert und ausgewertet, um die Versorgung permanent anzupassen.
An ingenious care concept is destined to keep effort and costs as low as possible. The hedges are pruned two or three times a year and can be reached via catwalks or a hand-driven façade access platform. A monitoring system documents figures for water and nutrient consumption and evaluates the findings, thus permanently adjusting supplies as required.

KLIMAERGEBNIS, KLIMA-
KONZEPT, KLIMAZIELE
CLIMATIC IMPACT, CLIMATE
CONCEPT, CLIMATE GOALS

Ziel ist die Verbesserung des Mikroklimas in der Stadt: Reduzierung des innerstädtischen Wärmeeffekts (Kühlungseffekt durch Abgabe von Feuchtigkeit an die Umgebungsluft), die Bindung von CO_2 und Feinstaub, Sauerstoffproduktion durch enorme Blattoberfläche sowie die Dämpfung von Stadtlärm.
The target is to improve the downtown microclimate: to reduce urban the heat effect (cooling effect by releasing moisture into the ambient air), to bind CO_2 and fine particulate matter, to foster oxygen production thanks to the immense surface of the leafage and absorb the noise of the city.

BESONDERHEIT
SPECIALTY

Der ökologische Nutzen der größten Grünfassade Europas entspricht dem Klimawert von rund 80 ausgewachsenen Laubbäumen.
The ecological benefit of Europe's largest greened façade corresponds to the climate value of about 80 fully grown deciduous trees.

FÜR DEN FALL: FAUNA
IN THE CASE: FAUNA

In der Regel werden Hainbuchenhecken von Insekten und Vögeln genutzt.
As a rule, the hornbeam hedges are used by insects and birds.

WAS ICH ERWÄHNEN
MÖCHTE ...
WHAT I WANT TO MENTION ...

Beratung für Vegetationsökologie: Albert Reif, Albert-Ludwigs-Universität, Freiburg, Professur für Standortskunde und Vegetationskunde
Phytotechnologie/Spezielle Bauwerksbegrünung: Karl-Heinz Strauch, Beuth Hochschule für Technik, Berlin, Fachbereich Life Science and Technology
Advisor on vegetation ecology: Albert Reif, Albert-Ludwigs-Universität, Freiburg, Professor of Land Evaluation and Vegetation science
Phytotechnology/special building greening: Karl-Heinz Strauch, Beuth Hochschule für Technik, Berlin, Dept. of Life Science and Technology

Chambre de commerce et d'industrie d'Amiens-Picardie

Chartier Corbasson Architectes
Corbasson + Tracer
Amiens, Frankreich
France

Der Verwaltungssitz der Chambre de commerce et d'industrie (CCI) d'Amiens-Picardie, ein Gebäude aus der Jahrhundertwende in Amiens, sollte um das Nachbargebäude erweitert werden. Das beide Gebäude zusammenfassende Grünkonzept basierte auf der Idee einer völligen Neudefinierung des Gebäudeensembles und sollte außerdem markantes Zeichen für bestehende Kontinuität in der historischen Umgebung und Region werden. Amiens ist bekannt für seine Hortillonages, einer mit Kanälen durchzogenen, ehemaligen Sumpfgegend mit viel Obst und Gemüseanbau. Mit dem CCI sollte einerseits die Natur in die Stadt geholt und andererseits der Gebäudekomplex in die Landschaft eingepasst werden – woraus sich die Felsformation an der Fassade ableiten lässt.

Der Architekt Thomas Corbasson versteht sich als ein Architekt, der mit Pflanzen gestaltet, und weniger als Landschaftsarchitekt. Ziel ist es, so Corbasson, Natur und Architektur nicht als Antipoden zu betrachten, sondern im Zusammenwirken bessere Gebäude und Städte zu schaffen.[38]

The administrative headquarters of Chambre de commerce et d'industrie (CCI) d'Amiens-Picardie, a building from the turn of the 20th century in Amiens, was to be extended to include the neighboring building. The greenery concept covered both buildings and was based on completely redefining the ensemble and also creating a striking symbol for the strong continuity in the historical surroundings and region. Amiens is renowned for its "hortillonages", a former swamp area bisected by canals with many orchards and vegetable plots. The CCI was intended both to bring nature into the city and to adapt the building complex to the countryside – the rock formation on the façade can be read in this light.

Architect Thomas Corbasson sees himself less as a landscape architect and more as an architect who designs with plants. The goal, says Corbasson, is not to view nature and architecture as opposites but through their interaction to create better buildings and cities.[38]

---

38   Thomas Corbasson, in: Almut Grüntuch-Ernst, IDEAS Institut for Design an Architectural Strategies (Hg.): Hortitecture.
     The Power of Architecture and Plants, Berlin 2018, S. 239; Thomas Schröpfer, Dense + Green, Basel 2016, S./p. 100–103.

BAUTYP, NUTZUNG *TYPE OF BUILDING, USAGE*	Verwaltungsgebäude *Administration building*
FERTIGSTELLUNG *COMPLETION*	2012
ARCHITEKTEN / *ARCHITECTS*	Chartier Corbasson Architectes
GRÜNPLANUNG *GREENERY PLANNERS*	Corbasson + Tracer
BAUHERR / *BUILDER*	Chambre de commerce et d'industrie d'Amiens-Picardie
ART DER BEGRÜNUNG, **METHODE** *TYPE OF GREENERY, METHOD*	Fassadenbegrünung *Façade greenery*
FLÄCHE DER BEGRÜNUNG *AREA GREENED*	Mehr als 75 % der Fläche wurden begrünt, das sind über 340 m². *More than 75% of the area was greened, or over 340m².*
TECHNIK *TECHNIQUE*	Das Modulsystem aus einer Gitterstruktur funktioniert wie „Pflanz-körbe", die das Pflanzsubstrat einfassen und sich an die Felsformation anpassen. Sie bilden zusammen ein Netz, eine „mur végétale". Eine formgebenden Metallkonstruktion bildet die Substruktion und ist vor die Fassade geblendet. Jedes vorfabrizierte Element musste an die Winkel der 17 m langen Struktur angepasst werden. *The modular system based on a grid structure functions like "plant baskets" that hold the plant substrate and adapt to the rock formation. Together they form a network, a "mur végétale". A defining metal structure provides the substructure and acts as a curtain façade. Each prefabricated element had to be adapted to the angles of the 17-meter-long structure.*

Plan:
© Chartier Corbasson Architectes

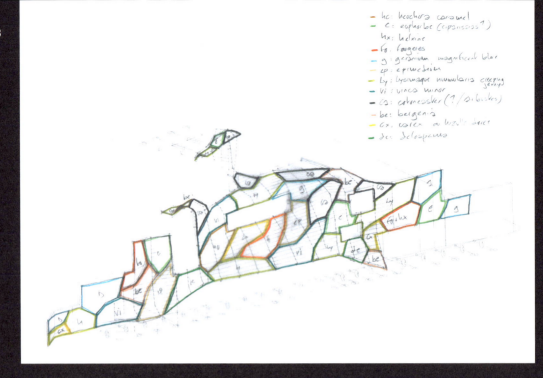

The handwritten legend in the plan reads:
- hc: heuchera caramel
- e: euphorbe (cipaussiss?)
- hx: helxine
- fo: faugeres
- g: geranium magnificent blur
- ep: epimedium
- Ly: Lysimaque nummularia creeping jenny?
- vi: vinca minor
- co: cotonosster (?/ arbustes)
- be: bergenia
- cx: carex ou briza brize
- dec: Selospama

PFLANZEN
PLANTS

Das Pflanzenspektrum variiert in den Blühphasen je nach Jahreszeit. Eingesetzt wurden Bodendecker wie Immergrün, Pfennigkraut oder Teppichmispeln, aber auch hängende Farne, Glockenblumen, Storchschnabel, Bergenien, Wolfsmilchgewächse oder Purpurglöckchen. Das Ziel war ein farbenreiches, „bukolisches" Spektrum zu schaffen (Thomas Corbasson)
The range of plants varies by season in terms of blossoming period. The spectrum includes groundcover and evergreens, moneywort or radicans, but also hanging ferns, bellflowers, geraniums, Bergenia, Euphorbia or Heuchera. The intention was to create a colorful, "bucolic" spectrum" as Thomas Corbasson put it.

KOSTEN DER EINRICHTUNG UND DER INSTANDHALTUNG
COSTS OF THE SYSTEM AND MAINTENANCE

Rund 20.000€ pro Jahr.
About €20,000 a year.

AUFWAND DER PFLEGE
OUTLAYS FOR CARING FOR THE PLANTS

Viermal im Jahr kümmert sich ein Gärtner um die Pflege.
A gardener cares for the plants four times a year.

KLIMAERGEBNIS, KLIMA-KONZEPT, KLIMAZIELE
CLIMATIC IMPACT, CLIMATE CONCEPT, CLIMATE GOALS

Das Ziel ist, die Luftqualität in Städten zu verbessern, das Erbe der Pflanzenvielfalt zu fördern und zugleich das historische Erbe in den Städten zu erhalten.
The goal is to improve the quality of air in cities, to promote the heritage of plant diversity, and also to maintain the historical heritage in our cities.

Tower 25 – The White Walls

Ateliers Jean Nouvel
Nikosia, Republik Zypern
Nicosia, Republic of Cyprus

Am Eleftheria-Platz, wenige hundert Meter von der Grenze der beiden Bundesstaaten entfernt, die die Stadt Nikosia zerschneidet, ragt das hell-glänzende Hochhaus „Tower 25" weit aus der umliegenden Bebauung. Je nach Himmelsrichtung unterscheiden sich die Fassaden. Die Südseite und prominente Schauseite ist mit tief einschneiden-den und unterschiedlich gestaffelten Terrassen ausgebildet, die üppig mit Hänge- und Kletter-pflanzen und Sträuchern bestückt sind. Im Osten und Westen ist die Fassade mit unregelmäßig platzierten quadratischen Aussparungen perfo-riert, hinter denen ebenfalls Pflanzen angesiedelt sind. Diese wuchern zum Teil wie zufällig aus den Fassadenöffnungen heraus. Aus der Entfernung wirken sie wie Flechten an der Gebäudeober-fläche. Ob im besten Fall als Statement oder Marke: Jean Nouvel setzt mit der begrünten Gebäudehülle durchaus einen Kontrast zum dicht bebauten Zentrum Nikosias mit weitflächig fehlenden Grünflächen.

On Eleftheria Square, only a few hundred meters from the border between the two Cypriot nations that cuts through Nicosia stands the bright high-rise "Tower 25", soaring up above its surroundings. The façades differ depending on which way they face. The south side and the prominent frontage with its deeply incised terraces which are staggered in different ways are opulently festooned with hanging and climbing plants. On the east and west side, the façades feature irregularly positioned square excisions behind which there are again plants. These grow exuberantly in part almost arbitrarily out of the openings. From a distance they resemble lichen on the building's surface. Most cer-tainly a great statement and branding, Jean Nouvel's use of the greened building envelope definitely con-trasts with the densely built-up center of Nicosia and its signal lack of larger green areas.

Photo: Yiorgis Gerolymbos

BAUTYP, NUTZUNG / *TYPE OF BUILDING, USAGE*
Mischnutzung: Einzelhandel, Wohnungen,
Büros
*Mixed usage: retail outlets, apartments,
offices*

FERTIGSTELLUNG / *COMPLETION*
2015

ARCHITEKTEN / *ARCHITECTS*
Ateliers Jean Nouvel

BAUHERR / *BUILDER*
Nice Day Developments

ART DER BEGRÜNUNG, METHODE
TYPE OF GREENERY, METHOD
Fassadenbegrünung / *Façade greenery*

FLÄCHE DER BEGRÜNUNG / *AREA GREENED*
An der Südfassade bedeckt eine vertikale
Landschaft etwa 80% der Fassadenfläche
des Gebäudes.
*On the south façade, vertical greenery
covers about 80% of the building's façade
surface.*

TECHNIK / *TECHNIQUE*
Modulsystem in Pflanztrögen
Modular system in planters

PFLANZEN / *PLANTS*
Zypriotische Kletter- und bodendeckende
Pflanzen.
Cypriot climbing and groundcovering plants.

BESCHREIBUNG / *DESCRIPTION*
Die vor- und rückspringenden Terrassen
schaffen durch die üppige Bepflanzung
beschattete Zonen an der stark besonn-
ten Südseite. Die Öffnungen der perfo-
rierten Ost- und Westfassaden sind zum
Teil verglast. Die offenen Bereiche
wurden von der Innenseite über zwei oder
mehr Stockwerke bepflanzt, so dass sie
halboffene und gut durchlüftete Grünräume bilden.
*The projecting and recessed terraces with
their opulent greenery create shaded areas
on the south side, which gets so much sun.
The openings in the perforated east and west
façades are in part glazed. The open areas
are greened on the inner side over two or
more stories to provide semi-open and well-
ventilated green spaces.*

Photo: Patrick Bingnham-Hall

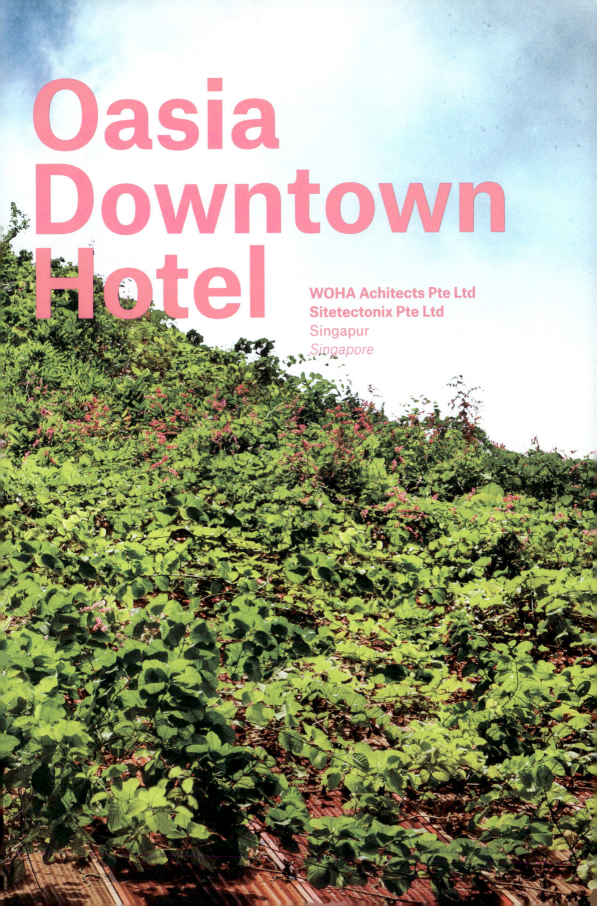

Oasia
Downtown
Hotel

WOHA Achitects Pte Ltd
Sitetectonix Pte Ltd
Singapur
Singapore

Die roten Farbtöne der Fassade und grünes Laub mit bunten Blüten vom Erdgeschoss bis zur Spitze des 27 geschossigen Hochhauses – das Oasia Hotel Downtown ist ein optischer Störer inmitten des Central Business District in Singapur, dicht bebaut mit Hochhäusern mit Stahl- und Glasfassaden. Über die kompletten Fassaden des Oasia Hotels Downtown zieht sich ein Aluminiumgitter. Dahinter liegen Pflanzgefäße, in denen über 20 verschiedene Kletterpflanzen wachsen, die sich an den Fassaden empor schlängeln. Zusätzlich sind auf vier Ebenen die gesamte Geschossfläche einnehmende, bepflanzte Terrassen in die Baustruktur eingefügt und urbane Gärten mit hoher Aufenthaltsqualität bilden. Über 1.000 Prozent des Fußabdrucks des Gebäudes auf der bebauten Fläche und eine hohe Biodiversität tragen positiv zum Ökosystem der Stadt bei. „Wir hegen die romantische Vorstellung, dass die Architektur die Natur an oberste Stelle stellt – somit lässt sich inmitten einer Großstadtumgebung zugleich Natur und Biodiversität genießen, und zwar in einem Zustand wie er vor der Stadtansiedelung existierte. Wenn wir das erreicht haben, ist es ein großartiger Ort.", so Richard Hassell. Studien belegen nicht nur ein um 30 °C niedrigere Temperaturmessung an der Fassade, sondern dokumentieren verschiedenste fauna-spezifische Ergebnisse – von Insekten bis zu seltenen Großvögeln.[39]

The red hues of the façade and the green foliage with the colorful blossoms run from the ground floor up to the top of the 27-story high-rise – the Oasia Hotel Downtown is the visual fly in the ointment of the Central Business District in Singapore, which is otherwise a dense fabric of towers with steel-and-glass façades. An aluminum grid runs across the entire frontage of die Oasia Hotel Downtown. Behind it lie planters in which over 20 different sorts of climbers grow that then creep their way up the façades. In addition, on four levels planted terraces are inserted into the structure of the building, running across the entire floor area; they form urban gardens that offer great rest and recreation. The city's ecosystem benefits from the fact that over 1,000 percent of the footprint of the building is greened in terms of built area and the hotel boasts a great biodiversity. "We have the romantic vision that architecture just pushes nature up on top of it – and so you have a whole city happening, but at the same time you have as much nature and biodiversity as you had before the city was there, and we think if we can achieve that it would be an amazing place.", so Richard Hassell. Studies prove that not only is the façade temperature 30 °C lower than that of adjacent buildings, but document all manner of fauna-specific events – ranging from seeing insects to large birds.[39]

---

39   Thomas Schröpfer, Dense+Green. Innovation Building Types for Sustainable Urban Architecture, Basel 2016, S./*p.* 267; Grüntuch-Ernst, Almut/IDEAS Institut for Design an Architectural Strategies (Hg./*Ed.*): Hortitecture. The Power of Architecture and Plants, Berlin 2018, S./*p.* 163.

BAUTYP, NUTZUNG	Mischnutzung: Hotel und Büros
TYPE OF BUILDING, USAGE	*Mixed usage: hotel and offices*
FERTIGSTELLUNG	2016
COMPLETION	
ARCHITEKTEN / *ARCHITECTS*	WOHA Achitects Pte Ltd
GRÜNPLANUNG	Sitetectonix Pte Ltd
GREENERY PLANNERS	
BAUHERR / *BUILDER*	Far East SOHO Pte Ltd
ART DER BEGRÜNUNG	Kletterpflanzen in 1.793 wandbasierte Pflanzentröge
TYPE OF GREENERY	**1.100(L) x 650(B) x 1.050(H)**
	Façade creepers in 1,793 wall-mounted planter boxes
	1,100(L) x 650(W) x 1,050(H)
FLÄCHE DER BEGRÜNUNG	1.100% des Grundrisses, 25.490m² Fassadenbegrünung sowie begrünte
AREA GREENED	Dachterrassen und offene Terrassen
	1,100% of site area, 25,490sqm of façade green, as well as greenery on its sky
	terraces
TECHNIK	Einfache Pflanzentröge auf jeder Ebene. Sie sind direkt hinter dem Alu-
TECHNIQUE	gitterrahmen der Fassade angebracht und über Wartungsstege ohne
	zusätzliche Ausrüstung leicht zugänglich.
	Simple planters on every level, sitting right behind the aluminium mesh façade,
	easily accessible via maintenance catwalk with no special equipment.
PFLANZEN	Insgesamt 54 Arten von Pflanzen und Bäumen (21 unterschiedliche
PLANTS	Fassadenkletterpflanzen, 33 Arten anderer Pflanzen und Bäume)
	Total of 54 species of plants & trees (21 species of façade creepers, 33 species
	of other plants and trees)
BEWÄSSERUNG	Automatisches Bewässerungssystem
WATERING SYSTEM	*Automatic irrigation*
AUFWAND DER PFLEGE	Die Begrünung ist das Aushängeschild des Hotels und somit lohnt sich
OUTLAYS FOR CARING FOR	der Pflege- und Wartungsaufwand. Teure Ausrüstung bzw. komplizierte
THE PLANTS	Technologie ist nicht erforderlich, aber angesichts der so großen begrün-
	ten Gesamtfläche ist Zeit und Arbeit erforderlich, um die Schönheit der
	Anlage aufrechtzuerhalten.
	The greenery is the hotel's calling-card and worth the upkeep & maintenance.
	No expensive equipment or complicated technology is needed but with such
	a huge green plot ratio, it does require time and care to remain beautiful.
KLIMAERGEBNIS, KLIMA-	Die grüne „Außenhaut" des Gebäudes funktioniert als Sonnenschutz und
KONZEPT, KLIMAZIELE	reduziert die thermische Last. Die Oberflächentemperatur liegt bei 25°C
CLIMATIC IMPACT, CLIMATE	– verglichen mit über 55°C bei einem der benachbarten Hochhäuser.
CONCEPT, CLIMATE GOALS	*The green "skin" of the building acts as a sun shade and reduces the thermal*
	load. The surface temperature is at approx. 25°C vs. over 55°C on a neighbour-
	ing building.
BESCHREIBUNG	Als grünes Hochhaus mitten im dichtbebauten Bankenviertel in Singapur
DESCRIPTION	stellt das Oasia Hotel Downtown einen Prototyp der Bebauungsintensi-
	vierung für Städte in den tropischen Breitengraden dar. Doch mit dem
	„lebendigen Hochhaus" wurde eine Turmgattung entwickelt, die stark
	von der üblichen, glatten und technoiden Erscheinung der Bürotürme
	abweicht.

Photos: Patrick Bingnham-Hall

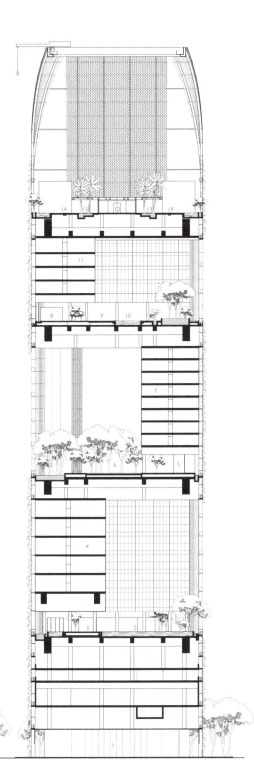

A verdant tower of green in the heart of Singapore's dense Central Business District (CBD), Oasia Hotel Downtown is a prototype of land use intensification for the urban tropics. But this tropical "living tower" offers an alternative image to the sleek technology of the genre.

BESONDERHEIT/*SPECIALTY*

Das Hotel zeigt, wie man mit einfachen Strategien eine sehr dichtbebaute städtische Umgebung verändern kann. Durch die Begrünung kehrt Biodiversität in die Stadt zurück und es entsteht eine biophilische Umwelt mitten im Bankenviertel von Singapur.

This hotel shows how we can chance a very densely built urban setting with very simple strategies. The greenery reintroduces biodiversity into the city and creates a biophilic environment in the middle of Singapore's Central Business District.

FÜR DEN FALL: FAUNA/*IN THE CASE: FAUNA*

Oasias Innen- und Außenfassaden wurden in einem bestimmten, dokumentierten Zeitraum von verschiedensten Tierarten besucht. Davon waren 50% Honigbienen, die in den Blüten der rosafarbenen Honolulu und Petra volubilis gesichtet wurden. Andere interessante Besucher waren Gelbbauch-Pirolen und Grünrücken-Nektarvögel. Ein Weißbauch-Seeadler kreiste sehr tief über dem Gebäude. Schließlich wurde überraschenderweise ein einfacher Bananenfalter (Hasora vitta) gesichtet, der üblicherweise nicht in bebauten Gegenden aufzufinden ist. Himalayageier unterbrachen ihren Vogelzug nach Süden und erholten sich hier vor ihrem Weiterflug. Eine vertiefende Studie zur Biodiversität führt auch eurasische Feldsperlinge, javanische Beos, Eidechsen, Heuschrecken und verschiedene Schmetterlinge auf.

Oasia's interior and external façades were visited by a wide variety of animal species in a specific period of time. 50% of them were honey bees found feeding on pink Honolulu and Petra volubilis flowers. Other interesting sightings at Oasia were of the Yellow-vented, Black-naped Orioles and Olive-backed Sunbird. A White-belied Sea Eagle was seen circling above the building very close to it. Finally, it was a surprise to record a Plain Banded Awl (Hasora vitta) butterfly – seen rather uncommonly in builtup areas. Himalayan Vultures stopped by the hotel and rested on their migratory flight. An indepth Biodiversity study also counted Eurasian Tree Sparrows, Javan Myna, Changeable Lizards, Grasshoppers and a variety of Butterflies.

Schnitt/*Section:* © WOHA Achitects Pte Ltd

Photo: VTN Architects

Urban
Farming
Office

VTN Architects
Ho-Chi-Minh-Stadt, Vietnam
Ho Chi Minh City, Vietnam

Vo Trong Nghia ist konsequent und übernimmt ausschließlich Aufträge, die Architekturbegrünung vorsehen. Mit dem eigenen Bürogebäude in einem neu erschlossenen Gebiet in Ho-Chi-Minh-Stadt setzen sie ein klares Statement. Nicht nur, dass die beiden Straßenfronten und das Dach vollständig begrünt sind, es wird auf vertikaler Ebene Landwirtschaft betrieben. Jährlich werden über eine Tonne Lebensmittel, Kräuter-, Obst- und Gemüsearten geerntet.

Das Konzept basiert auf einer zweiten Fassadenschicht aus einem modularen System aus Beton-Pflanzkübeln, die an einer Stahl-konstruktion aufgehängt sind, und in Größe und Abstand variieren. Den Bedingungen der jeweiligen Bepflanzung entsprechend, je nach Wachstum sowie Platz- und Lichtbedarf, kann die Positionie-rung der eingehängten Tröge flexibel verändert werden – dadurch variiert die Fassade permanent. Die straßenabgewandten Brand-wände sind zweischalige Ziegelwände, die durch eine zusätzlich isolierende Luftschicht getrennt und mit kleinen Öffnungen durchsetzt sind, die eine natürliche Querlüftung ermöglichen.

Die fortschreitende Industrialisierung Vietnams führt vor allem in den urbanen Agglomerationen zu einem anhaltenden Wachs-tum und einer immer stärkeren Verdichtung der Bebauung und damit zur Versiegelung des Bodens. Das Resultat sind Städte mit wenig Grünflächen bei gleichzeitiger starker Abgasbelastung. Vo Trong Nghia versucht dieser Entwicklung entgegenzuwirken und die Stadt mit jedem Neubau neu zu begrünen – und moderne und zugleich traditionell vernakuläre Bautradition zu verbinden.[40]

Photos: Hiroyuki Oki

40   Vo Trong Nghia, Häuser für Menschen und Bäume, in: Arch+ 226/2016, S./*p.* 196-198; VTN Architects, Urban Farming Office: www.vtnarchitects.net/urban-farming-office?pgid=kckc4elz-a9de0a7a-4e08-4eb2-9099-cf2a1fedf918; www.nytimes.com/2019/10/10/arts/design/vo-trong-nghia-architecture.html (10.11.2020).

Vo Trong Nghia stick to their policy and only take on jobs that involve greened architecture. They make a clear statement with their own office building in a newly accessed district in Ho Chi Minh City. Not just are both street façades and the roof completely greened, but the vertical level is actually used for farming. Each year, over a ton of food in the form of herbs, fruits and vegetables are harvested.

The concept is based on a dual façade layer involving a system of concrete planters that are hung from cables in a steel structure and vary in terms of size and the distance between them. In line with the conditions required for the particular plant, namely how it grows and the space and light requirements, the position of the planters can be flexibly changed – the façade itself varies thanks to these changes in where the planters are hung on the façade. The firewall that face away from the streets are two-layer brick walls, whereby the layers are divided by an insulating air gap and feature small openings that allow for natural cross ventilation.

Vietnam's ongoing industrialization has led above all in the urban conglomerations to continual growth and ever greater building densities, and with this to ever more earth being sealed. The result is cities with fewer green spaces and at the same time heavy exhaust emission levels. Vo Trong Nghia tries to help counteract this trend and to bring more greenery to the city with every new build, while combining modern and likewise traditional vernacular architectural traditions.[40]

BAUTYP, NUTZUNG *TYPE OF BUILDING, USAGE*	**Mehrgeschossiges, innerstädtisches Bürogebäude** *Multi-story downtown office building*
FERTIGSTELLUNG *COMPLETION*	**2020**
ARCHITEKTEN, GRÜN- PLANUNG & BAUHERR *ARCHITECTS, GREENERY PLANNERS & BUILDER*	**Vo Trong Nghia Architects**
ART DER BEGRÜNUNG, METHODE *TYPE OF GREENERY, METHOD*	**Fassadengrün (wandgebundenes System in Pflanzkübeln); Dachbegrünung** *Façade greening (wall-based system in planters); roof greening*
FLÄCHE DER BEGRÜNUNG *AREA GREENED*	**190% der BGF ist begrünt.** *190% of the GSA is greened.*
TECHNIK *TECHNIQUE*	**An die unverkleidete Stahlbetonkonstruktion schließt eine erste Fassadenschicht an, in deren Ebene sich die Verglasung befindet. Die äußere Ebene bildet ein modulares System aus Beton-Pflanzkübeln, die an einer Konstruktion aus Stahlseilen aufgehängt sind und je nach Bepflanzung in Größe und Abstand variieren.** *The unclad reinforced concrete structure includes a first façade layer in which the glazing is incorporated. The outer, curtain level consists of a modular system of concrete planters hung from a system of steel cables – they vary in size and distance from one another depending on the type of plant growing in them.*
PFLANZEN *PLANTS*	**Bepflanzung mit regionaltypischen Kräutern sowie und Obst- und Gemüsepflanzen entsprechend dem tropischen Klima Südvietnams.** *The plants are typical herbs from the region as well as fruits and vegetables in keeping with South Vietnam's tropical climate.*
BEWÄSSERUNG *WATERING SYSTEM*	**Regen und gesammeltes Regenwasser, das manuell verteilt wird.** *Rain and collected rainwater that is distributed manually.*
KLIMAERGEBNIS, KLIMA- KONZEPT, KLIMAZIELE *CLIMATIC IMPACT, CLIMATE CONCEPT, CLIMATE GOALS*	**Zwei Außenfassaden straßenwärts und das Dach wurden begrünt, sodass das Gebäude weitest möglich der Verbesserung des städtischen Mikroklimas dient, da die Pflanzen eine Kühlung und Reinigung der Luft bewirken. Die verglasten Flächen werden durch die vorgehängten Pflanzbehälter und die Bepflanzung weitgehend verschattet – dadurch wird die Hitzebildung reduziert. Die natürliche Querlüftung ermöglicht einen weitgehenden Verzicht auf künstliche Klimatisierung.** *Two outside surfaces and the roof have been greened so that the building as far as possible serves to improve the urban microclimate as the plants serve to cool and clean the air. The glazed surfaces are largely shaded by the curtain wall of cable-hung planters – which reduces heat build-up. The natural cross-ventilation renders artificial air conditioning as good as superfluous.*
BESONDERHEIT *SPECIALTY*	**Die Bepflanzung ist hauptsächlich auf Nutzpflanzen ausgerichtet. Die urbane Landwirtschaft („vertical farm") liefert Erträge von bis zu einer Tonne pro Jahr.** *Mainly, food crops are planted. The urban farm ("vertical farm") grows produce of up to one ton a year.*

Stadthaus M1

Barkow Leibinger
Raderschallpartner AG
Freiburg, Deutschland
Germany

Photo: Stefan Müller

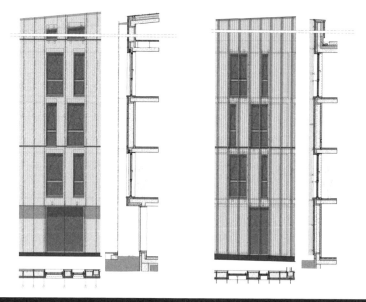

Schnittansicht / *Façade section:* Barkow Leibinger

Mit Konzepten zur Selbstverwaltung, Ökologie und Mobilität zeigt sich das Freiburger Viertel Vauban seit Jahren als unkonventioneller Vorreiter. Eine grüne Fassadenwand ist nun Aushängeschild und Bildmarke des Stadthauses M1. Dahinter verbergen sich zwei voneinander unabhängige Gebäude, ein Hotel und ein Wohngebäude.

Vor der Holzfinnenfassade an der Südseite der Gebäude mit Loggien und Balkonen ranken an Edelstahlseilen unterschiedliche Kletterpflanzen bald bis zu fünf Stockwerke hoch. Unabhängig vom durch Blüten und farbiges Laub abwechslungsreichen Fassadenbild wurde durch die Bepflanzung eine vorgeblendete klimatische Pufferzone geschaffen – ein durchaus relevanter Klimafaktor, da Freiburg im Vergleich zu anderen deutschen Städten über-durchschnittlich viele Sonnentage zählt.

The Freiburg district of Vauban has for years been an unconventional trailblazer with concepts for self-administration, ecology, and mobility. A green façade wall now acts as the calling card and brand for the M1 townhouse. Behind it there are actually two distinct buildings, the one a hotel, the other an apartment block.

In front of the building's south façade with its wooden fins, loggias and balconies, stainless steel cables guide a variety of climbing plants up to a height of five stories. The alternation of blossoms and colorful foliage brings great variety to the façade which, moreover, thanks to the plants functions as a climatic buffer zone curtain wall – which is definitely a relevant climatic factor as Freiburg enjoys more sunny days than other German cities.

Photo: Zooey Braun

BAUTYP, NUTZUNG *TYPE OF BUILDING, USAGE*	Mischnutzung: Wohnen, Gewerbe, Hotel *Mixed usage: Apartments, commerce, hotel*
FERTIGSTELLUNG *COMPLETION*	2013
ARCHITEKTEN / *ARCHITECTS*	Barkow Leibinger
GRÜNPLANUNG *GREENERY PLANNERS*	Raderschallpartner AG
BAUHERR / *BUILDER*	Freiburger Stadtbau GmbH
ART DER BEGRÜNUNG, **METHODE** *TYPE OF GREENERY, METHOD*	Bodengebundene Vertikal- begrünung mit Kletterpflanzen *Ground-based vertical* *greenery with climbing plants*
FLÄCHE DER BEGRÜNUNG *AREA GREENED*	1.756 m²
TECHNIK *TECHNIQUE*	Vertikalseile; Rankhilfen aus Edelstahl *Vertical cables; stainless steel guides for creepers*
PFLANZEN *PLANTS*	Gemischte Bepflanzung mit 25 verschiedenen Arten wie Kletterrosen, wildem Wein, Waldreben, Schlingknöterich, Geißblatt, Akebien und Glyzinien. *Mixture of 25 different types of plant, such as rambling roses, Virginia creeper, clematis, silver lace vine, woodbine, Akebia and wisteria.*
BEWÄSSERUNG *WATERING SYSTEM*	Automatisch gesteuerte Tropfbewässerung *Automatically controlled drip irrigation*
KLIMAERGEBNIS, KLIMA- **KONZEPT, KLIMAZIELE** *CLIMATIC IMPACT, CLIMATE* *CONCEPT, CLIMATE GOALS*	Im Sommer bildet die Bepflanzung einen natürlichen Filter und Sonnenschutz, während sie im Winter unbelaubt die passive Nutzung der Sonnenenergie ermöglicht. Der Bau unterschreitet die EnEV (Energieeinsparverordnung) 2009 primärenergetisch um 60%, im Bereich der Fassade um 30%. *In summer, the plants form a natural filter and protection from the sun, while in winter when they have shed their leaves, they enable passive use of sunlight. The building complies with EnEV (Law on Energy Saving) 2009 levels, coming 60% below the recommended level for primary energy sources, and 30% below that for the façade zone.*
BESCHREIBUNG *DESCRIPTION*	Das Stadthaus M1 – bestehend aus dem „Green City Hotel Vauban" und einem Wohngebäude – markiert den Eingang des Freiburger Quartiers Vauban, einem für seine ökologischen und nachhaltigen Ansätze bekannten Stadtteil von Freiburg im Breisgau. Das Stadthaus richtet sich zum Paula-Modersohn-Platz aus und gibt diesem eine räumliche Fassung. Der Durchgang zwischen den beiden Bauten und die Südseite mit ihren Loggien und Balkonen erhielt neben dem aktiven Sonnenschutz eine begrünte Seilfassade. *The M1 Townhouse consisting of the "Green City Hotel Vauban" and an apartment block constitutes the gateway to the Freiburg district of Vauban, a quarter famed for its ecological and sustainable approach. The townhouse faces onto Paula Modersohn Square and structures the latter. The passageway between the two buildings and the south façade with its loggias and balconies not only features active sun protection but also greenery that is guided by cables.*

Jobcenter am Altmarkt

Kuehn Malvezzi
Haas Architekten
atelier le balto
Oberhausen, Deutschland
Germany

Städte, die immer dichter werden und deren räumliche Ressourcen nach wirt-
schaftlichen Faktoren bewertet werden, stehen vor dem immer wieder kehren-
den Dilemma – wie innerstädtisch und jenseits kommerzieller Nutzung Räume
schaffen, die ökonomisch vertretbar sind und zugleich der Stadtgesellschaft
dienen? Im historischen Zentrum von Oberhausen entstand ein Jobcenter mit
einem darüber liegenden Gewächshaus, in dem Möglichkeiten urbaner Landwirtschaft erforscht und zugleich praktiziert werden. Zwei völlig konträre
Nutzungen in einem gesamtheitlichen Konzept und in einem Gebäude zu vereinen ist eine herausfordernde Bauaufgabe, die entsprechend unkonventionelle
Lösung erfordert. Darüber hinaus fügten die Architekten Kuehn Malvezzi und
die Landschaftsarchitekten atelier le balto noch ein weiteres Element hinzu:
Der vertikale Garten ist das räumlich erfahrbare Bindeglied zwischen dem
Bürogebäude mit Gewächshaus und dem traditionellen Altmarkt, auf dem an
sechs Tagen der Woche ein Markt stattfindet.

*Cities where building densities are increasing by the day and where spatial
resources are evaluated based solely on economic factors are forever facing the
same dilemma: How can spaces be created downtown that go beyond commercial usage yet are economically justifiable and serve the people of the city at the
same time? The historical heart of Oberhausen saw the development of a job
center topped by a greenhouse where the potential for urban agriculture is being
researched and practiced at the same time. Combining two entirely contradictory
uses within one holistic concept and one building is a challenging structural task
that calls for a suitably unconventional solution. On top of which, the architects
Kuehn Malvezzi and landscape architects atelier le balto have added another
element: The vertical garden creates a spatial experience, connecting the office
building to the greenhouse and the traditional Altmarkt square on which a market
is held six days a week.*

**Mischnutzung: Büro,
Forschung und Landwirtschaft**
*Mixed usage: office,
research and cultivation*

2019

**Kuehn Malvezzi
Haas Architekten (Gewächshausplaner/**
*greenhouse planners***)**

atelier le balto

Photo: © hiepler, brunier

**OGM Oberhausener Gebäudemanagement GmbH (gefördert im Rahmen
des Bundesprogramms Nationale Projekte des Städtebaus)**
*OGM Oberhausener Gebäudemanagement GmbH (with funding from the
Federal Government program for national urban development projects)*

**Gewächshaus: Rollbare Pflanztische, drei Klimakammern, verschiedene
Anbaumethoden**
Vertikaler Garten: Offenes Stahlgerüst als Rankhilfe sowie Pflanztröge
**Hofgarten: Topographie, die mit Höhenunterschieden bis zu 60 cm trocke-
nere und feuchtere Zonen ausbildet und für jeweils unterschiedliche Pflan-
zen ein geeignetes Habitat darstellt.**
*Greenhouse: castor-based planting tables, three climate chambers, different
planting methods*
Vertical garden: Open steel frame as a climbing aid and planters
*Inner courtyard garden: Topography that with its height differences of up to
60cm forms dryer or moister zones and provides a suitable habitat for respectively different types of plants.*

**Gewächshaus: Produktion auf 630 m² Nutzfläche, Forschung auf 160 m²
Nutzfläche; Vertikaler Garten: circa 200 m²; Hofgarten: circa 100 m²**
*Greenhouse: Production covering 630 m² of usable space, Research covering
160 m² of usable space; Vertical garden: approx. 200 m²; Inner courtyard garden:
approx. 100 m²*

Rankhilfen und Gewächshäuser / *Climbing aids and greenhouses*

Gewächshaus: Kräuter, Salate, Erdbeeren
**Vertikaler Garten: Kräftige Pflanzen wie Rostrote Weinrebe, Echter
Hopfen, Chinesischer Blauregen und Kletterhortensien wurzeln im Erd-
reich auf Platzniveau. Fingerblättrige Akebie, Kiwibeere oder auch
Clematis Montana sind filigranere Gewächse, die von Pflanztrögen aus
nach oben ranken.**
Hofgarten: Stauden, Sträucher, Farne und Gräser sowie Felsenbirnen

Greenhouse: Herbs, lettuce, strawberries
Vertical garden: Strong plants such as russet vines, real hops, Chinese Wisteria and climbing hydrangeas rooted in the earth at the ground level. Finger-leaf Akebia, Kiwi berries or Clematis Montana are all refined plants that climb out of planters upwards.
Inner courtyard garden: Shrubs, bushes, ferns and grasses as well as rock pears

BEWÄSSERUNG
WATERING SYSTEM

Das Regenwasser, das auf den Dächern anfällt, wird in einer Zisterne gesammelt und zum Gießen der Pflanzen verwendet. Das Grauwasser aus den Spül- und Waschbecken wird aufbereitet und als Betriebswasser teils in den Toilettenspülungen des Bürogebäudes und teils im vertikalen Garten wiederverwendet. Das Bewässerungssystem des Gewächshauses ist automatisiert. Der vertikale Garten und die Bepflanzung im Hofgarten werden temporär bewässert.

The rainwater that falls on the roofs is collected in a cistern and is used to water the plants. The grey water from sinks and washbasins is processed and used as operating water partly in the toilet flush systems in the office building and in partly in the vertical garden. The watering system in the greenhouse is automated. The vertical garden and the plants in the inner courtyard garden are watered temporarily.

KLIMAERGEBNIS, KLIMA-KONZEPT, KLIMAZIELE
CLIMATIC IMPACT, CLIMATE CONCEPT, CLIMATE GOALS

Gewächshaus: Die hier erstmals realisierte haustechnische Integration des Gewächshauses bedeutet, dass die verschiedenen Nutzungen voneinander profitieren. Die Abluft aus dem Bürogebäude wird in das Gewächshaus geleitet, wo Abwärme und CO_2-Gehalt u.a. das Pflanzenwachstum fördern.

Greenhouse: The integration of the greenhouse into the facilities technology achieved here for the first time means that the different usages benefit from one another. The office building's air extraction is directed into the greenhouse, where waste heat and CO_2 content etc. promote plant growth.

BESCHREIBUNG
DESCRIPTION

Die drei Elemente Bürohaus, Gewächshaus und vertikaler Garten sind in ihrer Gliederung modular aufeinander bezogen. Eine Struktur aus verzinktem Stahl nimmt das Grundmaß auf und variiert es in unterschiedlichen Bauteilen: vertikal als Teilung der Bürofenster, der gläsernen Gewächshauswand sowie des offenen Rankgerüsts; horizontal setzen sich die Plattformen des Gerüsts geschossweise in den umlaufenden Fenstersimsen fort. Die Verwendung standardisierter Bauteile ermöglicht eine sparsame Konstruktion und einen effizienten Betrieb.

The three elements, i.e. the office building, greenhouse and vertical garden, are divided up in modular fashion. A structure made of galvanized steel picks up on the basic dimensions and varies them in different sections of the building: vertically in the division of the office windows, the glazed wall of the greenhouse and the open trellis; horizontally in the platforms of the frame, which continue the line of the all-round window ledges on a floor-by-floor basis. The use of standardized modules makes for thrifty construction and efficient operation.

BESONDERHEIT
SPECIALTY

Der vertikale Garten war nicht Teil des Raumprogramms in der Wettbewerbs-Auslobung, sondern wurde als zusätzliches Element vorgeschlagen – und realisiert –, das Stadt und Dachgewächshaus miteinander verbindet sowie zur Nachbarbebauung vermittelt.

The vertical Garden was not part of the spatial program in the competition brief but was proposed as an additional element – and realized – connecting the city and the roof greenhouse as well as the neighboring buildings.

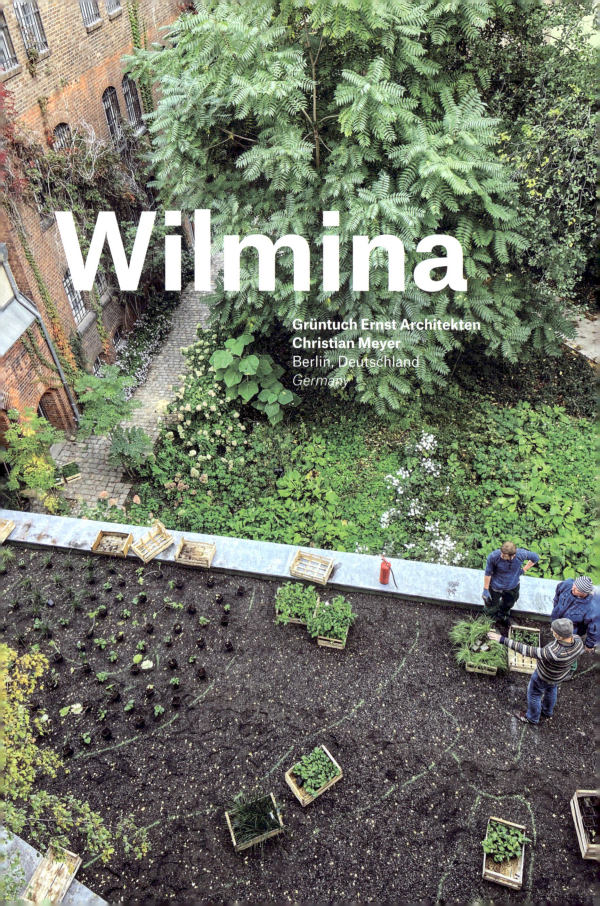

Wilmina

Grüntuch Ernst Architekten
Christian Meyer
Berlin, Deutschland
Germany

Die Transformation vom ehemaligen Frauengefängnis in Charlottenburg zum Hotel ist radikal. Nicht nur, dass das Gebäude aus dem 19. Jahrhundert in der Raumstruktur von einer nutzungsbedingt eher antisozialen Raumkonfiguration geprägt war und nun in seiner neuen Funktion als Hotel einladend wirken sollte – Efeu hatte über weite Teile die Fassaden überwuchert und ruderaler Wildwuchs den Innenhof für sich eingenommen. Das Grünkonzept betriff drei Bereiche: Der Bewuchs des Hofes wurde zum Teil belassen und ehemals versiegelte Flächen wurden aufgebrochen und neu bepflanzt. Der weitläufige Efeubewuchs an den Fassaden, der in Teilen herabzustürzen drohte, wurde zurückgeschnitten und an den Hofseiten mit weiteren Rankpflanzen ergänzt. Auf den Dachflächen, u.a. über dem Schleusenhof, wurden Dachgärten angelegt.

Die Architekten Grüntuch Ernst übertrugen die Balance zwischen Bestandserhalt und Wiederbelebung sowie zwischen Konservierung und Sanierung von der Herausforderung des Gebäudes auf die Grünflächen. Sie schufen auch durch die Einbeziehung der Bestandsbegrünung einen Komplex, der zu 30 Prozent der Gebäudehülle begrünt ist. Ein Konzept, das im Sinne der Begrünung der Städte Schule machen könnte.

The transformation of the former women's prison in Charlottenburg into a hotel is truly radical. It is not just that the 19th-century building was defined in light of its use by an essentially antisocial spatial configuration and now needed to be inviting in its new function as a hotel. Ivy had run wild over large parts of the façades and rampant ruderal plants had as good as taken over the inner courtyard. The greening concept covered three areas: The plants in the courtyard were partially left in place and formerly sealed surfaces broken open to create space for new plants. The extensive ivy on the façades, which in part threatened to crash down off the walls, was cut back and supplemented on the courtyard sides with other climbing plants. Roof gardens were arranged on the roof areas, incl. over the lock gate.

Architects Grüntuch Ernst translated the balance between maintaining the old and giving it new life, between conservation and modernization onto the green areas, too. By including the existing greenery they also created a complex that covers as much as 30 percent of the building's shell. It is a concept that could become a role model when it comes to greening cities.

BAUTYP, NUTZUNG *TYPE OF BUILDING, USAGE*	Hotel *Hotel*
FERTIGSTELLUNG *COMPLETION*	2020/2021
ARCHITEKTEN / *ARCHITECTS*	Grüntuch Ernst Architekten
GRÜNPLANUNG *GREENERY PLANNERS*	Grüntuch Ernst Architekten Christian Meyer
BAUHERR / *BUILDER*	Wilmina GmbH
ART DER BEGRÜNUNG, **METHODE** *TYPE OF GREENERY, METHOD*	Renaturierte Hofflächen, Dach- und Fassadenbegrünungen *Renatured courtyards areas, roof and façade greenery*
FLÄCHE DER BEGRÜNUNG *AREA GREENED*	Dachfläche: 250 m², Fassadenbegrünung: 1.000 m². Über 30 % der Gebäudehülle begrünt *Roof surface: 250 m², façade greenery: 1,000 m². Over 30 percent of the building's envelope is greened*
TECHNIK *TECHNIQUE*	Intensiv- und Extensivbegrünung; Bodengebundene Fassadenbegrünung *Intensive and extensive greenery; ground-based façade greenery*
PFLANZEN *PLANTS*	Neben Gehölzen, Knollen- und Zwiebelgewächsen, Farnen, Stauden und Gräsern wurde die bestehende Bepflanzung (Bäume, Efeu) einbezogen. *Alongside shrubs, tubers and bulb-based plants, ferns, bushes and grasses, the existing plants (trees, ivy) were incorporated into the new scheme.*
BEWÄSSERUNG *WATERING SYSTEM*	In Teilbereichen automatische Bewässerung *In subsections automatic watering*
KLIMAERGEBNIS, KLIMA- **KONZEPT, KLIMAZIELE** *CLIMATIC IMPACT, CLIMATE* *CONCEPT, CLIMATE GOALS*	Regeneration für das urbane Mikroklima und die Nutzer *Regeneration for the urban microclimate and the users*
BESCHREIBUNG *DESCRIPTION*	Der begrünte Garten des sanierten und erweiterten Bestandsgebäudes liegt im inneren des Blocks. Das seit Jahrzehnten ruderal überwachsene Bestandsgrün wurde erhalten und Betonflächen abgebrochen, sodass entsiegelte Hofbereiche renaturiert werden konnten. Ein Sonderbereich wurde mit seltenen Farnen und Reben inszeniert. Das Konzept konzentrierte sich neben der intensiven und extensiv Begrünung der Flachdachbereiche auf den Erhalt der bestehenden Efeubegrünung der Fassaden. *The greened garden of the modernized and expanded old build is on the inside of the block. The existing ruderal plants that have grown there down through the decades were kept and concrete paving removed so that open courtyard areas could be renatured. A special segment was staged to feature rare ferns and vines. The concept focuses not only on intensive and extensive greenery for the flat roofs but also on preserving the existing ivy on the façades.*

Ökohaus

Eble & Sambeth
Hans Loidl
John Wilkes
Frankfurt / Main, Deutschland
Germany

Im Rahmen der städtebaulichen Quartierserneuerung einer Industriebrache am Westbahnhof in Frankfurt-Bockenheim sollte eine „grüne Oase" entstehen, so die Architekten Elble & Sambeth, die beim Wettbewerb 1988 für ein Verlags- und Bürogebäude als Sieger hervorgegangen waren. Dem Bauprojekt gingen langwierige Verhandlungen mit der Commerzbank AG Frankfurt voraus. Diese hatte sich jahrelang um ein Grundstück nahe dem Hauptbahnhof bemüht, das dem Verlag Kühl KG gehörte. Das Ergebnis war ein Tausch zwischen zwei Interessensgruppen: Als Gegenleistung für die begehrte Liegenschaft verpflichtete sich die Bank zum Neubau am Frankfurter Westbahnhof. Ganz im Zeichen der Umweltschutzbewegung der 1980er-Jahre lag der Fokus auf baubiologischen und ökologischen Aspekten – hinsichtlich der Nutzergemeinschaft aus Verlag und verschiedenen alternativen Gruppen aus Überzeugung. Die Bank wiederum verfolgte einen Imagewechsel mit umweltpolitischem Engagement. Das Passivhaus mit Solarhaus und Kerngebäude setzte in der Materialwahl und einem umfassenden Wasser- und Raumklimakonzept auf ressourcenschonendes und energieeffizientes Bauen.

The plan was, said architects Elble & Sambeth, to create a "green oasis" as part of renewing the urban fabric of a dilapidated industrial quarter at Westbahnhof in Frankfurt's Bockenheim district when commenting on their winning entry in the 1988 competition for a publishing and office building. The construction project had been preceded by arduous negotiations with Commerzbank AG Frankfurt which had for many years sought to acquire the land owned by publisher Kühl KG close to the main railway station. The result was a swap between two different interest groups: In return for the cherished piece of land, the bank committed to a new build at Frankfurt's Westbahnhof. Firmly under the sign of the environmental protection movement of the 1980s, the focus was on building biology and ecological aspects – out of conviction on the part of the users from the publishing house and the different alternative groups. The bank for its part wanted to change its image and emphasize eco-political commitment. The new build met the passivhaus standard with solar powering and the core building emphasized sparing resources and energy-efficient construction in terms of the choice of materials used and the comprehensive water and ambient climate concept.

Photo: Moritz Bernoully

Das Ökohaus – heute Ökohaus Arche – war auch im Hinblick auf das Begrünungskonzept ein Pilotprojekt. Nicht nur Dachgärten und intensive Dachbegrünung prägen das Bild von außen, vor allem im Inneren der beiden Glashallen zeigt sich nach 25 Jahren ein üppiger Bewuchs auf mehreren Ebenen. Aus der Wahl der mittlerweile hochstämmigen Pflanzen weht der Geist der 90er-Jahre. Der gelenkte Wasserlauf durch die große Glashalle erzeugt zusammen mit der Bepflanzung ein spezifisches Raumklima, das durch das Plätschern des Bachlaufs unterstrichen wird. Der hohe Aufwand in der Instandhaltung und der Gewächshausatmosphäre an immer mehr werdenden heißen Sommertagen werden durch langjährige Nutzer und eine hohe Mieterzufriedenheit aufgewogen – nicht zu vergessen, dass das Ökohaus auch heute noch ein Statement für mutige Konzepte ist.[41]

41 Roman Hollenstein, Kunstchronik 2/1992, S./p. 28–39; DBZ 1/1993, S./p. 65–68.

The Ökohaus is today called the Ökohaus Arche and was in its day a pilot project in terms of building greenery. Not only the roof gardens and intensive roof greenery define its outside appearance, but above all in the interior with the two glass halls after 25 years there is opulent greenery over several levels. The choice of what are now tall plants attests to the spirit of the 1990s. The water course designed to run through the large glass hall combines with the plants to generate a specific ambient climate that is emphasized by the burbling of the brook. The heavy workload required to maintain the systems and the glasshouse atmosphere on the increasing number of hot summer days are offset by the many years of benefits and great satisfaction among the tenants – not to forget that to this day the Ökohaus makes a statement on courageous concepts.[41]

BAUTYP, NUTZUNG *TYPE OF BUILDING, USAGE*	Mischnutzung: Büro, Gewerbe, Dienstleitung, Veranstaltungsräume, Restaurant *Mixed usage: Office, commerce, services, events rooms, restaurant*
FERTIGSTELLUNG *COMPLETION*	1992
ARCHITEKTEN / *ARCHITECTS*	Eble & Sambeth
GRÜNPLANUNG *GREENERY PLANNERS*	Hans Loidl John Wilkes (Wassergestaltung / *water design*)
BAUHERR / *BUILDER*	Commerzbank AG, Frankfurt (bis zur Übergabe / *until handover*); Kühl KG, Frankfurt
ART DER BEGRÜNUNG *TYPE OF GREENERY*	Intensive Dachbegrünung; umfassendes Begrünungskonzept in den beiden großen Glashäusern *Intensive roof greenery; greening concept for both large glass halls*
BEWÄSSERUNG *WATERING SYSTEM*	Nicht alle Dachflächen sind begrünt, um Regenwasser für ressourcen- sparende Brauchwasser- und Grauwassersysteme einzusetzen. Das über- schüssige, auf den Tonnendächern gesammelte Dachwasser wird über einen Pflanzfiltertrog in einer Zisterne gesammelt. Das Dachwasser vom Glashaus fließt über den Pflanzfilter des südwestlichen Schrägdaches direkt in das Feuchtbiotop vor dem Haupteingang. *Not all areas of the roof are greened in order to use rainwater for resource- sparing service water and grey water systems. The surplus roof water is col- lected on the barrel roofs and held in a cistern fed through a plant filter trough. The water from the roof of the glass house runs through the plant filter of the sloping roof in the southwest directly into the wetland biotope in front of the main entrance.*

Wasserkonzept
Water concept

Klimakonzept
Climate concept

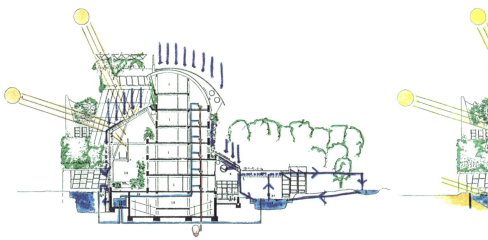

TECHNIK
TECHNIQUE

Das straßenseitige, südliche Glashaus und das rückwärtige, nördliche Glashaus stehen in klimatischer Wechselwirkung. Im Sommer wird die aufsteigende Warmluft durch die Kaminwirkung unter dem Dach abgeführt. Kühle, frische Luft aus dem nordöstlichen Glashaus – gespeist durch die Abkühl-Pflanzenfilterfassade – strömt nach. Solarglas-Lichtlenksysteme in den Fensterscheiben verhindern die Überhitzung. In der Übergangszeit und im Winter wird die temperierte Warmluft unter dem Dach technisch durch Ventilatorensysteme in das Erdgeschoss der Glashäuser niedergeblasen.

Die Glashäuser sind nicht beheizt. Sie sind als rein passive Klimavorzonen und Puffer ausgelegt. Durch die Transmissionswärmeverluste der Kernhäuser und durch die hohen Speichermassen in Wänden und der Rampe ist ein Absinken in die Nähe des Gefrierpunktes nicht zu erwarten. Dadurch sind ideale Voraussetzungen für Innenraumbepflanzung gegeben.

The southern glasshouse facing the street and the one behind facing north interact climatically. In the summer, the chimney effect ensures the rising hot air is sucked out of the building under the roof. Cool fresh air from the northeast glasshouse – fed by the cooling plant filter façade – flows in behind it. Solar-glass-heliostats in the windowpanes prevent overheating. Between seasons and in the winter, a ventilator system blows the tempered warm air under the roof back down to the ground floor of the glasshouses.

The glasshouses do not have a heating system and are designed as purely passive climate zones and buffers. Given the transmission heat losses of the core buildings and the higher storage masses of the walls and the ramp, the temperature is very unlikely to drop anywhere close to freezing point. This creates ideal conditions for indoor plants.

PFLANZEN
PLANTS

Vielfältige Innenraumbepflanzung von hochstämmigen Birkenfeigen bis zu Palmen, Farnen und Moosen.
A wide variety of indoor plants ranging from tall weeping figs to palms, ferns and mosses.

Konzeptschnitte / *Concept sections:* Eble & Sambeth

Energiekonzept
Energy concept

LITERATURVERZEICHNIS
BIBLIOGRAPHY

Ahrendt, Dorothee/Aepfler, Gertraud: Goethes Gärten in Weimar, Leipzig 2009

Althaus, Christoph: Fassadenbegrünung. Ein Beitrag zu Risiken, Schäden und präventiver Schadensverhütung, Berlin/Hannover 1987

Ambasz, Emilio: Nature and architecture. Emilio Ambasz and Fukuoka's ACROS centre 25 year later: www.ambasz.com/fukuoka-25th-anniversary (2.12.2020)

Ansel, Wolfgang/Meier, Reimer: DDV-Praxisratgeber. Das 1x1 der Dachbegrünung, Nürtingen 2016

Ansel, Wolfgang/Meier, Reimer/Dickhaut, Wolfgang/Kruse, Elke/Baumgarten, Heiner: Leitfaden Dachbegrünungen für Kommunen, Nürtingen 2011

Ansel, Wolfgang/Reidel, Petra: Moderne Dachgärten – kreativ und individuell, Stuttgart 2012

Arup: Cities Alive – Green building Envelope, Berlin 2016: www.arup.com/perspectives/publications/research/section/cities-alive-green-building-envelope (2.12.2020)

BASt Bundesanstalt für Straßenwesen (Hg.): Fachtagung Luftqualität an Straßen, Bergisch Gladbach 2008

Baumann, Rudi: Begrünte Architektur. Bauen und Gestalten mit Kletterpflanzen, München 1983

BBSR Bundesinstitut für Bau-, Stadt- und Raumforschung (Hg.): Stadtgrün in der Städtebauförderung, Bonn 2020

BBSR Bundesinstitut für Bau-, Stadt- und Raumforschung (Hg.): Wachstumsdruck in deutschen Städten, Bonn 2017

Becker, Annette/Cachola Schmal, Peter: Stadtgrün. Europäische Landschaftsarchitektur für das 21. Jahrhundert, Basel 2010

Becsei, Stephan/Hackenbracht, Christine: Rankraum. Filigrane grüne Architektursysteme, Köln 1986

Bergdoll, Barry/Ambasz, Emilio: Emerging Nature – Precursor of Architecture and Design, Zürich 2017

Berndt, Heide: Die Natur der Stadt, Frankfurt 1978

BfN Bundesamt für Naturschutz: FloraWeb: www.floraweb.de/index.html (30.11.2020)

Blanc, Patrick: Les murs végétaux de la nature à la ville, Neuilly-sur-Seine 2008

Blanc, Patrick: Vertikale Gärten. Die Natur in der Stadt, Stuttgart 2009

BMUB Bundesministerium für Umwelt, Naturschutz, Bau und Reaktorsicherheit: Nationale Strategie zur biologischen Vielfalt, Kabinettbeschluss vom 07. November 2007: www.bfn.de/fileadmin/BfN/biologischevielfalt/Dokumente/broschuere_biolog_vielfalt_strategie_bf.pdf (30.11.2020)

Brandhorst, Stefan: Pflege und Wartung wandgebundener Fassadenbegrünungen, 7. FBB-Symposium Fassadenbegrünung 2014: www.gebaeudegruen.info/fileadmin/website/downloads/bugg-symposien/Fassadenbegruenungssymposium/7_FBB-Fassadenbegruenungssymposium_2014.pdf (2.12.2020).

Brandwein, Thorwald: Bemessungsdaten, Tabelle zu den Lasteinflüssen von Fassadenbegrünungen: www.biotekt.de/fassadenbegruenung/kletterhilfen-rankgitter (30.11.2020)

Brandwein, Thorwald: Statistisches über Brände mit Kletterpflanzen und Strategien zu ihrer Vermeidung: www.fassadenbegrünung-polygrün.de/wp-content/uploads/2014/11/Text-Brand_Strat_Wien-2014_ISO.pdf (2.12.2020)

Brenneisen, Stephan/u.a. (Hg.): Ökologischer Ausgleich auf dem Dach: Vegetation und bodenbrütende Vögel, Zürich 2010

BuGG Bundesverband GebäudeGrün e.V.: Fachinformation „Positive Wirkungen von Gebäudebegrünungen (Dach-, Fassaden- und Innenraumbegrünung)": www.gebaeudegruen.info (1.12.2020)

BuGG Bundesverband GebäudeGrün e.V.: Fachinformation „Solar-Gründach": www.gebaeudegruen.info (1.12.2020)

Dettmar, Jörg/Pfoser, Nicole/Sieber, Sandra: Gutachten Fassadenbegrünung: Gutachten über quartiersorientierte Unterstützungsansätze von Fassadenbegrünungen, Darmstadt 2016: www.umwelt.nrw.de/fileadmin/redaktion/PDFs/klima/gutachten_fassadenbegruenung.pdf (2.12.2020)

Doernach, Rudolf/Heid, Gerhard: Das Naturhaus. Wege zur Naturstadt, Frankfurt am Main 1982

Enzi, Vera: Fassadenbegrünungen – Innovation und Chancen, Wien 2010

Enzi, Vera/Scharf, Bernhard: Das Haus im Grünen Pelz, Bürogebäude der MA 48, Einsiedlergasse 2, 1050 Wien, in: Wettbewerbe 303/2012, S./*p.* 14–19

EU Kommission: Grüne Infrastruktur (GI) – Aufwertung des europäischen Naturkapitals, Mitteilung 2013: eur-lex.europa.eu/legal-content/DE/TXT/?uri=CELEX%3A52013DC0249 (30.11.2020)

Europäische Union: Eine grüne Infrastruktur für Europa, Belgien: ec.europa.eu/environment/nature/ecosystems/docs/GI-Brochure-210x210-DE-web.pdf (30.11.2020)

Fabbrizzi, Fabio: Architettura verso natura, natura verso architettura, Florenz 2003

FBB Fachvereinigung Bauwerksbegrünung: Ergebnisse der bundesweiten Umfrage zur Förderung von Gebäudebegrünung der FBB 2016: www.gebaeudegruen.info/gruen/dachbegruenung/wirkungen-vorteile-fakten/foerderung-2016 (30.11.2020)

FBB Fachvereinigung Bauwerksbegrünung: Fortschreibung von Publikationen zur Gebäudebegrünung: www.gebaeudegruen.info/gruen/publikationen (3.12.2017)

Finke, Cerstin/Osterhoff Blottner, Julia: Fassaden begrünen – Ratgeber für Gestaltung, Ausführung und Pflanzenwahl, Taunisstein 2001

FLL Forschungsgesellschaft Landschaftsentwicklung Landschaftsbau e.V. (Hg.): Das begrünte Haus – Bedeutung u. konstruktive Hinweise, Karlsruhe 1983

FLL Forschungsgesellschaft Landschaftsentwicklung Landschaftsbau e.V. (Hg.): Die wertsteigernde Wirkung von städtischen Grünflächen auf Immobilien. Dokumentation des Symposiums am 26. März 1999 in Berlin, Bonn 1999

FLL Forschungsgesellschaft Landschaftsentwicklung Landschaftsbau e.V. (Hg.): Richtlinie für die Planung, Ausführung und Pflege von Fassadenbegrünung mit Kletterpflanzen – Fassadenbegrünungsrichtlinien, Bonn 2000

Frahm, Jan Peter: Feinstaubreduktion an Straßenrändern durch Moosmatten, in: BASt Bundesanstalt für Straßenwesen (Hg.) 2008

Franke, Erhard: Stadtklima. Ergebnisse und Aspekte für die Stadtplanung, Stuttgart 1977

Freie Hansestadt Hamburg, Behörde für Umwelt und Energie (Hg.): Hamburgs Gründächer. Eine ökonomische Bewertung, Hamburg 2017

Freie Hansestadt Hamburg, Behörde für Umwelt und Energie (Hg.): Dachbegrünung. Leitfaden zur Planung, Hamburg 2019

Friedensreich Hundertwasser: Baummieter sind Botschafter des freien Waldes in der Stadt, in: Goritz 2002

Gollwitzer, Gerda/Wirsing, Werner: Dachgärten + Dachterrassen, München 1962

Gollwitzer, Gerda/Wirsing, Werner: Dachflächen bewohnt, belebt, bepflanzt, München 1971

Goritz, Christoph: Auseinandersetzung mit einer Wechsel-beziehung, Leipzig 2002

Gotheins, Marie Luise: Geschichte der Gartenkunst, Jena 1926

Green City Begrünungsbüro: Kostenfreie Beratung für Immobilien im Münchener Stadtgebiet: www.greencity.de/projekt/begruenungsbuero (30.11.2020)

Grub, Hermann: Unternehmen Grün – Ideen, Konzepte, Beispiele für mehr Natur in der Arbeitswelt, München 1990

Grüntuch-Ernst, Almut/IDEAS Institut for Design an Architectural Strategies (Hg.): Hortitecture. The Power of Architecture and Plants, Berlin 2018

Gunkel, Rita: Fassadenbegrünung – Kletterpflanzen und Klettergerüste, Stuttgart 2004

Guttmann, Rainer: Hausbegrünung – Kletterpflanzen am Haus und im Garten, Stuttgart 1985

Haeupler, Henning/Muer, Thomas: Bildatlas der Farn- und Blütenpflanzen Deutschlands, Stuttgart 2007

Hansen, Richard/Stahl, Friedrich: Die Stauden und ihre Lebens-bereiche in Gärten und Grünanlagen, Stuttgart 2016

Hegger, Manfred/u.a.: Energie Atlas, Nachhaltige Architektur, München 2007

Heinigk, Alexander/Roethele, Erich: Besonders ökologisch, 9.11.2008: www.p-stadtkultur.de/besonders-darmstadt-7 (2.12.2020)

Hoffmann, Ot: Handbuch für begrünte und genutzte Dächer. Konstruktion – Gestaltung – Bauökologie für flache und geneigte begehbare, befahrbare begrünte Dächer, Stuttgart 1987

Hopkins, Graeme/Goodwin, Christine: Living Architecture, Green Roofs and Walls, Clayton 2011

Junklewitz, Dirk: Nachruf, 1.7.2017: biotope-city.com/de/2019/07/01/ein-pionier-interview-mit-ot-hofmann (2.12.2020)

Karlsson, Martin/Ziebarth, Nicolas R.: Population health effects and health-related costs of extreme temperatures: Comprehensive evidence from Germany, in: Journal of Environmental Economics and Management, 91/2018, S./p. 93–117

Köhler, Manfred: Ökologische Untersuchungen an extensiven Dachbegrünungen – Sonderdruck aus „Verhandlungen Gesellschaft für Ökologie", Band XVIII, Essen 1989, S./p. 249–255

Köhler, Manfred: Fassaden- und Dachbegrünung, Stuttgart 1993

Köhler, Manfred: Green facades – a view back and some visions, in: Urban Ecosystems 11/2008, Art. 423

Köhler, Manfred: Living Walls – die neue Dimension der Fassaden-begrünung, in: Neue Landschaft 11/2010, S./p. 39–44

Köhler, Manfred: Veröffentlichungen zu Fassadenbegrünungen, 2011

Köhler, Manfred: Handbuch Bauwerksbegrünung, Planung – Konstruktion – Ausführung, Köln 2012

Köhler, Manfred/Nistor, Christian: Wandgebundene Begrünungen – Quantifizierung einer neuen Bauweise in der Klima-Architektur, Neubrandenburg 2015

Kolb, Walter: Dachbegrünung – Planung, Ausführung, Pflege, Stuttgart 2016

Kolb, Walter/Schwarz, Tassilo: Grün auf kleinen Dächern. Dachbegrünung für jedermann, München/Wien 1993

Kolb, Walter: Abflussverhältnisse extensiv begrünter Flachdächer, in: Zeitschrift für Vegetationstechnik 3/1987, S./p. 111–115

Koschak, Michaela: Ein Rekord nach dem anderen: Was war das für ein Sommer?, 30.08.2019: www.t-online.de/nachrichten/panorama/id_86353720/wetter-in-deutschland-hitzerekorde-was-war-das-denn-fuer-ein-sommer-.html (2.12.2020)

Krawina, Josef/Loidl, Hans: Vertikale Begrünung von Bauwerken, Kriterien und Lösungsprinzipien für stadtklimatisch effektive, standortgerechte und architektonisch vertretbare Bepflanzung von Fassaden im Stadtgebiet, Wien 1990

Kruschke, Per/Althaus, Dirk: Ökologisches Bauen, Gütersloh 1982

Kühn, Norbert: Neue Staudenverwendung, Stuttgart 2011

Kuttler, Wilhelm: Klimatologie, Paderborn 2009

Kuttler, Wilhelm: Urbanes Klima, Teil 2, in: Gefahrstoffe – Reinhaltung der Luft, Umweltmeteorologie 9/2010, S./p. 378–382

Lambertini, Anna: Vertikale Gärten, München 2009

Lassalle, François: Pariser Vorgehen für die Gebäudebegrünung. Konkretisierung eines politischen Willens, WGIC 2017: www.gebaeudegruen.info/fi leadmin/website/downloads/wgic_vortraege/Lassalle_Francois.pdf (2.12.2020)

Le Corbusier: Fünf Punkte zu einer neuen Architektur, in: Die Form. Zeitschrift für gestaltende Arbeit 2/1927

Liesecke, Hans-Joachim: Untersuchungen zur Wasserrückhaltung extensiv begrünter Flachdächer, in: Zeitschrift für Vegetations-technik 2/1988, S./p. 56–66

Liesecke, Hans-Joachim/u.a.: Grundlagen der Dachbegrünung: Zur Planung, Ausführung und Unterhaltung von Extensivbegrünungen und einfachen Intensivbegrünungen, Berlin 1989

Lubell, Sam: Designed for Serenity, With Nature in Mind. Vo Trong Nghia's firm meditates every day, which helps in their approach to refining urban environments, in: New York Times, 10.10.2019: www.nytimes.com/2019/10/10/arts/design/vo-trong-nghia-architecture.html (2.12.2020)

Ludwig, Karl: Kletterpflanzen, Auswahl, Planung, Pflege, München 1994

Maier-Solgk, Frank: Von den Hängenden Gärten zur zeitgenössischen Hortitecture, in: Schweizer 2020

Margolis, Liat/Robinson, Alexander: Living Systems, Innovative Materialien und Technologien für die Landschaftsarchitektur, Basel 2007

Migge, Leberecht: Das grüne Dach, in: Das neue Frankfurt. Internatio-nale Monatsschrift für die Probleme kultureller Neugestaltung Bd. 12 (1927), Frankfurt am Main 1926–1931

Minke, Gernot/Witter, Gottfried: Häuser mit grünem Pelz, Frankfurt 1982

Mollenhauer, Felix/Mann, Gunter: Kosten-Nutzen-Betrachtungen von Dachbegrünungen, in: Gebäude-Grün 4/2018, S./p. 20–23

Ohlwein, Klaus: Grüner Wohnen. Gebäudebegrünung eine Notwendigkeit, Köln 1984

Oswalt, Philipp: Implantationen, Natur in der zeitgenössischen Architektur, in: Arch+ 142/1998, S./p. 74–78

Ottelé, Marc: The Green Building Envelope – Vertcal Greening, Dissertation Universität Delft 2011

Ottelé, Marc/u.a.: Vertical greening systems and the effect on air flow and temperature on the building envelope, in: Building and Environment 46/2011, S./*p.* 2287–2294

Pfoser, Nicole/Jenner, Nathalie/Henrich, Johanna/Heusinger, Jannik/Weber, Stephan: Leitfaden Gebäude, Begrünung und Energie – Potenziale und Wechselwirkungen, Bonn 2014

Pfoser, Nicole: Vertikale Begrünung, Stuttgart 2018

Pfoser, Nicole: Fassaden und Pflanzen, Potenziale einer neuen Fassadengestaltung: tuprints.ulb.tu-darmstadt.de/5587 (1.12.2020)

Pfoser, Nicole/Janner, Nathalie: Gebäude, Begrünung, Energie – Potenziale und Wechselwirkung, Bonn 2014: www.fll.de/leitfaden-gebaeude-begruenung-energie-potenziale-und-wechselwirkungen (30.11.2020)

Preiss, Joachim: Programm Fassadenbegrünungen in Wien, ExpertInnenworkshop, Vilm 2013

Preiss, Joachim (Hg.)/u.a.: Leitfaden Fassadenbegrünung – Stadt Wien: www.wien.gv.at/umweltschutz/raum/pdf/fassadenbegruenung-leitfaden.pdf (1.12.2020)

Ruby, Andreas und Ilka (Hg.): MVRDV Buildings, Basel 2013

Scharf, Bernhard: Living Walls – more than scenic beauties, in: IFLA – International Federation of Landscape Architects, Landscapes in Transition 2012

Schmidt, Marco: Gebäudebegrünung und Verdunstung, in: Garten + Landschaft 1/2008, S./*p.* 15–18

Schröpfer, Thomas: Dense+Green. Innovation Building Types for Sustainable Urban Architecture, Basel 2016

Schulte, Andreas: Living Walls erobern die Städte, Funktion und System der neuen „Fassadengärten", in: Neue Landschaft 5/2012, S./*p.* 54

Schweizer, Stefan: Die hängenden Gärten von Babylon. Vom Weltwunder zur grünen Architektur, Berlin 2020

Sieferle, Rolf Peter: Rückblick auf die Natur: Eine Geschichte des Menschen und seiner Umwelt, München 1997

Slessor, Catherine: Total Landscape, in: The Architectural Review 1/2000, S./*p.* 64–67

Stadt Frankfurt: Klimaplanatlas 2016 für Frankfurt: frankfurt.de/themen/klima-und-energie/stadtklima/klimaplanatlas (2.12.2020)

Stadt Wien: Planungsgrundlagen zur Bebauungsbestimmung „Begrünung der Fassaden": www.wien.gv.at/stadtentwicklung/strategien/pdf/planungsgrundlagen-bebauungsbestimmung-fassadenbegruenung.pdf (2.12.2020)

Stadt Zürich: Grün am Baum. Magazin zur Ausstellung, Zürich 2018

Statistikstudie zum Sommer 2003, 23.03.2007: www.spiegel.de/wissenschaft/mensch/statistik-studie-hitze-sommer-2003-hat-70-000-europaeer-getoetet-a-473614.html (2.12.2020).

Sukopp, Herbert/Wittig, Rüdiger: Stadtökologie: Ein Fachbuch für Studium und Praxis, Stuttgart 1998

Taudte-Repp, Beate: Die „Vertikalen Gärten" von Patrick Blanc, in: Becker/Cachola Schmal 2010, S./*p.* 26–31

Ungers, Oswald Mathias: Fassadengestaltung Kaufhaus Woolworth in Berlin-Wedding, in: db 10/1979, S./*p.* 42–47

URA Urban Redevelopment Authority: LUSH 3.0, 2017: www.ura.gov.sg/Corporate/Guidelines/Circulars/dc17-06 (2.12.2020)

Vo Trong Nghia: Häuser für Menschen und Bäume, in: Arch+ 226/2016, S./*p.* 196–198

Vo Trong Nghia Architects: Urban Farming Office: www.vtnarchitects.net/urban-farming-office?pgid=kckc4elz-a9de0a7a-4e08-4eb2-9099-cf2a1fedf918 (1.12.2020)

Volm, Christine: Innenraumbegrünung in Theorie und Praxis, Stuttgart 2002

Wieland, Dieter/ Bode, Peter M./ Disko, Rüdiger: Grün kaputt. Landschaften und Gärten der Deutschen, München 1983

Wölfl, Klaus: Dachbegrünung erhöht Erträge der Photovoltaik: www.zinco.de/dachbegrünung-erhöht-erträge-der-photovoltaik (30.11.2020)

Weitere Webseiten:
BfN Bundesamt für Naturschutz: www.bfn.de (2.12.2020)

BuGG Bundesverband GebäudeGrün e.V.: www.gebaeudegruen.info (2.12.2020)

Deutscher Wetterdienst: www.dwd.de (2.12.2020)

FassadenGrün: www.fassadengruen.de (2.12.2020)

Frankfurt frischt auf: www.frankfurt-greencity.de/de/thema/frankfurt-frischt-auf-50-klimabonus (2.12.2020)

GRÜNSTATTGRAU Forschungs- und Innovations GmbH, Wien: gruenstattgrau.at (1.12.2020)

Hundertwasser-Haus: www.hundertwasser-haus.info (2.12.2020)

Hundertwasser-Stiftung: www.hundertwasserfoundation.org (2.12.2020)

URA Urban Redevelopment Authority: www.ura.gov.sg (2.12.2020)

DANKE! / *THANKS!*

Das Projekt konnte nur durch die großartige Unterstützung Vieler verwirklich werden!
The project could only be realized with the great support of many!

Beate Alberternst (Team „Lebendige Dächer", Botanischer Garten Frankfurt / Main), **Nils Andreas** (Samen Andreas, Frankfurt / Main), **Francesca Cesa Bianchi** (Stefano Boeri Architetti), **Alexander von Birgelen** (Hochschule Geisenheim), **Stephan Boehme** (s.boehme & co. KGaA, Frankfurt / Main), **Lin Bolt** (WOHA), **Katharina Böttger** (Historisches Museum Frankfurt / Main), **Cinthia Buchheister** (Arup), **Peter Dommermuth** (Umweltamt Frankfurt / Main), **Torben Giese** (StadtPalais – Museum für Stuttgart), **Nina Gorgus** (Historisches Museum Frankfurt / Main), **Almut Grüntuch-Ernst** (Grüntuch Ernst Architekten), **Hans Georg Dannert** (Umweltamt Frankfurt / Main), **Johann Eisele** (Eisele Staniek+), **Gerd Heinemann** (Ökohaus Arche, Frankfurt / Kühl Verwaltung GmbH & Co Verlags KG), **Mai Hoan** (VTN Architects), **Pan Hoffmann** (Architekt / *architect*, Darmstadt), **Horst Ewerling** (Team „Lebendige Dächer", Botanischer Garten Frankfurt / Main), **Andreas König** (Team „Lebendige Dächer", Botanischer Garten Frankfurt / Main),

Rouja König (ingenhoven architects), **Ralf Kremser** (Team „Lebendige Dächer", Botanischer Garten Frankfurt / Main), **Martin Malzahn** (Landschaftsarchitekt / *Landscape architect*, Osnabrück), **Gunter Mann** (BuGG Bundesverband GebäudeGrün e.V.), **Gayle Mault** (Heatherwick Studio), **Petra Messerschmidt** (Eble Messerschmidt Partner, Tübingen), **Christian Mettlach** (WICONA), **Lara-Maria Mohr** (Umweltamt Frankfurt / Main), **Stefan Nawrat** (Team „Lebendige Dächer", Botanischer Garten Frankfurt / Main), **Peter Jan van Ouwerkerk** (ingenhoven architects), **Isabel Pagel** (MVRDV), **Peter Pätzold** (Bürgermeister, Referat Städtebau, Wohnen und Umwelt, Stuttgart), **Nicole Pfoser** (Hochschule für Wirtschaft und Umwelt, Nürtingen-Geislingen), **Joachim Preiss** (Umweltamt Wien), **Martin Reuter** (ingenhoven architects), **Joachim Stroh** (ZinCo, Nürtingen), **Peter Takasz** (IKEA Stiftung, Hofheim-Wallau), **Schirin Taraz** (WOHA), **Reinhard Tiemann** (Bgrünt², Mainz), **Markus Welsch** (Perspectus Films, Berlin)

AUTOREN / *AUTHORS*

Soweit nicht anders angegeben:
Unless indicated otherwise:
Hilde Strobl
in Zusammenarbeit mit / *in collaboration with*
Jonas Malzahn

IM GESPRÄCH MIT ...
IN CONVERSATION WITH ...

Biographische Hinweise zu den Personen finden sich auf den angegebenen Seiten:
Biographical information on the people can be found on the pages indicated:

Wilhelm Kuttler (S. / *p.* 14)
Hans-Georg Dannert (S. / *p.* 21)
Rudi Scheuermann (S. / *p.* 26)
Nicole Pfoser (S. / *p.* 33)
Alexander von Birgelen (S. / *p.* 93)
Schirin Taraz (S. / *p.* 171)
Martin Reuter (S. / *p.* 250)

WARUM, WIE UND WOFÜR GEBÄUDEGRÜN?
BUILDING GREENERY – WHY, HOW, AND TO WHAT END?

wurden von folgenden Fachexperten beantwortet:
were answered by the following experts:

Alexander Hildebrand
ist Raumbegrüner und Florist. Er ist Geschäftsführer von Pflanzen-Forum und Element Green Rhein/Main.
specialized in greening spaces and is a florist. He is Managing Director of Pflanzen-Forum und Element Green Rhein/Main.

Werner Jager
ist Geschäftsführer Technisches Marketing beim Aluminiumsystemhaus WICONA. Der Schwerpunkt seiner Tätigkeit liegt in der Entwicklung und Vermarktung nachhaltiger und ressourcenschonender Aluminiumlösungen.
is Managing Director Technical Marketing at the aluminium system house WICONA. The focus of his activities is on the development and marketing of sustainable and resource-saving aluminium solutions.

Gunter Mann
ist promovierter Biologe und hauptamtlich Präsident des Bundesverbands GebäudeGrün e.V. (BuGG). Er ist seit 27 Jahren in der Gebäudegrün-Branche tätig und veröffentlichte zahlreiche Fachbeiträge und Publikationen.
holds a Ph.D. in biology and is full-time president of Bundesverband GebäudeGrün e.V. (BuGG). He had been active in the building greenery segment for 27 years now and has published countless specialist articles and publications.

Lara-Maria Mohr
ist Geografin und Projektleiterin für das Programm „Frankfurt frischt auf" im Umweltamt der Stadt Frankfurt am Main. Ihre Themenschwerpunkte sind Gebäudebegrünung, Stadtgeografie, Klimawandel und Klimaanpassung.
is a geographer and project manager for the program "Frankfurt frischt auf" in the Environmental Agency of the City of Frankfurt am Main. Her main topics are greening buildings, urban geography, climate change and climate adaptation.

Joachim Stroh
verantwortet seit 1994 die Öffentlichkeitsarbeit der ZinCo GmbH. ZinCo ist einer der marktführenden Systemanbieter für die Nutzung der Dachlandschaft.
has since 1994 headed the PR desk at ZinCo GmbH. ZinCo is one of the leading suppliers of systems for creating usable roof worlds.

Gerhard Zemp
ist Architekt, Gartenbauingenieur und Co-Gründer von aplantis, Bern, einem Architekturbüro für Gebäudebegrünung. Er ist seit 20 Jahren in der Gebäudegrün-Branche tätig und veröffentlichte zahlreiche Fachbeiträge und Publikationen.
is an architect, horticultural engineer and co-founder of aplantis, Bern, an architectural office for building greening. He has been active in the building greening industry for 20 years and has published numerous specialist articles and publications.

IMPRESSUM AUSSTELLUNG
IMPRINT EXHIBITION

**EINFACH GRÜN – Greening the City im/*at* Deutsches Architekturmuseum (DAM)
in Frankfurt am Main
16. Januar 2021 bis 20. Juni 2020/*January 16, 2021 – June 20, 2021***

Direktor/*Director:* **Peter Cachola Schmal**
Stellvertretende Direktorin/*Deputy director:* **Andrea Jürges**
Kuratoren/*Curators:* **Hilde Strobl, Rudi Scheuermann**
Kuratorische Assistenz/*Curatorial assistence:* **Jonas Malzahn**
Volontärin/*Volunteer:* **Katleen Nagel**
Ausstellungsdesign/*Exhibition design:* **Mario Lorenz** DESERVE
Illustrationen/*Illustrations:* **Geka Pahnke**
Ausstellung Grünplanung und Umsetzung/*Exhibition greenery and implentation:*
    Gerhard Zemp, aplantis AG, Bern; **Alexander Hildebrand**, Pflanzen-Forum GmbH, Bodenheim
Filmschnitt/*Film editing:* **Moritz Bernoully**
Kuratorin Architekturvermittlung/*Education curator:* **Rebekka Kremershof, Flora Ciupke**
Öffentlichkeitsarbeit/*Public relations:* **Brita Köhler, Anna Wegmann**
Verwaltung/*Administration:* **Inka Plechaty, Jacqueline Brauer**
Registrar: **Wolfgang Welker**
Übersetzungen/*Translations:* **Jeremy Gaines**
Führungen/*Guided tours:* **Yorck Förster**
Call for Projects, Mediengestaltung/*Media Design:* **Urban Media Project**
DAM Corporate Design: Gardeners, Frankfurt am Main
Aufbau/*Installation:* **Ulrich Diekmann, Enrico Hirsekorn, Jannik Hofmann, Leo Laduch,
    Eike Laeuen, Anke Menck, Jörn Schön, Ömer Simsek, Houaida Soubai, Gerhard Winkler**
    unter der Leitung von/*Under the direction of* **Christian Walter**
Haustechnik Museum/*Museum technic:* **Joachim Müller-Rahn**
Ausstellungsproduktion/*Exhibition production:* **Inditec GmbH**, Bad Camberg;
    Metallbau Lill, Taunusstein

IMPRESSUM KATALOG
IMPRINT CATALOGUE

**Einfach Grün – Greening the City
Handbuch für Gebäudegrün**

*Simply Green – Die Stadt begrünen
Manual for Building Greenery*

Hilde Strobl, Peter Cachola Schmal, Rudi Scheuermann (Hg./*Ed.*)

© Deutsches Architekturmuseum (DAM), Frankfurt am Main, 2021
Erscheinungsdatum/*Release date:* 15.1.2021; 304 Seiten/*Pages*

ISBN 978-3-939114-10-9

Redaktion/*Editing:* **Hilde Strobl, Jonas Malzahn**
Redaktionelle Assistenz/*Editoral assistance:* **Katleen Nagel**
Design und Gestaltung/*Graphic design and typesetting:* **Christoph Sauter**
Illustrationen/*Illustrations:* **Geka Pahnke**
Lektorat/*Copyediting:* **Ilka Backmeister-Collacott**
Übersetzungen/*Translations:* **Jeremy Gaines**
Druckerei/*Printing company:* **DZA Druckerei zu Altenburg GmbH**
Umschlag/*Cover:* **Gmund** Bio Cycle, Chlorophyll (aus 50% Grünschnitt oberbayerischer Wiesen/
    from 50% green cut of upper bavarian meadows), FSC®
Schrift/*Font:* Atlas Grotesk

KOOPERATION & FÖRDERER
COOPERATION & SPONSORS

Ausstellung und Publikation sind eine Kooperation mit der Forschungsabteilung des internationalen Planungs- und Beratungsbüros Arup „Green Building Envelopes" und dem Umweltamt der Stadt Frankfurt am Main.
Exhibition and publication are a cooperation with the research department of the international design and consultancy practice Arup "Green Building Envelopes" and the Environmental Agency of the City of Frankfurt am Main.

Ausstellung und Publikation wurden gefördert durch
Exhibition and publication are sponsored by

s.boehme & co.

Gesellschaft der Freunde des DAM
WICONA Hydro Building Systems Germany GmbH
Bundesverband Gebäudegrün e.V. (BuGG)

Die Begrünung der Ausstellung im Innen- und Außenbereich wurde unterstützt von
The greening of the exhibition inside and outside was supported by

Helix Pflanzen GmbH, D-Kornwestheim
Hutzel Hydrokulturen GmbH, D-Bad Iburg
Mobilane GmbH, D-Heusenstamm
Skyflor – Creabeton Matériaux AG/SA, Ch-Lyss
Therme Group, AT-Wien
Wallflore Systems, NL-Zwolle
ZinCo GmbH, D-Nürtingen